Cervantes's
Theory of the Novel

Cervantes's
Theory of the Novel

by

E.C. RILEY

Juan de la Cuesta
Newark, Delaware

Juan de la Cuesta—Hispanic Monographs
270 Indian Road
Newark, Delaware 19711
(302) 453-8695
Fax: (302) 453-8601

MANUFACTURED IN THE UNITED STATES OF AMERICA

ISBN: 0-936388-56-0

PREFACE

CERVANTES, who did more to create the modern European novel than any other writer before the eighteenth century, speculated a good deal about the problems of literature. He hinted indeed that he had views about one type of novel which he might have expressed at length. The Priest in *Don Quixote* remarks:

If this were the right occasion and my audience so desired, I could say things about the qualities that books of chivalry ought to have in order to be good ones—things that might perhaps be profitable and even pleasing to some people. But I hope the time will come when I can communicate them to someone who can remedy the situation. (I. 32)

Unlike Lope de Vega or Torquato Tasso, Cervantes never wrote down his ideas in anything resembling a treatise, but directly and indirectly he made a great many critical and theoretical comments in the course of his writings. Those in *Don Quixote* alone would make up a slim but substantial treatise. Yet no one has so far studied his ideas about literature comprehensively and in detail. Except in general outline and in certain limited connexions, the nature and scope of the theory fragmentarily revealed in Cervantes's scattered comments and its exact relevance to his own writings have remained uncertain.

This book is an attempt to make good the deficiency only in part. My first object has been to present a more complete picture of his theory of prose fiction than has so far appeared. I have sought to elucidate his views, which are by no means always clear, and put them in their critical and historical context, by setting them against those of contemporary and earlier writers. Some considerations on the problem of his principal sources will be found in Chapter I. I have not dealt with his general aesthetic, his judicial criticism as such, or his views on the drama, except in so far as they are related to my subject. His poetic theory has come under discussion to the extent that it is inseparable from any sixteenth-century theorizing on the novel. I have not been concerned to interpret his novels in the light of his doctrines, but I have examined his practice where this has helped to clarify the theory. As it happens, his theory and his imaginative writing are in certain respects literally inseparable. In the last chapter I have considered three features of *Don Quixote* which are among other things illustrations of this inseparability, and which only in recent years seem to have attracted much attention. They are included not only because they throw some more light on the subject of this book, but also because an approach to them through Cervantes's theory makes them more meaningful.

Attempts to define 'the novel' in any but the broadest terms have always seemed to me futile. At best they usually apply to the *modern* novel. I shall understand by the word: a prose narrative written as fiction. It may be distinguished, imprecisely, from the *novela corta* and the short story by its length. There are, of course, hybrids, and one of these, the pastoral novel, will be included with prose fiction for my purposes.

Cervantes was a great novelist, not a highly original theorist. His basic precepts were as derivative as those of Sir Philip Sidney, say. But he was certainly one of the first European writers to theorize on the novel to any considerable extent, and some of his views have implications of immediate importance to the theory of prose fiction. Moreover, I know of no writer who vitalized critical problems as he did. *Don Quixote* itself is a work of criticism in a very peculiar sense.

The eternal gap between literary theory and practice, which tended to be especially wide where Spanish writers of the Golden Age were concerned, is obvious enough in his novels. One should guard, however, against drawing analogies with his dramatic theory and practice, where the disparity is much greater. I believe that special circumstances have to be taken into account there: notably that he was working in a highly conventionalized medium where he never felt sure of himself and where audience-requirements, to which he was always very sensitive, were particularly exacting.

I am aware of having seemed at times to impose on Cervantes's sporadic comments an appearance of ordered thought which they certainly do not present when encountered in his books. But they add up to a theory, and their summation has not been made according to any modern theory of the novel, which could only be misleading, or theoretical views of my own, as far as these could be eliminated, but in general accordance with Spanish and Italian critical writing of the sixteenth and early seventeenth centuries. The standardized character of much of this has simplified the task, and may not be unwelcome to the English reader, since English criticism of the period shares common, Italian, ground with Spanish and French. On the other hand, the unsystematic form in which Cervantes chose to give expression to his ideas and his reluctance to draw conclusions also make his theory less clear-cut than one could wish. It lacks definition, in the photographic sense. There are inconsistencies and loose ends. To have tied these up would have made a neater package of his theory, but at the expense of authenticity. It should be added that the literary theories which have been abstracted for the purposes of this study cannot be wholly disengaged from the rest of Cervantes's thought without some violence. The questions with which we shall be dealing are often particular, artistic aspects of matters of wider import. The problem of the relation of poetry to history is the most obvious and striking example.

No one, least of all a foreigner, can approach a subject like Cervantes without some diffidence. Nor can one contemplate the massive Cervantine bibliography without alarm and the realization that some relevant work or other will remain unread. The remoter corners of Cervantes criticism produced few surprises, however, and it is clear that relatively little has been written on him as a theorist and critic. On the whole, the most important writing on his literary theory is the best known and is comparatively modern: Menéndez y Pelayo's few pages on the subject in his *Historia de las ideas estéticas en España* (ed. Buenos Aires, 1943), vol. ii;[1] A. Bonilla's 'Las teorías estéticas de Cervantes' in *Cervantes y su obra* (Madrid, 1916); the observations of R. Schevill and A. Bonilla in the introductions to the complete works; G. Toffanin, *La fine dell'umanesimo* (Turin, 1920), ch. 15; C. De Lollis, *Cervantes reazionario* (ed. Florence, 1947); Américo Castro, *El pensamiento de Cervantes* (Madrid, 1925), ch. 1, probably still the best introduction to the subject; parts of M. Casella's *Cervantes: Il 'Chisciotte'* (Florence, 1938, 2 vols.); W. C. Atkinson, 'The Enigma of the *Persiles*', *BSS* xxiv (1947), and 'Cervantes, El Pinciano and the *Novelas ejemplares*', *HR* xvi (1948); the introduction to A. del Campo's edition of the *Viaje del Parnaso* (Madrid, 1948); A. G. de Amezúa, *Cervantes creador de la novela corta española*

[1] References throughout are to the editions I have used.

(Madrid, 1956–8), vol. i, ch. 8; and J.-F. Canavaggio's substantial article, 'Alonso López Pinciano y la estética literaria de Cervantes en el *Quijote*', *ACerv* vii (1958). The only complete book devoted to the subject known to me is S. Salas Garrido's *Exposición de las ideas estéticas de Cervantes* (Malaga, 1905), which may most charitably be described as useless.

Most full-scale critical studies and many lesser ones include some mention of Cervantes's theories or seek to relate them to his writings. There have also been some more or less summary expositions, such as J. A. Tamayo's 'Ideas estéticas y literarias de Cervantes', *RIEs* vi (1948), R. del Arco's 'Estética cervantina en el *Persiles*' (ibid.) and 'Las artes y los artistas en la obra cervantina', ibid. viii (1950), to mention only some of the more recent. A number of critical writings that do not deal specifically with Cervantes's literary theories have been particularly enlightening. I refer especially to studies, some of which are cited in this book, by Ortega y Gasset, Madariaga, Bataillon, Hatzfeld, Casalduero, Spitzer, A. A. Parker, Mia Gerhardt, Levin, Ángel del Río, Avalle-Arce, Rosales, and the later essays of Castro now collected in *Hacia Cervantes* (Madrid, 1957). A few others have appeared since the work was prepared for the press.

Quotations are translated into English, both to avoid giving the effect of a linguistic potpourri, and because neither the readers of Cervantes nor those interested in the development of ideas on the novel are confined to speakers of Spanish. The translations are my own, with a few rare exceptions from ancient classical authors. The originals of the more significant passages will be found in the footnotes. I have modernized their spelling and punctuation where necessary. Page-references to Cervantes's works in the footnotes are to the *Obras completas* edited by Schevill and Bonilla (Madrid, 1914–41), except for *Don Quixote*. Here, they are to the critical edition of F. Rodríguez Marín (Madrid, 1947–9), ten volumes.

I owe a debt of gratitude to many colleagues and other friends who have helped me while I was working on this book. In particular I should like to thank Professor A. E. Sloman and Professor P. E. Russell who read it at earlier stages of its preparation and made many valuable suggestions. I am very grateful to Mr. T. G. Griffith and Mr. G. H. McWilliam for their help with the sixteenth-century Italian theorists, and to Professor W. B. Stanford and Mr. J. V. Luce for dealing with some queries about classical sources. My thanks too are due to P. José López de Toro, Subdirector of the Biblioteca Nacional, Madrid, and to the Sección Cervantina of that library for the facilities and courtesies extended to me; to Professor G. L. Stagg for some useful bibliographical information; to Professor K. Whinnom for his comments on Chapter I; to Mr. G. D. Trotter for the time, care, and energy he has given to reading the proofs; and to Miss Margaret Larminie for her patience and typewriting skill.

E. C. R.

Trinity College, Dublin

Note to the 1992 Edition

The text is that of the third (1968) printing of the Clarendon Press, Oxford, edition. A few small emendations have been either incorporated into the text or are listed on the next page.

My thanks are due to Tom Lathrop for proposing the republication of this book.

E.C.R.

Author's 1992 Emendations

p. 151, line 7

reads: telling which one finds in contemporary...
should read: telling which one finds in Cicero, Castiglione, and
   contemporary...

p. 156, last line

reads: limits: to say that a woman is an angel...
should read: limits: to say that a woman is more beautiful than an
   angel...

p. 157, footnote 1

reads: tados: decir que una mujer es un ángel...
should read: tados: decir que una mujer es más hermosa que un
   ángel...

p. 186, line 20

reads: The only other instance of its...
should read: The other main comparable instance of its...

p. 210, lines 30,31

reads: exact in all things' (I. 16), a 'trustworthy author' (II. 61), the
   'flower of historians' (I. 52), and so on. On the other hand
   he is...
should read: exact in all things' (I.16), a 'trustworthy author' (I.
   52), the 'flower of historians' (II. 61), and so on. On the
   other hand he is...

Additions to List of Works Cited:

Fernández, Jerónimo, *El libro primero del valeroso e invencible
   principe don Belianis de Grecia.* Burgos, 1547.
Ortega, Melchor, *Felixmarte de Hyrcania.* Valladolid, 1556.

CONTENTS

ABBREVIATIONS

ACerv	*Anales cervantinos.* Madrid.
BAE	*Biblioteca de Autores españoles.* Madrid.
BH	*Bulletin Hispanique.* Bordeaux.
BHS	*Bulletin of Hispanic Studies.* Liverpool.
BRAE	*Boletín de la Real Academia española.* Madrid.
BSS	*Bulletin of Spanish Studies.* Liverpool.
CL	*Comparative Literature.* Eugene, Oregon.
Clav	*Clavileño.* Madrid.
DQ	*Don Quixote.*
HR	*Hispanic Review.* Philadelphia.
MPh	*Modern Philology.* Chicago.
NBAE	*Nueva Biblioteca de Autores españoles.* Madrid.
NRFH	*Nueva revista de filología hispánica.* Mexico.
RFE	*Revista de filología española.* Madrid.
RIEs	*Revista de ideas estéticas.* Madrid.
RLC	*Revue de Littérature Comparée.* Paris.
RR	*Romanic Review.* New York.
SRen	*Studies in the Renaissance.* New York.
UISLL	*University of Illinois Studies in Language and Literature.*

I

INTRODUCTORY

1. *Cervantes and the Literary Theory of his Time*

As I am extremely fond of reading, even the scraps of
paper in the streets . . . . CERVANTES

IN the sixteenth and early seventeenth centuries there was,
strictly speaking, no theory of the novel. That is to say, what
there was did not exist in its own right. The theoretical
observations on prose fiction occasionally to be found in critical
and moralistic writings, plays, novels, authors' prologues, and the
like were nearly all adapted from poetics, which in their turn
contained a strong leavening of rhetorical theory. The novel took
over a theory in essentials ready-made, and the fit was not all that
could be desired. It was the newest of the genres, having scarcely
existed in Antiquity, and its prestige was low. The persistence
with which moralists in the sixteenth century deplored the reading
of novels, especially by young girls, testifies to their popularity,
but the official disesteem in which they were held and the scarcity
of ancient models largely account for the lack of critical attention
given to the art of the novel. One finds scattered comments on the
romances of chivalry, on the Italian *novelle*, on pastoral and Byzantine
romances; manuals of courtly behaviour included hints on how
to tell a good story in polite company; but prose fiction, unlike
poetry and the drama, could boast no full-scale treatise. Probably
the first piece of theorizing in Spain that systematically expounded
the principles of a type of prose fiction was Francisco de Lugo y
Dávila's brief introduction to his *Teatro popular* (Madrid, 1622).[1]
It is a rather mechanical but by no means uninteresting application
of Aristotelian poetic theory to the *novela*.

Literary theory in Golden-Age Spain made slow progress until
the last quarter of the sixteenth century. Earlier developments,

---

[1] I have used the edition of Madrid, 1906.

however, had contributed to the marked acceleration which then took place. Humanists had paid some attention to imaginative literature as a part of general education. Rhetorics had been appearing in the vernacular.[1] Commentaries on writers of Antiquity led to the systematic criticism of Garcilaso, who acquired all the status of a classic within fifty years of his death. From the scholar's study poetic theory made its way into the circles of poets. The significant moment of the transition was when Fernando de Herrera followed up El Brocense's mainly philological commentary on Garcilaso's works with the publication of his own copiously annotated edition at Seville in 1580. This, the work of a poet as well as a scholar, pointed the direction that poetic theory in Spain was to follow, despite its somewhat limited subject. Sánchez de Lima's *Arte poética*, published at Alcalá de Henares in the same year, was hopelessly old-fashioned beside it, although it was to have a successor, much superior and more inspired in its Platonism, in Carvallo's *Cisne de Apolo* (Medina del Campo, 1602).

The main impetus came from Italy. It was not an accident that the increase in critical consciousness among Spanish writers of the last two decades of the sixteenth century (a development apparent among English writers of the same period) coincided with the divulgation of Aristotelian poetic doctrines from Italy. Aristotle's *Poetics* had been known to Italian scholars from the beginning of the century, and the process of wedding its principles with those of Horace's *Ars poetica* was completed by 1555.[2] But it was Robortelli's commentary on the work in 1548[3] that sparked off the series of treatises and commentaries which transformed European criticism. The Aristotelian poetic doctrines lent themselves with remarkable immediacy to a critical preoccupation with ends and means which stemmed from the realization that, in this new era of the printing press and religious convulsion in Europe, literature was a powerful social force for good and ill. Theoretical considerations never exercised so tight a hold on Spanish writers as they did on the Italians, and in the 1590's Spain

[1] Fr. Miguel de Salinas, *Retórica en lengua castellana* (Alcalá de Henares, 1541); Pedro de Navarra, *Diálogos de la diferencia del hablar al escribir* (Tolosa, [1560?]); R. de Espinosa de Santayana, *Arte de retórica* (Madrid, 1578); Juan de Guzmán, *Primera parte de la retórica* (Alcalá de Henares, 1589).

[2] M. T. Herrick, 'The Fusion of Horatian and Aristotelian Literary Criticism', *UISLL* xxxii (1946).

[3] F. Robortelli, *In librum Aristotelis de Arte Poetica explicationes* (Florence, 1548).

was a generation behind Italy in these matters, but their influence mounted steadily in the lifetime of Cervantes.

Although no Spanish translation of the *Poetics* was published until 1626,[1] its contents were widely known well before then. Herrera was evidently familiar with them, but they were first propagated in a manner comparable with that of the Aristotelian treatises of Italy by López Pinciano's dialogue, the *Filosofía antigua poética* (Madrid, 1596). The comparative novelty of the *Poetics* in Spain at this time is reflected in the book by a comment of the cultured Don Gabriel that this work of Aristotle's is new to him.[2]

El Pinciano's lucid and intelligent treatise has long been assumed by most critics to have been the chief source of Cervantes's theory. Some, notably Toffanin, De Lollis, and Castro, have given equal or more prominence to the Italians. The fact is, however, that no one has yet established that source with certainty.

There are three main difficulties in tracing the derivation of Cervantes's theory. He refers to no authority, except to a few standard ancient authors like Plato, Horace, and Ovid. Secondly, extensive passages transposed with minimal alteration from the works of literary theorists or other authors are lacking. Few passages can be assigned to a specific source with as much assurance as the portions of neo-Platonic doctrine in the *Galatea* and elsewhere can be assigned to León Hebreo and a few Italian writers. It is conceivable that Cervantes took pains to disguise his borrowings, but the indications are that he relied on his memory. His voracious appetite for books—for which we have the evidence in his works as well as his own admission—was clearly accompanied by an excellent literary digestion.

The third difficulty is that the principal literary tenets were common currency. Writers repeat them again and again. The mere coincidence of a major theme in Cervantes and another writer is therefore rarely significant. Critics who have asserted the debt of Cervantes to El Pinciano have failed to take proper account of this. The fact that Cervantes and El Pinciano both refer to the

[1] A. Ordóñez das Seijas y Tovar, *La Poética de Aristóteles dada a nuestra lengua castellana* (Madrid, 1626).

[2] A. López Pinciano, *Filosofía antigua poética* (ed. Madrid, 1953), i. 192. The second edition of the work was that of Valladolid, 1894.

division of styles, for instance, or show a fondness for the idea that poetry embraced philosophy and the other arts and sciences, offers no certainty at all that the former was indebted to the latter for these notions.[1] Such subjects as the prose epic, invention, imitation, the end of poetry, the complexity of truth, and the superiority of poetic over historical truth were all too widely discussed for these two writers' common concern with them to be evidence, by itself, of indebtedness.[2] Many other theorists were exercised by the same problems.

Clemencín[3] seems to have been the first commentator to note the resemblance between the literary doctrines expounded by the Canon of Toledo at the end of *Don Quixote* I. 47 and those in the *Filosofía antigua poética* and in the *Tablas poéticas* of Francisco Cascales (Murcia, 1617).[4] Menéndez y Pelayo merely said that Cervantes's theories were 'the same, exactly the same as those expounded by any poetics of the time, Cascales's or El Pinciano's'.[5] More serious attempts to define the debt to El Pinciano have been made by Bonilla, Atkinson, and Amezúa.[6] But all along too much has been taken for granted. It simply begs the question to suggest that the mere existence of El Pinciano's work is sufficient to 'absolve from any need to turn to Italy'.[7]

The most serious attempt which has yet been made, that of J.-F. Canavaggio in his detailed comparative study, 'Alonso López Pinciano y la estética literaria de Cervantes en el *Quijote*', is ultimately impaired by the same defect. His conclusion, that 'we are obliged to concede to El Pinciano a preferential place among the possible sources of the literary aesthetic in the *Quixote*',[8] is cautious and qualified, but the fact is that, the other contenders having been eliminated before the start, there is no one left to whom El Pinciano is to be preferred. The author gives good reasons why the *Filosofía antigua poética* is worth studying in

---

[1] As affirmed, respectively, by A. Cotarelo Valledor, *Cervantes, lector* (Madrid, 1943), p. 33, and Bonilla, *Cervantes y su obra*, pp. 91–92.

[2] As supposed by Atkinson, 'Cervantes, El Pinciano and the *Novelas ejemplares*', pp. 195–6.

[3] *El ingenioso hidalgo Don Quijote de la Mancha* . . . Comentado por D. Diego Clemencín (ed. Madrid, 1894).

[4] My references are to the second edition of the *Tablas poéticas* (Madrid, 1779).

[5] Menéndez y Pelayo, *Ideas estéticas*, ii. 267.

[6] Amezúa, *Cervantes creador*, i. 362 ff. Also see Castro, *Pensamiento*, pp. 44–45, n. 5.

[7] See Atkinson, op. cit., p. 194.

[8] Canavaggio, op. cit., p. 107.

relation to *Don Quixote*,[1] but the extent of the debt to El Pinciano cannot be measured except against the debt, if any, to other authorities. Consequently, too much weight is again given to coincidences of view on major topics, coincidences which could be multiplied with other writers. Nevertheless, Canavaggio well shows how much their works have in common; the mere number of correspondences does impress. This contributes to my own belief that Cervantes was indeed indebted to El Pinciano—a conclusion, however, which can only be legitimately reached after widening as far as possible the field of comparison and narrowing the conception of what constitutes a significant coincidence of view. Even so, one is only dealing, at best, with probabilities.

Vilanova has discerned the influence of Cascales's *Tablas* in the last novel of Cervantes, *Persiles y Sigismunda*.[2] The treatise was written by 1604, according to his biographer, although not published until 1617;[3] so conceivably Cervantes could have read it. On the other hand, the correspondences between the ideas of Cervantes and Cascales can easily be paralleled by those between the ideas of Cervantes and the Italians, on occasion more closely. Cascales himself was heavily indebted to the Italians—probably to a greater extent than was El Pinciano. The influence of Cascales must be considered unlikely until more persuasive evidence has been produced.

The uncertainty attaching to the name of El Pinciano attaches to the Italians of the sixteenth century for the same reasons and to the same extent. Toffanin's observations that Cervantes was in Italy during the years between the appearance of Castelvetro's *Poetica d'Aristotele volgarizzata ed esposta* (Vienna, 1570)[4] and Alessandro Piccolomini's *Annotazioni nel libro della poetica d'Aristotele* (Venice, 1575), and that his problems were the same as those that troubled Torquato Tasso, have been taken up by De Lollis, Castro, and others. C. Guerrieri-Crocetti has seen in Cervantes the influence of Giraldi Cinthio.[5] The names of Robortelli, Fracastoro,

---

[1] Ibid., p. 23.

[2] A. Vilanova, 'Preceptistas españoles de los siglos XVI y XVII', in *Historia general de las literaturas hispánicas*, ed. Días-Plaja (Barcelona, 1949–58), iii. 628.

[3] J. García Soriano, *El humanista Francisco Cascales* (Madrid, 1924), p. 44.

[4] References are to the second edition, Basle, 1576.

[5] C. Guerrieri-Crocetti, *G. B. Giraldi e il pensiero critico del sec. XVI* (Milan, 1932), p. 441.

Minturno, Maggi, J. C. Scaliger, Muzio, Bernardo Tasso, Varchi, Patrizi, and others have also figured in the general comparisons.

Cervantes had four different sources from which to derive principles for the novel: a documentary source (standard poetics, rhetorics, and critical writing), verbal intercourse with other writers, the observations of his own reading of prose fiction, and his own experience as a novelist. The first is manifestly the most important as regards his direct statements of theory. Nothing is known about the second. We can deduce a very little about the other two and permit a reasonable conjecture on occasion. Independent reflection on his reading may account for Cervantes's preoccupation with certain problems. The artlessness and irresponsibility of many chivalresque novelists, and the contrast between their works and the *Orlando furioso*, for instance, might well have set him wondering about the principles of literary fiction. And, of course, what looks like influence can be more than one sort of accident, especially where similar temperaments in the same period are concerned.

Apart from the highly original way in which much of Cervantes's theory intervenes in his novels, the very fact that it is expressed in stray comments and sporadic passages gives his views a significance they would not have had if he had covered all the ground in a comprehensive treatise. A writer of fiction is not bound to express views on his subject. Though many of them are commonplaces and some are *idées reçues* of no great consequence, they occur too frequently and in a good many cases with too much emphasis to be dismissed as a species of otherwise meaningless intellectual ornament. The theoretical statements of a writer who had no patience with affected erudition and pedantry at least deserve serious scrutiny.

It has seemed to me more important to try to elucidate Cervantes's theory than to concentrate on finding out exactly where it came from. By a comparison of theoretical statements, however, we can draw some provisional conclusions about the main sources of his theory of prose fiction, which will be better than assumptions. The field of literary theory down to Cervantes's time is vast and other precedents for his views no doubt remain to be pointed out. A full study of his dramatic and poetic theory may also yet reveal that he read other theorists and confirm his debt to those mentioned here. There is no external evidence: we can only compare texts.

First, there are resemblances of general theme. Here, only when both parties treat the subject, or aspects of it, with some uncommon emphasis or in some unusual way, can the resemblance be considered significant. Secondly, there are textual resemblances between particular passages. Though fortuitous coincidence cannot be ruled out here either, these offer the more reliable indications; but only close similarity of wording, the concurrence of a number of points in a brief space, or the exceptional nature of the particular idea expressed entitles us to infer that Cervantes appropriated it from the other writer in question.

Since Italians and Spaniards alike were indebted to the literary theory of Antiquity, and to some extent that of the Middle Ages, Cervantes could have repaired to ancient sources directly or become acquainted with their doctrines through his contemporaries. No doubt some standard works like Quintilian's *Institutio oratoria*, Cicero on oratory, and perhaps the *Rhetorica ad Herennium* and Horace's *Ars poetica*, figured as part of his formal education. At all events, directly or indirectly, it is Aristotelian, Horatian, and Platonic ideas that provide the foundation of his theory. From Aristotle's *Poetics* or treatises based on it derive many of his most important principles and the greatest single issue, the nature of truth in poetic fiction.

The author of *Don Quixote* shares with the late Greek critics, Plutarch, Dio Chrysostom, and Lucian, a preoccupation with the relationship of history and poetic fiction. I see no obvious reminiscences of the first two writers, but it should be remembered how popular Plutarch was in the later sixteenth century. There are echoes of Lucian, who is generally believed to have had some influence on Cervantes's work in other respects. I incline to think, though, that such resemblances as may be detected between their critical views are the result of indirect influence or are coincidental. Parodies such as the *True History* apart, the specifically critical writings of Lucian do not figure in the more popular sixteenth-century Italian translations or in the brief Spanish selection of *Diálogos* (León, 1550). But all his works were available in Latin and we should not rule out the possibility that Cervantes read the influential treatise on *The Way to Write History*.

The theories of J. C. Scaliger, Piccolomini, the younger Tasso, and probably Fracastoro and others were well known to El Pinciano. No doubt it was through him that some of their doctrines were transmitted to Cervantes (less probably through Cascales). But there are passages in Cervantes which seem to derive from Italian writers without intermediary. The characteristics of the ideal romance listed in *Don Quixote* I. 47 recall Giraldi Cinthio and, more particularly, Tasso on heroic poetry—the former in his *Discorso intorno al comporre dei romanzi* (Venice, 1554) and the latter in the *Discorsi dell'arte poetica e in particolare sopra il poema eroico* and the *Discorsi del poéma eroico*.[1] The enumeration itself resembles those catalogues of items suitable for heroic poems, found in Italian works of theory but not in El Pinciano. Similarly, Cervantes's comment on the variety of incident to be expected on long journeys is more conspicuously close to an observation of Tasso's than to a comparable observation of El Pinciano's. The Italian poet's obsessive concern with verisimilitude and the marvellous reappears with not very much less urgency in Cervantes. So does his desire to reconcile epic and romance. Direct literary influence may be suspected to have played a part here, but it can be no more than a suspicion where such general matters are concerned.

There are some interesting coincidences with Piccolomini's *Annotazioni*. A comic homily in Cervantes on the correct way to describe the charms and attributes of a mere serving-wench echoes a distinction made by Piccolomini. His recognition of the part played by the intelligence of the reader in the functioning of verisimilitude could have derived from the same author. So could his use in the *Persiles* of two cosmological examples of an unconvincing fact.

The particular claims of Vida, Robortelli, Fracastoro, Scaliger, Minturno, Castelvetro, Patrizi, and others, much as they did to shape literary theory, are less apparent. A slight exception might be made in favour of Castelvetro, however. Though many of his views are utterly unlike those of Cervantes, the unusual importance he gives to history as the bedrock of poetry has a certain parallel with the way that Cervantes anchors poetry to history in the novel.

El Pinciano's claims, without being unique, are of course strong. Apart from numerous general topics, such as his notable definition of the object of poetry, certain particular passages, such

[1] Both in T. Tasso, *Opere* (ed. Florence, 1724), vol. iv.

as those on *admiratio* and the comic, the achievement of literary perfection through imitation and verisimilitude, and the comparison of the novels of chivalry with the Milesian fables, are close enough in detail to passages in Cervantes to suggest indebtedness. His remarks on allegory might well have made Cervantes cautious about its use in the novel. And it is not unlikely that his generally rational approach to literature had some effect on Cervantes, though this is not susceptible of proof.

What shows every sign of being a piece of borrowing from Carvallo's *Cisne de Apolo* occurs in the *Addendum* to Cervantes's poem, *Journey to Parnassus*, the *Adjunta al Parnaso*. Its subject is, precisely, the limits of poetic borrowing—which is just the sort of joke that Cervantes enjoyed. His formulation of the important distinction between the purposeful and the unpurposeful absurdity may well have been suggested to him by Carvallo also.

I am aware of no specific debt to Herrera, apart from the well-known sentence in the dedication of *Don Quixote* I, probably appropriated from the dedication of Herrera's edition of Garcilaso. But there are possible reminiscences of two other notable works of the time. Huarte de San Juan's internationally known *Examen de ingenios* is generally regarded as having influenced Cervantes, and though his book is only marginally connected with literary theory, the influence evidently extends to Cervantes's ideas about literary creation. (Castiglione's *Il Cortegiano* stands in a similarly marginal relation to Cervantes's literary theory.) The other book is the *Galateo español*, the hispanicized version of Giovanni della Casa's no less widely known manual, by Gracián Dantisco, some of whose comments on style show a verbal resemblance to those of Cervantes.

If the influence of the sixteenth-century humanists had not been so diffused, one would be very tempted to include the great name of Luis Vives among the major sources too. As it is, he played at least an indirect part in shaping Cervantes's theory of the novel. Cervantes's distrust of poetic distortions recalls Vives more than anyone. In addition to this, the passage in *Don Quixote* I. 47 illustrating the absurdities in the novels of chivalry directly resembles one in the *De institutione feminae christianae*, which was translated into the vernacular and much read in Spain.[1]

---

[1] The case of Juan de Valdés is more doubtful. It is generally agreed that Cervantes is unlikely to have known the *Diálogo de la lengua*. Certain similarities in their

To sum up, Cervantes's theory of prose fiction is predominantly neo-Aristotelian, in the manner of the major Italian and Spanish poetics of the later sixteenth and early seventeenth centuries, though compounded with neo-Platonist doctrines and other ingredients.[1] He probably made more use of poetics than of rhetorics, and of works in the vernacular than works in Latin, although not necessarily to the exclusion of either. More specifically, just one thing is certain: if he was indebted to El Pinciano, there are other authorities, both Italian and Spanish, whose claims are as good. The most striking correspondences are with El Pinciano, Tasso, Carvallo, Piccolomini, Huarte, Giraldi Cinthio, Gracián Dantisco, Vives, and possibly Castelvetro, in something like that order of priority.[2] It is conceivable, but unlikely, that he read Cascales's *Tablas poéticas* in manuscript. There remain incidental parallels with the critical opinions of other writers who are not major sources, but whose words Cervantes might have recalled from his extensive reading.[3] His own reading of fiction and his experience as a writer must be allowed for in his theory, but they influenced his imaginative writing more than they did his statements of principle. He sought, I think, a confirmation of the validity of those principles, even though he was capable of exploiting their often mutually contradictory character.

It is no easier to say when Cervantes would have read such books as provided the basis of his critical opinions. From the first part of *Don Quixote* (1605) until *Persiles y Sigismunda*, published

views are plain, however, and it seems at least worth noting that Don Quixote's definition of the *vulgo* virtually reproduces that of Valdés. Perhaps it was more common than one supposes, though I have found no other sixteenth-century example of it.

[1] Casella's view is eccentric. He considers that Cervantes's literary theory is 'traditional, Platonic-Augustinian and scholastic', like Dante's, Boccaccio's, and Ariosto's, and basically opposed to the new, Aristotelian 'estetica classicheggiante' emanating from the universities (*Il 'Chisciotte'*, ii. 29, 401, and *passim*).

[2] Grouped below for convenience of reference are the page numbers in this book where the more significant correspondences occur: El Pinciano—pp. 58, 92-93, 181, 186-7; Tasso—pp. 104, 117, 124; Carvallo—pp. 22, 63; Piccolomini—pp. 159, 183, 189; Huarte—pp. 68, 76, n. 3; Giraldi—pp. 104, 126; Gracián Dantisco—p. 149; Vives—p. 181-2. In addition, there are some striking instances of the practical application of a theoretical idea, whether intended or not, by Cervantes. Cf. Piccolomini—p. 47 (and see p. 220); Tasso—p. 190; Castelvetro—p. 211.

[3] e.g. El Brocense—see pp. 77-78; Ercilla—p. 123; D. Hurtado de Mendoza—p. 147; Cabrera de Córdoba (whom Cervantes praises in the *Parnaso* II. 27)—p. 171, n. 2; see also p. 173, n. 3.

posthumously in 1617, his theory of the novel shows in general remarkably little change. In this, as in other respects, it must be sharply differentiated from his dramatic theory. The difference in attitudes to the *comedia* expressed in *Don Quixote* I. 48 and in the prologue to the *Ocho comedias y ocho entremeses* (*Eight Plays and Eight Interludes*) (1615) does not, I believe, represent such a volte-face as it appears to do, but there was plainly a reaccommodation of views. Where his theories of poetry and prose fiction are concerned, the greatest difference is between his first novel the *Galatea* (1585) and *Don Quixote* I. For while it is perfectly clear that he was well acquainted with Aristotelian theory when he wrote the *Quixote*, no such conclusion can be drawn from the critical comments (which are much fewer) in the *Galatea*.

The task of comprehending his theory is simplified as a result. But a complication arises from the deep-rooted ambivalence which is fundamental to his writing. We shall speak of this at more length later on. It permitted him to hold contradictory or divergent principles simultaneously. More of the disparities in his views spring from this than from changes of mind. No doubt some of the inconsistencies to be found even in a single work do in fact represent changes of mind, but we must assume that if he felt strongly enough to alter his words before the book went to the press, he did so. His treatment of pastoral, sometimes respectful and affectionate, sometimes derisive, offers one of the clearest illustrations of this ambivalence. His love–hate relationship with the chivalresque novel is another. If we do not make full allowance for Cervantes's capacity for divided sympathies we shall never begin to understand his theory—or the rest of his writing either.

For a considerable part of the time between December 1569 and September 1575 Cervantes was in Italy, where the literary debates were in full swing. If this, as one would expect, was when he acquired the familiarity he shows later with Aristotelian theory, it is very odd that it should not appear in the *Galatea*. There is some important aesthetic theorizing in that novel, but the specifically literary theory—nearly all in the prologue and Book VI— recalls, not Spanish or Italian Aristotelian theory, but rather the *Arte poética* of Sánchez de Lima, with its enthusiastic, half-apologetic justification of poetry. The preoccupation with the 'truth' of the story which he shows throughout the *Quixote*, the

Persiles, and on occasion in the *Exemplary Novels*, is absent. The
only approach to it is in an observation in verse to the effect that
the substance of a true story lies in its truth and not in the mode
of its telling. He shows some slight concern with the problems of
relevance and brevity, but the amount of critical comment on the
stories in the *Galatea* and the generally detached air of critical
awareness of what he is writing are slight in comparison with
what the *Quixote* or the *Persiles* can offer.

The natural, though not inevitable, conclusion is that the
decisive event was his reading of El Pinciano's book, which
appeared in 1596. But this leaves Tasso's two major treatises out
of account. Tasso probably began the *Discorsi dell'arte poetica* in
1565, and they were first published in 1587. The rewritten and
amplified version, the *Discorsi del poema eroico*, was composed
between 1575 and 1580 and first published in 1594. If Cervantes
became familiar with the contents of the first in literary circles in
Italy, we must still inquire why its influence should not appear in
the *Galatea* but only, apparently, in subsequent novels. It is therefore more likely that he read one or both of Tasso's published
treatises later in Spain, which he could have done perfectly well.
There seems to be no way of knowing whether he read Tasso or
El Pinciano first. The *Novelas* are little help here. Only four of
them contain any statements of theory to speak of.[1] Their dates of
composition are not accurately known in most cases, and they
could have been revised at any time down to 1612—which the
evidence of the two different versions of *Rinconete y Cortadillo* and
El celoso extremeño (*The Jealous Extremaduran*) suggests is more
likely than not.

Cervantes, then, almost certainly became acquainted with the
most advanced poetics of his day during the twenty years between
the *Galatea* and *Don Quixote* I. This was just the period when the
impact of critical theory from Italy was coming to be generally
felt by Spanish writers. In the dozen years from 1605 until his
death in 1616, during which time nearly all his works were
published, it is difficult to trace any marked evolution in his
theory. However, his critical interest in problems affecting the

[1] *La gitanilla, El licenciado Vidriera, La ilustre fregona, El coloquio de los perros*. The
interpretation of the *Novelas* in *terms* of theory is another matter, but still a highly
uncertain one. The principal objections to Atkinson's thesis in 'Cervantes, El
Pinciano and the *Novelas ejemplares*' have been ably put by Amado Alonso in *NRFH*
iv (1950), 184–5.

novel shows no sign of diminishing—if anything, the reverse—
and one or two developments on a broad scale can be noted. His
concern with the nature of truth in literary fiction, which impinges
on every major aspect of his theory, evidently increases. So do his
scruples, which are a part of that concern, about the use of
rhetorical language. At the same time, in the *Coloquio de los perros*
(*The Dogs' Colloquy*) and the *Persiles* he shows an inclination to
push experimentally towards the limits of what he considers
novelistically permissible—in theoretical parlance, to explore the
domain of verisimilitude and see to what extent the exceptional
and the marvellous could be included in it.

His views on the problem of unity evidently fluctuate too. Both
his practice and the critical opinions he expresses show a stiffening
of principle in *Don Quixote* II as compared with *Don Quixote* I,
and a relaxation again in the *Persiles*. The last development I am
once more inclined to attribute to a desire to experiment, though
under the aegis of the precepts of epic.

It is a reasonable conjecture that a latent critical bent and the
wide reading of good and bad books led Cervantes to speculate on
the principles of literary fiction. If this was the case, he probably
did not advance far in the formulation of his views. Defences of
poetry like Sánchez de Lima's *Arte poética* may have helped. His
interest in critical questions seems to have been stimulated, at
some time after the publication of the *Galatea*, by reading some
Aristotelian theorist. Very probably this was El Pinciano. But if
he read the Spanish doctor's work, it is no less likely that he also
read those of a number of Italian authorities. We cannot tell
which happened first. There is not the slightest reason why
Cervantes should have come to know the work of Italian theorists
only as a young man in Italy. In the case of Tasso's *Discorsi* this is
even highly unlikely. It is tempting to see the dominant influence
of El Pinciano in *Don Quixote* I and that of Italian writers like
Tasso, who make a good deal of the importance of variety and
marvellous things in epic, in the *Persiles*; but Italian critical
influence is certainly apparent in Part I of the *Quixote* too. El
Pinciano's work could have led Cervantes to other theorists, or
other theorists have led him to El Pinciano. The former seems
the more likely course. He may well have widened his reading of
epic theory especially for the purpose of writing the *Persiles*—
a novel for which he did a good deal of reading of all kinds.

2. *Art and the Rules*

> Art is nothing else but the right reason about things to
> be made.   ST. THOMAS AQUINAS

Only in modern times has poetic theory been content with analysis. From the Hellenistic age until the romantic era it generally served a doctrinaire purpose, although it became increasingly analytical from the mid-seventeenth century. But whatever else poetry was during these many centuries, it was seen in some degree as an art that was susceptible of systematization and subject to rules.

In the Middle Ages and long after the Renaissance, the distinction between *ars* and *scientia* was extremely hazy. Poetry was traditionally called a 'science' by the Provençal poets, by fifteenth-century Spanish poets like the Marquis of Santillana, and by many other writers later, including Cervantes. There were, however, attempts to distinguish art from science, making the latter something more exact than the former. The writer of a useful little handbook of the year 1600, one Gutiérrez de los Ríos, explains that the word 'art' has a particular sense in which the 'sciences' are not included, and a general one in which they are. In matters in which art is concerned there is room for opinion; but in those arts which are sciences there can be no room for opinion or any variation, since science treats what is eternal and true.[1] Some sense of this distinction, of which Cervantes elsewhere shows himself aware,[2] is betrayed in *Don Quixote* when Don Diego de Miranda momentarily doubts whether poetry can really be called a science (II. 16); but generally speaking Cervantes does not use the words with particular discrimination. He inherited the centuries-old conception of poetry as a science, and to take him to task, as Menéndez y Pelayo did, for allowing himself to be misled by it and tyrannized over by the rules, was a surprisingly incorrect (and regrettably authoritative) statement of Cervantes's position.[3] His attitude to the rules in fact was much less simple and uncompromising than many critics, limiting their considerations

---

[1] G. Gutiérrez de los Ríos, *Noticia general para la estimación de las artes* (Madrid, 1600), pp. 9–11. See also J. L. Vives, *De tradendis disciplinis* 1, *Opera* (Basle, 1555), i. 440.
[2] *Galatea* I; i. 72.
[3] Menéndez y Pelayo, *Ideas estéticas*, ii. 269.

to *Don Quixote* I. 47–48 and a few other well-known passages, have assumed.

Deference to authority meant, in the first instance, deference to the authority of the ancients. The attitude to this in Cervantes's day is a subject too large and complex for consideration in a few words, but the most important development was the gradual encroachment of a critical spirit based on reason and a certain amount of observation, a spirit which in the late sixteenth century lived in awkward partnership with authority. 'Aristotle, our master, perpetual dictator of all good arts!' exclaimed Scaliger, who in a number of fundamental matters emphatically contradicted him.[1] Herrera, whose admirable commentary was a tissue of Quintilian, Cicero, and other authorities ancient and modern, said of the ancients:

> They were men like ourselves, whose senses and judgements are subject to deception and debility; and thus they could and did err, although this does not wipe out their excellence, for no certainty has been granted humankind in these things.[2]

As a contemporary rhetorician put it: 'Reason convinces because it is reason, and authority convinces because it is reason plus authority.'[3] Allusions to the ancients in Cervantes's writings show that he shared the general respect for them. At the same time, he could make fun of excessive or spurious deference to them. Don Quixote's cult of chivalresque authority is a gentle parody of the whole procedure.

While few theorists might be bold enough to declare with Scaliger, 'We undertake to create a poet',[4] it is certain that art was universally identified to a greater or lesser extent with the 'rules'. The rigorous Cascales in the prologue to his *Tablas* clinches the argument for the necessity of poetics with the Aristotelian reminder that poetry, being an art, depends upon precepts. And even Vives, the enemy of pedantry and pettifogging rules in rhetoric, sees art as a collection of universal precepts.

So while the customary division of Spanish critics of the Golden Age into *preceptistas* and *anti-preceptistas* holds good in a

---

[1] J. C. Scaliger, *Poetices libri septem* (ed. [Heidelberg], 1581), VII. 932.

[2] F. de Herrera, 'Contestación a Prete Jacopín', in *Controversia sobre sus anotaciones a las obras de Garcilaso de la Vega* (Seville, 1870), pp. 84–85.

[3] Juan de Guzmán, op. cit., fol. 120ᵛ.

[4] Scaliger, op. cit. II. 200.

rough and ready way, it is very imprecise. One can easily discern the extremes, but many writers—among them Cervantes—were much less clearly placed. From both sides there was some inclination towards the centre. The classically disposed El Pinciano admitted the limitations of the rules and said there were poets without poetics and that occasionally one could achieve beauty while departing from the rules of art.[1] On the other side Lope de Vega, who, among the great writers, most nearly achieved a state of unfettered romanticism and who professed to put natural genius above the rules of art, was, as is well known, by no means able to get them out of his system. An informed and competent critic, he was far more pedantic than Cervantes—as a glance at the prologue to his *Jerusalén conquistada* is sufficient to show. He implicitly identified art and the rules in his repeated admission that Spanish *comedias* did not 'follow art'. He more than once paid court to those ancient authorities whose precepts he had 'locked away six times over'.[2] And he too showed some disposition to find a middle way between the demands of art and those imposed by the vulgar audiences of his *comedias*.[3]

Spain's major contribution to European literary criticism in this period was undoubtedly an embryo romantic theory of the drama, but it is a mistake to read into it modern notions of artistic liberty, as was done by literary historians of the nineteenth century. They over-romanticized Spain's Golden Age, and the general reaction against neo-classical 'principles left behind it some tenacious misconceptions. One of these, still commonly encountered, was the notion that a preoccupation with classical literary principles was synonymous with pedantry—a notion much more applicable to the year 1800 than to 1600. The fundamental characteristic of the period known as 'baroque' was, to put it in its simplest terms, a tension between stabilizing classical and dynamic romantic forces. It was not confined to Spain: contemporary England, for example, offered a close parallel. But the phenomenon has been a constant of Spain's cultural history; at any rate, since the petrification of the national genius in the

---

[1] El Pinciano, op. cit. iii. 228, 296.

[2] Thus Lope de Vega in *Respuesta a un papel en razón de la nueva poesía*: 'pues la autoridad de Quintiliano carece de réplica'; and, referring to St. Augustine, 'pienso que su opinión, ninguno será tan atrevido que la contradiga' (*BAE* xxxviii. 138, 139).

[3] Lope de Vega, *Arte nuevo de hacer comedias en este tiempo*, ed. Morel-Fatio, *BH* iii (1901), verses 153-6.

baroque—Spain's greatest—period, Spaniards have by and large been too classical to be romantic and too romantic to be classical.

Saintsbury accurately observed that in their attitude to the rules Golden-Age writers were, for the most part, 'much rather inclined to divide their attentions, or, as the impudent old Greek definition has it, "to keep the wife for convenience and decency, the mistress for pleasure" '.[1] The tension between discipline and impulsive creativeness is very perceptible in Cervantes. It need not surprise us, therefore, that there should be in his works contradictions, ambiguities, and shifting opinions in the matter of the rules, though they are more evident where the drama is concerned than in the novel.

The claims of the rules varied from one genre to another, and the novel, as the newest of them, was the least subject to their dictates. Cervantes certainly had *preceptista* inclinations, but it is equally certain that what he emphasized in the classical precepts were really important and abiding principles of art. He passed by huge stretches of contemporary theory without comment; he never even mentioned catharsis. At the same time he took pleasure, apparently, in experimenting in regions where the jurisdiction of established rules seemed doubtful and remote. At times his critical demon seems to delight in showing up their limitations and contradictions. But for him as for everyone else art did mean rules. The novel was a form of art and so the Priest condemned chivalresque novelists because they failed to 'pay heed to any discourse of reason, art or rules by which they might have been guided and become famous prose-writers' (*DQ* I. 48).

In Italy there had been an attempt to free the *romanzo* from the poetic precepts of Aristotle and other authorities. Giraldi Cinthio declared:

I have often laughed at people who have wanted to subject the writers of *romanzi* to the laws of art prescribed by Aristotle and Horace, without considering that neither the one nor the other knew our language, or this type of composition.[2]

---

[1] G. Saintsbury, *A History of Criticism and Literary Taste in Europe* (Edinburgh, 1900–4), ii. 342.

[2] 'Io mi sono molte volte riso di alcuni, c'hanno voluto chiamare gli scrittori dei romanzi sotto le leggi dell'arte dateci da Aristotile e da Orazio, non considerando che nè questi nè quegli conobbe questa lingua, nè questa maniera di comporre' (*Dei romanzi*, pp. 44–45).

Minturno compromised, seeing the *romanzo* as defective in form
but often excellent in execution.[1] Later theorists such as Tasso
quite abandoned any idea of its immunity.[2] The novel of chivalry
was the Spanish equivalent of the *romanzo*, and there is a moment
when Cervantes seems to argue its independence on the same
grounds as Giraldi; but the note of irony, as so often, makes his
meaning uncertain. He speaks of 'the books of chivalry, which
Aristotle never thought of, of which St. Basil had nothing to say,
and of which Cicero had never heard' (*DQ* I, prol.). There even
seems to be an implicit extension of the idea to his own great
work. But if he was arguing this, the moment did not last. He did
in fact judge the novels of chivalry by Aristotelian principles—
even if he himself sometimes kicked against the pricks. In the
Quixote II. 44 he fidgets under the necessity of keeping his story
within the limits prescribed by the rule of unity and is provoked
for a moment into that splendid outburst when he says that the
author 'is confining himself closely within the narrow limits of
the action, even though he has ability, sufficiency, and wit to talk
of the whole universe'. At one point in the dramatic theorizing
in his play *El rufián dichoso*, indeed, Cervantes uses the great anti-
classicist argument that times change and that so therefore must
the rules—an argument nearly as old as the rules themselves.[3]
But he does not apply it to the novel.

For Cervantes, who ridicules all sorts of pedants, rules without
talent will not produce art. Yet he wastes little time in making
fun of the rules themselves. His targets are much more often the
incompetents who ignore the important principles of literary
creation. The poet in the hospital, described by Berganza in the
Coloquio, complains that he can find no patron to sponsor his work,
despite the fact that he has observed the injunction of Horace not
to bring it out until a decade has passed. The poet clearly knows
his Horatian rules, but Cervantes is not concerned with mocking
them (except possibly the nine-year rule); his ridicule is directed
at the conceit and lack of judgement of an obviously stupid writer.
His folly consists in the conviction that he has met the requirements of a good poem (requirements which Cervantes believes

---

[1] A. S. Minturno, *L'Arte poetica* (Venice, 1563), p. 30.

[2] Tasso, *Del poema eroico* III. 73 ff.

[3] e.g. Tacitus, *Dialogus de oratoribus*, § 19; Quintilian, *Institutio oratoria* II. xiii. 2.
Cf. J. de la Cueva, *Ejemplar poético*, Clásicos castellanos (Madrid, 1941), III, verses
523–5.

in): that he has composed a poem of which the subject is grand, the invention admirable and original, the verse grave, the episodes entertaining, the division of parts marvellous; that his poem is 'lofty, sonorous, heroic, delightful and substantial'. As the reader infers, the poem is in fact nothing of the sort. Its subject, far from being great, consists of the pseudo-heroic nonsense Cervantes most despises, written in heroic verses of ridiculous substantival proparoxytones.

Cervantes was undoubtedly aware too that there were limits to what could be systematized in poetry, for he acknowledges in the *Viaje del Parnaso* IV the 'inscrutable *je ne sais quoi*' of poetry.

Castro long ago pinpointed the following passage for its importance as a summary of Cervantes's main artistic beliefs:

for my pen has always shied away from things that smack of the impossible; those with a glimmering of possibility, which are sweet and mild and sure, explain my harmless scribbling. Never does my narrow wit open its doors indiscriminately [*a disparidad*], but those things that are concordant [*consonancia*] find them always wide open. How can an absurdity please, unless it is committed deliberately, guided by a seemly humour? For that is when falsehood satisfies: when it looks like truth and is written in a delightful way that will please both the simple and the discreet.[1]

In a comparable passage of his play *La entretenida* Cervantes describes what is concordant as the product of a discerning (*discreto*) talent, and what is incongruous (*disparidad*) as that of a foolish mind.[2]

---

[1] 'que a las cosas que tienen de imposibles
siempre mi pluma se ha mostrado esquiva;
   las que tienen vislumbre de posibles,
de dulces, de suaves y de ciertas,
explican mis borrones apacibles.
   Nunca a disparidad abre las puertas
mi corto ingenio, y hállalas contino
de par en par la consonancia abiertas.
   ¿Cómo pueda agradar un desatino,
si no es que de propósito se hace,
mostrándole el donaire su camino?
   Que entonces la mentira satisface,
cuando verdad parece, y está escrita
con gracia, que al discreto y simple aplace.' (*Parnaso* VI. 84–85)

[2] 'El discreto es concordancia
que engendra la habilidad;
el necio, disparidad
que no hace consonancia.' (*La entretenida* I, p. 27)

Concordancia or *consonancia* in Cervantes's literary theory means the harmony established in the mind of the reader by a rapport with the work. It is ruptured by the *disparatado* or incongruously absurd. So *disparate* is no heedless term of abuse, but one of the most meaningful in his critical vocabulary.[1] It frequently occurs in his criticism, and it is the keyword in the condemnation of the romances of chivalry. The core of his theory is in these two passages, and his words may be counted among the most intelligent statements in the literary theory of the age. The major requirements of credibility, harmony, and pleasing style can be seen as subservient to two greater principles, which form the backbone of his critical thought—reason and purpose. Without these there can be for him neither shape nor significance in a work of art. We shall see them running right through his critical opinions. His highest aim in the novel was one of reconciliation: to impose minority standards on majority tastes, to make romance reasonable.

His concept of *consonancia* animates his views on verisimilitude and formal unity. These two become inseparably linked because he sees defective verisimilitude (a matter of substance) as an aesthetic blemish (a matter of form). Intellectual and aesthetic satisfaction are combined, he sees, in the mind of the reader. A work of art thus becomes a complex of delicate relationships between the author, the work, and the reader. Awareness of this— for which some thanks are due to rhetoric—is one of the major contributions of the sixteenth century to literary criticism. In Cervantes's novels the awareness shows itself in his critical detachment, the realization of his power to control and manipulate his creation, and his sensitivity to the reader's reactions.

Of all the lessons that Cervantes may have learnt from El Pinciano or the Italians the most important was that the writer must be completely aware of what he is doing. It occurs in the form of an anecdote in *Don Quixote* II. 3:

'Let me say now', declared Don Quixote, 'that the author of my history was not a sage, but some ignorant chatterer who haphazardly and without any rational method set about writing it, leaving it to turn out any way it might—just like Orbaneja, the painter of Úbeda,

---

[1] 'Es lo mismo que dislate . . . cosa despropositada, la cual no se hizo o dijo con el modo debido y con cierto fin' (S. de Covarrubias, *Tesoro de la lengua castellana o española*, ed. Barcelona, 1943).

who, when asked what he was painting, replied, "Whatever it turns out to be." If he were painting a cock, it would be so ill depicted that it was necessary to write beside it in Gothic letters, "This is a cock." And so it must be with my story, which will need a commentary if it is to be understood."[1]

The anecdote must have made some impression on Cervantes, because he repeats it in chapter 71. The incompetent painter who calls it to mind there is compared with Orbaneja, who in turn is compared with Avellaneda; all three are for the same reason bad artists. The idea of purposeful creation also lies behind the irony and the semi-serious apologetics of the prologue to *Don Quixote* I. This contains much criticism of pedantic irrelevancies, and culminates in a summary of what is required if the novel is to be a good one. 'Depict what you intend', the author is told, 'as nearly as you possibly may.'

As long as the author knows what he is doing and where he is going, Cervantes concedes him a good deal of liberty. He is even allowed to perpetrate what would be outrages in other circumstances. 'How can an absurdity [*un desatino*] please, unless it is committed deliberately, guided by a seemly humour [*el donaire*]?' These words help to elucidate a claim, made earlier in the same poem, that in his *Novelas* he had opened a way whereby the Castilian language might depict an absurdity (*un desatino*) appositely (*con propiedad*).[2] The general idea behind the passages is clear, but the terminology offers certain difficulties. *Desatino*, according to Covarrubias's dictionary of 1611, is a *desconcierto* or something done without discourse of reason and consideration. This, it seems, Cervantes allows when it is in fact committed deliberately, and in the manner indicated by the word *donaire* in the first passage, or *propiedad* in the second. *Donaire* commonly signifies a jest; it can also be used for a pleasing and seemly stylistic quality. Either sense is possible and Cervantes may well

---

[1] '— Ahora digo — dijo don Quijote — que no ha sido sabio el autor de mi historia, sino algún ignorante hablador, que a tiento y sin algún discurso se puso a escribirla, salga lo que saliere, como hacía Orbaneja, el pintor de Úbeda, al cual preguntándole qué pintaba, respondió : "Lo que saliere." Tal vez pintaba un gallo, de tal suerte y tan mal parecido, que era menester que con letras góticas escribiese junto a él: "Este es gallo." Y así debe de ser de mi historia, que tendrá necesidad de comento para entenderla' (*DQ* II. 3; iv. 92–93).

[2]   'Yo he abierto en mis *Novelas* un camino,
              por do la lengua castellana puede
              mostrar con propiedad un desatino.' (*Parnaso* IV. 55)

have combined them. *Propiedad* may be translated 'appositeness', or 'decency' in the sense that English theorists like Puttenham used the word. It was a term often associated with decorum, and it presupposes an appeal to the judgement. The full idea then seems to be that only an artist's rational purpose, realized in a pleasant and apposite or humorous manner, can make a discordant absurdity agreeable, and therefore artistically acceptable. Some form of artistic error is certainly meant in the first of the two passages, and most probably in the second, referring to the *Novelas ejemplares*, although certain critics have read them differently. In the second, the *desatino* Cervantes is most likely to have in mind is the fantastic phenomenon of talking dogs in the *Coloquio*, something for which he takes great pains to provide possible explanations.

This distinction between the calculated and the uncalculated absurdity is one of the most important in Cervantes's literary theory. It derives originally (probably via Aquinas) from the dictum in Aristotle's *Nicomachean Ethics* that 'in art voluntary error is not so bad as involuntary'.[1] But, unless Cervantes arrived at it independently, the most likely immediate source is a passing remark of Carvallo's: 'Diligent contrivance [*industria*] often excuses what would otherwise be an error.'[2]

Ortega y Gasset put his finger on the great weakness of the novel of chivalry when he observed that, unlike its progenitor epic, it betrayed a lack of belief in the reality of what it related.[3] If this is true of *Amadís de Gaula*, it is even more so of a *Don Belianís de Grecia* or a *Don Olivante de Laura*. One of the most disconcerting things about the romances is indeed their authors' inability either to treat them as pure fiction or to sustain the illusion that they were fact. The flagrant confusion of history and fiction, the declarations that the stories were literally true and the devices used to enhance this pretence, the affirmations of the edifying nature of their works: all this might have been justified by some clear purpose. But it is lacking. The authors' outrageous remarks about their stories, and their handling of them, often show the

---

[1] Aristotle, *Nicomachean Ethics*, trans. Rackham, Loeb Classical Library, VI. v. 7. See Margaret Bates, 'Cervantes' criticism of *Tirant lo Blanch*', *HR* xxi (1953), 142.
[2] '. . . la industria excusa muchas faltas que sin ella lo serían' (op. cit., fol. 171ᵛ).
[3] J. Ortega y Gasset, *Meditaciones del 'Quijote'* (ed. Madrid, 1957), p. 163.

oddest mixture of ingenuousness and irony—a sort of half-conviction symptomatic of the degeneracy of the genre. It is difficult to interpret some of their preposterous claims (we shall record a few in Chapter V) as anything but bungled irony—quite unlike the clear sharp irony of Lucian or of Rabelais with his 'tant véritables contes'. When one also takes into account the many burlesque names ('Pintiquiniestra', 'Contumeliano de Fenicia', 'Cataquefarás', 'Quirieleisón') and the self-criticism in the first of the *Amadis* sequels, *Las sergas de Esplandián*,[1] it becomes clear that this is a half-hearted self-mockery and a crude pre-Cervantine irony. The floundering authors hardly seem to know their own sentiments or what effect they are producing. Here, in fact, are some of the purposeless *desatinos* or *disparates* that so irritated the author of the *Quixote*.

His impatience with their ambiguities I think owes a good deal to his having learnt the lesson that his predecessors had not. The author of *Don Quixote*, it will be remembered, is also the author of *La casa de los celos*. This very bad early play is paralysed by his ambiguous treatment of both the chivalresque and pastoral; he does not seem to know how far he is ridiculing them and how far he is not, or how to harmonize the two attitudes. With *Don Quixote* he learnt how to turn uncertainty into irony, and irony into a powerful tool for the novelist.

It is in the light of the principle that the purposeful absurdity alone is permissible that the paradoxical judgement on *Tirante el Blanco*[2] must be read. This used to be considered 'the most obscure passage in the *Quixote*' and has accumulated a large critical bibliography. Since the observations of Sanvisenti were followed up by a number of other critics (though certainly not all of them), there can no longer be any reasonable doubt of its interpretation.[3] In

---

[1] Garci Rodríguez (or Ordóñez) de Montalvo, *Las sergas de Esplandián*, *BAE* xl, chs. 98, 99.

[2] Johannot Martorell, *Tirant lo Blanch*—completed by Martí Johan de Galba (Valencia, 1490). Cervantes probably knew the inaccurate Castilian translation of Valladolid, 1511. My references are to the Castilian version in *Libros de caballerías españoles*, ed. F. Buendía (Madrid, 1954).

[3] See B. Sanvisenti, 'Il passo più oscuro del *Chisciotte*', *RFE* ix (1922); he did not quote the supporting tercet from the *Parnaso*. Schevill and Bonilla were the first to do so, in their edition of the *Quixote* (Madrid, 1928–41), i, note on the passage in I. 6; but they missed the point. Of the critics who have furthered the elucidation, F. Maldonado de Guevara has made the most exhaustive inquiry into the implications of the passage, in 'El dolo como potencia estética', *ACerv* i (1951).

the scrutiny of Don Quixote's library the Priest begins by warmly praising the novel:

Give it here, my friend; for I recall that I have found in it a treasure of contentment and a mine of recreation. Here we have the valiant knight Don Quirieleisón de Montalbán and his brother Tomás de Montalbán and the knight Fonseca, with the battle that brave Tirante fought with the wolfhound; the witticisms of the damsel Placerdemivida, and the frauds and amours of Widow Reposada; and my lady the Empress, who was in love with Hipólito, [Tirante's] squire. I tell you honestly, my dear fellow, that in its style this is the best book in the world. Here knights eat and sleep and die in their beds and make their wills before dying, and other things quite unknown to all the rest of the books of this kind. (*DQ* I. 6)

Then, strangely, he condemns the author:

For all that, I tell you that the man who composed it deserved to be sent to the galleys for the rest of his life, because he did not perpetrate all those absurdities in a calculated manner [*de industria*].[1]

In the light of the dictum in the *Parnaso* the paradox becomes perfectly clear. The book is commended for its undeniable high qualities (its unusual lack of extravagance, its humour, and lively characters); but the author is severely judged for wanting clarity of purpose. *De industria* implies more effort, ingenuity, and contrivance than the phrase *de propósito* used in the *Parnaso*. Carvallo's observation on the calculated error springs to mind.

A reading of the book reveals clearly enough what Cervantes meant. *Tirante el Blanco* must be one of the most disconcertingly ambiguous novels of chivalry ever written. The hero (perhaps the most realistic of all chivalresque heroes), an outstanding general and a gallant lover, is involved, at the court of Constantinople, in a protracted bedroom farce that is very funny, but also egregiously indecent. In terms of classical literary theory, this is a violent and—what really matters to Cervantes—an uncalculated breach of decorum. Even the modern reader must regard it as more than a combination of the comic and the serious: it is a confusion of literary attitudes. How can one continue to take Tirante seriously, as one is clearly meant to do, after he has been

---

[1] 'Con todo eso, os digo que merecía el que lo compuso, pues no hizo tantas necedades de industria, que le echaran a galeras por todos los días de su vida' (*DQ* I. 6; i. 206).

bundled under the bedclothes, sat on by the Princess Carmesina, and narrowly escaped being sat on by the Empress? How could anyone in the Counter-Reformation take this lascivious hero for the paragon of virtues the author obviously intended? The other characters are no better either. The peerless princess is a flirt. Placerdemivida, who later becomes a queen and is described by Tirante as a lady of consummate discretion and blameless life, acts as a shameless Celestina. The elderly Empress gladly allows herself to be thrown to the floor and enjoyed by the squire Hipólito, and the two of them are too busy to weep for the recently deceased Tirante, Carmesina, and Emperor when they have the chance of a night in bed together. There is good reason for interpreting the word 'absurdities' in this context in *Don Quixote* as 'obscenities'.

But apart from this, Cervantes must have judged such improprieties as artistic blots. Consider, as a last example, this incident, in which there is no question of indecency. The Countess of Warwick is lamenting the imminent departure of her husband. To supplement her own show of grief, she drags her infant son to her by the hair, boxes his ears, and exclaims, 'Child, weep for the dolorous departure of your father and keep your grieving mother company!' The child, understandably enough, begins to cry, and presently the Earl, his wife, and all the duennas and ladies of the court are howling in sympathy.[1] The novel is full of good things; it marks a significant stage in the history of prose fiction; and it deserves consideration as a forerunner of the *Quixote* itself. Its vivid detailed writing remarkably anticipates the realism of the modern novel in many ways. But the fumbling comic irony is at variance with the otherwise serious and elevated tone of the book. Martorell's ambiguity has induced some modern critics to take *Tirante* as a parody and others as a fundamentally serious work. Each view is just half-right. It is a testimony to the critical perceptiveness of Cervantes, and the mark of the difference between the two writers, that he condemned his predecessor for not knowing clearly what he was doing—in a passage that is itself a piece of mischievous and, we may surely suspect, calculated ambiguity.

Cervantes emerges neither as a rigorous *preceptista* nor as an iconoclastic innovator. Not even in the drama, I believe, does his

[1] Martorell, op. cit., p. 1064.

literary theory rest fundamentally on the argument that 'times change' and so must the rules of art. He belongs, rather, with those for whom art has certain universal and immutable principles together with accidental conditions, which alone are subject to change. In this he resembles Tasso, who, unlike him, expressed his views systematically, and said:

art, being constant and fixed, cannot include within its rules that which depends on the instability of custom, and is changeable and uncertain.[1]

The objections of Cervantes to the novels of chivalry above all show his insistence on rational purpose and artistic awareness. Reason in any case could not be divorced from the conception of art, as contemporary definitions make quite clear.[2] He was a writer of fiction and so not concerned with the codification of every nicety, at which no doubt his sharp critical sense, which was quite capable of turning on itself, would have rebelled. His principles of art express the critical and classical side of his mind, which should not be underrated just because he was a writer with a great and sometimes sprawling imagination. We must now say something about this two-sided temper of his.

3. The Author-Critic

> Not every critic is a genius, but every genius is a born critic.　　　　　　　　　　　　　　LESSING

The legend of Cervantes as the careless, smiling genius has been generally supplanted by a better appreciation of his reflective and critical capacities. Indeed the danger nowadays is of over-endowing him with scrupulous percipience. Cervantes is not Calderón, or Corneille; but he is a writer in whom a great fund of invention is accompanied by a strong critical instinct. Madariaga and others have shown how fundamental this dualism of creator and critic

---

[1] Tasso, *Del poema eroico* III. 77.
[2] León Hebreo: 'La arte es el hábito de las cosas factibles, según la razón' (*Diálogos de amor*, Austral, Buenos Aires, 1947, p. 41); El Pinciano: 'Arte es hábito de efectuar con razón verdadera' (op. cit. i. 76).

is to his writing.[1] In a study of his novelistic theory we must necessarily dwell on the second faculty, but we can no more keep his imaginative writing distinct from his criticism than he was able to keep his criticism out of his works of fiction. He is not alone among Golden-Age writers in showing this temperamental dualism: it is evident in Lope de Vega, for instance, though the effects are quite different in his case. In Cervantes the union is particularly strong. Without it *Don Quixote* could not have been written.

His literary theories and judicial criticism appear in his books in various conventional and unconventional forms. They occur outside the work proper, in prologues and dedications. They figure directly and in allegorical form in the *Viaje del Parnaso* and its *Adjunta*, and in the earlier *Canto de Calíope* in the *Galatea*. They are expressed in comments made by the author (or pseudo-author) within the work, and in comments, arguments, and dissertations by his characters. Finally, they appear integrated with the fiction itself. Like Aristophanes, but on a grander scale and in a more complex manner, Cervantes uses literary criticism as part of the substance of a work of entertainment.

The first prologue to *Don Quixote* offers a simple illustration of his technique in this respect. Cervantes there depicts himself in the usual writer's posture, the paper in front of him, his pen on his ear, his elbow on the desk, resting his cheek on his hand, wondering what to say. A friend, who is a 'humorous and intelligent' fellow, and probably none other than Cervantes's critical self, comes in and offers his advice. His arguments so impress the author that he decides to make his prologue out of them. Instead of writing a neat critical essay or jotting down his random reflections, Cervantes concocts a scene in which the author's preoccupations and problems are discussed. The significant fact about this prologue, however, is not that he has presented critical matters in the form of an animated dialogue, which was common enough, but that his starting-point is to visualize himself thinking about them. The characteristic and original art of Cervantes begins with an act of detachment from himself and his work.

The dualism of creator-critic takes other forms and has other

[1] S. de Madariaga, *Don Quixote: An Introductory Essay in Psychology* (Oxford, 1935), chs. 1 and 2.

effects. Often these different faculties do not come to terms at all, as happens to some extent in the *Persiles*. Sometimes, when a particular judgement or conclusion is to be expected, Cervantes will not or cannot commit himself. He makes good capital out of his abstentions, but his ambiguities and evasions are frequently the result of uncertainty. In a few of the literary problems that most absorb him, like that of making the idealized hero or heroine human and credible, he wants to have things both ways. A favourite means of dodging the issue of credibility is to plant it squarely before one, make his characters discuss it, and then, having lulled the inattentive reader into thinking it has been dealt with, to pass on, leaving it exactly as it was. He has thus introduced into his story something about which he evidently has artistic scruples and, by implicitly criticizing its admission, glossed over a possible impropriety. The trick was well known in rhetoric even in Aristotle's day:

The corrective for every excess is the notorious one—to censure oneself at the same time: the thing seems to be true, since at all events the speaker knows what he is doing.[1]

Cervantes repeatedly takes the precaution of disarming possible criticism by being the first to criticize himself. He will put into the mouths of his characters an excuse or apology that would be far less acceptable if it came from him. Or one person will rebuke another for something that is ultimately the author's responsibility. These are two ways in which he commonly anticipates criticism for irrelevance or prolixity. Comments of approval, on the other hand, can be used to fabricate a favourable, if fictitious, audience-reaction. Even fictitious applause for one of his own stories helps to enhance it in the eyes of the reader. Half-humorously he advertises his own wares. In *Don Quixote* he goes so far as to construct a complete alibi, and remains at a safe distance while responsibility for the whole book is borne by Cide Hamete Benengeli. Of course, none of these devices can possibly deceive the reader. When used with discretion, however, they do win his sympathy, or at least his tolerance. Cervantes's ambiguity in these equivocal procedures, even when he is covering up a real doubt, is unlike that of the romancers he condemned. Rarely

---

[1] Aristotle, *Rhetoric*, trans. Jebb (ed. Cambridge, 1909), III. vii. 8-9.

are his mystifications not deliberate. They are subterfuges artfully employed.

One of the difficulties of determining his literary opinions with any exactness is that a large proportion of the views that appear in his works are not expressed by himself, but by his characters. With Cervantes above all writers, we must be careful about imputing to the author the opinions of his invented personages. On the other hand, there is no need to go to the extreme of discounting all those opinions that are not expressed directly as his own. There are some reliable guides. Sometimes the views of his characters coincide with those he expresses personally elsewhere. Again, when a number of sensible characters in different works take the same line in a matter, we can reasonably presume it is the author's own. Moreover, he does not often fail to give some indication of the general standard of a character's integrity or intelligence, which is some help in estimating the value to be attached to the opinion.

In so far as he has anything that can be called a critical method in his novels, it resembles that of the dialogue. The *Coloquio de los perros*, where Berganza narrates and Cipión makes critical comments, is the logical outcome of Cervantes's own capacity for simultaneous invention and self-criticism. Though the method itself is conducive to inconclusiveness, the usefulness of approaching such a subject as the chivalresque romances from numerous points of view is considerable. Even Don Quixote is able to show up the limitations of some of the arguments the Canon of Toledo uses against them.

The Canon and the Priest are the foremost spokesmen in the *Quixote*. Don Quixote himself is important when he can be relied on; so is Sansón Carrasco. The Canon's views are rather more liberal than the Priest's. The close correspondence between those of the Canon in I. 47 and Cervantes's own is shown by the evidence of the *Persiles*. The Priest, I think, generally speaks with the voice of the author's strictest critical conscience. At the same time we must allow for his speaking in character—as the local ecclesiastic in Don Quixote's immediate entourage. This is not to suggest that his views are not enlightened. They are.

Even when we can feel tolerably sure of having disposed of this sort of difficulty, the ambiguity in Cervantes's own opinions often remains. The notorious judgement on *Tirante el Blanco*, sparing the book and condemning the author, was one example. The ironic treatment of Antonio de Lofraso's *Diez libros de fortuna de amor* (Barcelona, 1573) is another.

'By the holy orders I have received,' said the Priest, 'since Apollo was Apollo, and the Muses were Muses, and poets were poets, no book so droll and absurd as this has ever been written. In its way, it is unique and the best of those of its kind that have seen the light of day; and he who has not read it cannot say that he has ever read anything really enjoyable.' (*DQ* I. 6)

By the standards of the Priest or Cervantes the book is undoubtedly a bad one, yet the Priest puts it to one side with every sign of pleasure and does not send it to the bonfire. For although absurd (*disparatado*), it is droll (*gracioso*) and 'in its way' the best of its kind in the world. The miserable author is treated with just the same mixture of affection and contempt in the *Viaje del Parnaso* III. He narrowly escapes being thrown overboard to placate Scylla and Charybdis. Mercury intervenes just in time, saying it would be a serious matter of conscience to jettison 'so much poetry'. But he bullies him in his turn, and confusingly describes him as subtle and sincere and a poor, lying, ignorant fellow. Lofraso's view of the Muses, when the ship's company sights Parnassus, is significantly grotesque: he spies five of them on foot and the remainder on all fours. Finally, in the battle of Parnassus, he turns out to have been conscripted on the wrong side, being really one of the enemy (VII).

In literary terms, Lofraso possesses talents he never learnt how to use. Cervantes, I think, regards his book with the same sort of pleasurable amusement that modern admirers of Mrs. Amanda M. Ros feel for her novels. Like her, he gave pleasure in not quite the way that was intended—

Long live Lofraso, as long as Apollo lights the day, and as long as men have a discreet and sprightly fantasy! (*Parnaso* III)

It is Cervantes's own 'discreet and sprightly fantasy', intervening in the application of his principles of art, that so often results in these ambivalent attitudes and divided judgements.

But he had a way of reconciling opposites, and even incompatibles. (Lope was far more inclined than he to let his thought fly to pieces, following its disparate directions.) To some extent the author of the *Quixote* pursued that golden mean everyone has recognized in his works, but he also tried to bind these opposites together in an artistic whole, 'weaving of contraries one fabric' (to borrow a line from his beautiful sonnet in the *Galatea*).[1] This use of antithesis is fundamental not only to his style but to the whole technique of construction in *Don Quixote*. In stylistic matters he had perhaps more latitude, but for opinions and judgements, not to say *Weltanschauung*, he needed a binding agent. He found it in irony.

By this I mean what is unhelpfully called 'romantic irony'. We can use Wellek's definition of the term as employed by Friedrich Schlegel (who so admired *Don Quixote*), since it is applicable in all its breadth to Cervantes:

> Irony is his recognition of the fact that the world in its essence is paradoxical and that an ambivalent attitude alone can grasp its contradictory totality. For Schlegel irony is the struggle between the absolute and the relative, the simultaneous consciousness of the impossibility and the necessity of a complete account of reality. The writer must thus feel ambivalent toward his work: he stands above and apart from it and manipulates it almost playfully.[2]

Detaching himself from what he writes, Cervantes puts mutually contradictory ideas together; neither affirming nor denying, he chooses both and chooses neither. This makes sympathy and criticism possible simultaneously. And because the irony is all-embracing it includes the author within its range. Cervantes discovered in irony the novelist's most valuable tool. As a purely critical instrument it is of limited usefulness, for the questions are left unanswered. But its very undecidedness has one important consequence: it clears the way for another, and newer, sort of criticism. The multiplicity of possible perspectives makes a fresh and complex view of things possible, a view more nearly in the round. It does not pinpoint the truth of the matter, but circumscribes the operative area. Irony allows Cervantes to criticize while he writes, and to present different points of view with considerable impartiality. Its chief importance is artistic, however; he is not an innovator in critical method so much as in his use of irony as a novelistic technique.[3]

---

[1] *Galatea* V; ii. 110.
[2] R. Wellek, *A History of Modern Criticism* (London, 1955), ii. 14.
[3] Cervantes's irony is more acknowledged than studied. But there are important

He keeps up what is almost a running commentary on his own fiction in *Don Quixote*. Criticism is repeatedly suggested, when not made outright. For example, the responsibility for perhaps boring people with a lengthy dissertation on the mythical Golden Age is placed on Don Quixote. Not only Cervantes but even Benengeli stands clear, describing the long harangue as something 'that might well have been done without' (I. 11).

The irony that he uses so successfully in the *Quixote*, however, is apt to be a disconcerting intrusion in the *Persiles*, which stands in relation to the earlier novel rather as Flaubert's *Salammbô* does to *Madame Bovary*. His criticism here is at times too sharp for the fragile texture of the imaginative illusion. It takes one of its more successful forms in the malicious commentary of the short-lived, evil-speaking Clodio; for although he has a knack of fastening on unpleasant truths, he can still be dismissed as a bad character. His comments on the persons with whom he is implicated are not 'literary' criticism from his point of view, but from the reader's they amount to as much. He ridicules the folly of Arnaldo's pursuit of Auristela. He casts doubt on the alleged brother-sister relationship of the hero and heroine, adding that even if it is true he cannot approve of this 'fraternity' wandering together over land and sea, through deserts and fields and inns and taverns. How do they imagine they will get small change for the priceless jewels they use as currency? Do they think they will always find kings and princes to entertain them? What of Transila and her astrologer father? What tales will the 'barbarian' not tell when he returns! Characteristically, Cervantes retracts the last implied criticism, anxious as he is to make these astonishing tales acceptable to the reader (II. 5).

Cervantes was first and foremost a critic of himself. No one knew better than he, for instance, that his natural inclination to poetry was not equalled by the ability to write it. Nor was he such a bad critic of the works of others as is still sometimes suggested. The pages of indiscriminate praise lavished on poets of the most unequal merit in the *Canto de Calíope* and the *Viaje del Parnaso* have nothing to do with criticism. They are celebration, not critical assessments. Panegyric, abuse, and personal considerations continually interfere with criticism in the Golden Age. When

observations in A. Castro's 'Los prólogos del *Quijote*', *Hacia Cervantes*, and in A. del Río's 'El equívoco del *Quijote*', *HR* xxvii (1959).

Cervantes was uninfluenced by these, as in his pronouncements on the chivalresque novels, he made judgements that were generally sound and sometimes shrewd.

What was particularly needed for the growth of literary 'self-consciousness' as we find it in Cervantes's novels was for writers to make their characters detach themselves from, and comment on, stories or verses included in the same book. This is a feature of the Italian *novelle* and their Spanish imitations. To a certain extent it therefore derives from Boccaccio's use of a 'framework' for his tales. Between the stories and the reader Boccaccio interposes a fictitious audience, and, though very briefly, he nearly always remarks the audience's reactions. Straparola, Parabosco, Lucas Hidalgo, and Eslava, to mention only a few of his Italian and Spanish imitators, do this too, with more or less elaboration. The same sometimes occurs in long novels where stories are woven in with the main narrative or where part of this is narrated by one of the characters. It is especially a feature of pastoral novels, where the shepherds and nymphs applaud each other's songs and stories. In Sannazaro's *Arcadia*, for example, Galicio's song pleases everyone 'in different ways', which are specified and testify to a certain artistic discrimination.[1] And in the augmented edition of Montemayor's *Diana* the wise Felicia and all the company compliment the beauteous Felismena on the 'grace and well-chosen words' with which she has told the tale of Abindarráez.[2]

Renaissance pastoral had a good deal to contribute to the growth of literary self-consciousness. This was a consequence of its very nature, which was essentially lyrical. Because it was lyrical, author and reader enjoyed a communion of emotions with the characters; and so, where the pastoral novel was concerned, they could participate much more intimately in the work than was usual in ordinary prose fiction. Thus the world of pastoral fiction, so incomprehensibly unreal to the modern mind, was probably that into which the educated sixteenth-century reader entered most easily. But not only were emotions shared; the author attributed to his

[1] 'Alcuni lodarono la giovenil voce piena di armonia inestimabile; altri il modo suavissimo e dolce, atto ad irretire qualunque animo stato fusse più ad amore ribello; molti comendarono le rime leggiadre, e tra rustici pastori non usitate; e di quelli ancora vi furono, che con più ammirazione estolsero la acutissima sagacità del suo avvedimento' (J. Sannazaro, *Arcadia*, ed. Turin, 1948, p. 29).

[2] J. de Montemayor, *Los siete libros de la Diana*, Clás. cast. (Madrid, 1946), p. 221, note.

characters critical standards and an artistic sensibility which he could rely on being shared by his cultivated readers or audience. A certain critical attitude was inherent in pastoral: the idea of shepherds *competing* in song was older than Virgil. In the Renaissance, pastoral characters (so readily identified with persons outside the fiction) intervened between author and public by assuming, with their songs and stories, the roles of artist and audience. It is true that these disguised courtiers indulged in more complimentary courtesies than real criticism, but the injection of what was at least a critical awareness into prose fiction had a stimulating effect on the early development of the modern novel.

It is consequently not too surprising to find in these authors an occasional, if often tacit, acknowledgement of the unreality of their fiction.[1] A sporadic note of irony, even, can be heard in Spanish pastoral—a note much more subtle and better controlled than in the novel of chivalry. When the beautiful Selvagia in the *Diana* sheds tears, all the others join in, this 'being an occupation in which they were highly experienced'.[2] In Cervantes's own *Galatea* VI, where his customary amused detachment and ironic criticism are conspicuously slight, the shepherds and their ladies turn to parlour games as a new diversion and so as 'not to weary their ears listening eternally to lamentations and doleful songs of love'. In Gálvez de Montalvo's *Pastor de Fílida*[3] there is unabashed ridicule of the genre, and we are already on the road to Sorel's *Berger extravagant*.

There is good reason to believe, as Castro has maintained, that Cervantes learnt much about novelistic technique from pastoral. Writing his own *Galatea* was no doubt a fruitful experience. Not least, it would have instructed him in that innocent complicity of writer, reader, and characters which he exploits to the utmost in *Don Quixote*. The critical awareness of his characters there is a projection of his own. And this in its turn is part of an ironic detachment that not only permits him to manipulate his creation in an extraordinary fashion, but has major artistic consequences.

---

[1] This is the implication of the phrase 'rime leggiadre . . . tra rustici pastori non usitate', in p. 33, n. 1, for instance.

[2] Montemayor, op. cit., p. 59.

[3] L. Gálvez de Montalvo, *El pastor de Fílida*. Cf., for example, the verses on p. 146 of the edition of Madrid, 1589.

4. *Literature and Life in* Don Quixote

The true hero is a poet, whether he knows it or not; for
what is heroism if not poetry?   UNAMUNO

The interaction of literature and life is a fundamental theme of
Don Quixote.[1] The subject is not literary theory itself (no one
would be so foolish as to suggest that *Don Quixote* was a sort of
dramatized treatise), but it is useful to approach it from the standpoint of Cervantes's novelistic theory, with which it is firmly
connected. This may throw more light not only on the theory,
but on the motivation and methods of the author in what looks
at times like a waggish, bewildering, and complicated game or a
protracted private joke. We must confine ourselves to the literary
and artistic aspects of matters susceptible of unlimited philosophical extension. The epistemological questions which the
Quixote poses are also literary problems of professional interest to
Cervantes as a novelist.

There is a basic preoccupation with literary fiction in the expressed purpose of the book and in the most elemental conception
of the hero. However far the author transcended his purpose, his
declared aim was to debunk the novels of chivalry. Whatever else
the hero may be, he is, quite simply, a man who cannot distinguish
between life and literary fiction:

everything that our adventurer thought, saw or imagined seemed to
him to be done and to happen in the manner of the things he had
read. (I. 2)

The discussion of history (matters of fact) and poetry (fiction) in
II. 3, as Toffanin first showed, springs therefore, like other such
passages, from the very heart of the novel.[2]

The critique of the novels of chivalry is made in two ways: by
more or less direct judgements within the fiction, and also *as* the

---

[1] Ortega first saw its importance, op. cit., 'Meditación primera'. See also: A. Castro,
'Cervantes y Pirandello', *La Nación* (Buenos Aires, 16 Nov. 1924), *Pensamiento,*
pp. 30 ff., and many observations in his later essays in *Hacia Cervantes*; J. Casalduero,
Sentido y forma del 'Quijote' (Madrid, 1949), *passim*; Leo Spitzer, 'Perspectivismo
lingüístico en el *Quijote*', *Lingüística e historia literaria* (Madrid, 1955); M. I. Gerhardt's
substantial critical study, '*Don Quijote': la vie et les livres* (Amsterdam, 1955); R. L.
Predmore, *El mundo del 'Quijote'* (Madrid, 1958), ch. 1; and Harry Levin's perceptive
essay, 'The Example of Cervantes', *Contexts of Criticism* (London, 1957).

[2] Toffanin, *Fine dell' umanesimo*, ch. 15.

fiction. Criticism in fictional form is conventionally parody, and
to some extent the *Quixote* is parody, but it is unusual in containing the object of the parody within itself, as a vital ingredient. The
novels of chivalry exist in the book in just the same way as
Rocinante or the barber's basin. They are so palpably present that
some of them can be burnt. Cervantes's originality lies not in
parodying them himself (or only incidentally), but in making the
mad Knight parody them involuntarily in his efforts to bring
them, by means of imitation, literally to life.

A more essential characteristic of Don Quixote's delusions than
the fact that they have to do with chivalry is their bookish, fabulous
nature. The golden age of chivalry that he wanted to resurrect
had little to do with the real Middle Ages; it was an age that never
was, the imaginary storybook age of 'Once upon a time'. History
only inspired him when it merged distantly with fiction as legend.
Byron's foolish remark that Cervantes 'smiled Spain's chivalry
away' is a confusion of history and literature not far removed from
that of the mad Knight himself. Quixote's Utopian and messianic
ideals may have proved more important in the end, but it was
fabulous romance, Cervantes tells us in the first chapter, that
originally captivated his fancy:

His imagination became filled with everything he had read in his
books, with enchantments, affrays, battles, challenges, wounds,
gallantries, amours, torments and impossible extravagances [*disparates
imposibles*]. (I. 1)

In 1752 Mrs. Lennox published her *Female Quixote* about a lady
whose head had been turned by heroic romances, and a modern
Cervantes could as easily create a twentieth-century Quixote
obsessed, say, with science fiction. Don Quixote the reader of
popular romances is the grandfather of Emma Bovary and Joyce's
Gertie McDowell. What distinguishes him from them is an
obsession with the most impossibly fabulous form of fiction that
could be imagined.

His imitation of the heroes of chivalresque novels aims at such
completeness that it becomes an attempt to live literature. He is
not inspired to a vague sort of emulation, nor does he merely
ape the habits, manners, and dress of knights errant; he does
not simply adapt chivalresque ideals to some other cause, like
St. Ignatius Loyola; he is not even acting a part, in the usual sense.

He is content with nothing less than that the whole of the fabulous world—knights, princesses, magicians, giants and all—should be part of his experience. Once he believes he really is a knight errant, and believes in his world of fiction, he steps off the pinnacle of inspired idealistic emulation into madness. He cannot play his part as he would like except in this fabulous world. In this sense he is trying to live literature.

His choice of literature is a debased and supremely fictitious form of epic; he its idealized and superhuman hero. He has epic aspirations to honour and glory through hardship and danger, the chivalric ideal of service and the hero's urge to shape the world to his pattern. He goes farther than that: in effect he is trying to cast off his earthly, historical existence and live in the rarefied region of poetry. (Since Cervantes's story of this endeavour is itself a poetic fiction—since what is 'life' in the story is a literary creation by Cervantes—we begin to see some of the complications of the novel.) Don Quixote is trying to turn life into art while it is yet being lived, which cannot be done because art, and idealistic art more than any, means selection, and it is impossible to select every scrap of one's experience. Life is one thing and art is another, but just what the difference is was the problem that baffled and fascinated Cervantes. If the Knight is like the wise man of Epicurus who would rather 'live poems' than write them, his efforts to do this literally are madness. Unamuno identified poetry and heroism in a wide sense, but they cannot be literally identical, if words mean anything at all.

Now the obvious and practicable way for Don Quixote to imitate the books of chivalry would have been through a recognized artistic medium—to have written romances himself, for instance. In fact, he was initially tempted to do so. He many times felt the urge to complete the unfinished novel *Don Belianís de Grecia* and would undoubtedly have done so, and very well too, 'if other and continual thoughts of greater moment had not prevented him' (I. 1). The books had too strong a hold on him. He was impelled to take up not the pen but the sword.

Don Quixote is, among a great many other things, an artist in his own peculiar way. His medium is action and, secondarily, words. Consciously living a book and acting for a sage enchanter to record, he is in a sense the author of his own biography. Even when he has abandoned the idea of conventional literary expression he retains many of the writer's characteristics. He composes verse on occasion. He imitates the archaic language of the novels of chivalry. At the start of his venture he anticipates his chronicler by putting the scene of his departure into verbal form—ornate, elevated language which makes a magnificent ironic contrast with the style used by the real author. His fantasies in I. 21 and I. 50 and his description of the battle of the flocks are brilliant pastiches, scarcely more absurd than the sort of writing that inspired them. He is repeatedly stimulated by literature. Cardenio's verses found in the Sierra Morena immediately induce in him thoughts of imitation; Cardenio's reference to *Amadis* occasions his disastrous interruption; the dramatized ballad of Gaiferos and Melisendra provokes him to violence.

His artistic instinct does not desert him in action, though it seldom has a chance to operate fruitfully. He takes much trouble over his preparations. Like a well-instructed writer he thinks long before he chooses names.[1] When conditions are particularly favourable, as on the occasion of the penance in the Sierra Morena, he is most attentive to detail and concerned with effect. This is art in action, if it is also madness. But the idea of bringing art into the business of living was not foreign to Cervantes's contemporaries. The lesson of Castiglione's much-read work was that the life of the perfect courtier should be a veritable work of art. It is perhaps not too fanciful to see the urge to render art in action, which may lie among the motive forces of heroism itself, as one of the distinguishing marks of the Spanish genius. It is realized in two of the most individual forms of Spanish art: the dance and the bullfight, where stylization combines with improvisation and author with actor. In the same way Don Quixote must improvise to meet the situations life offers him, without departing from the conventions laid down by his chivalresque models; and he creates, in part at least, the story of which he is the hero. The difference is that life is long and a dance is short and the world is not contained in a bullring. But the impulse which prompts the Knight to shape his life into an epic and that which puts beauty into the dancer's and the matador's every movement is the same.

[1] M. T. Herrick, 'Comic Theory in the Sixteenth Century', *UISLL* xxxiv (1950), 63, observes that Donatus, Servius, Robortelli, and Castelvetro all attached importance to the choice of appropriate names in the writing of comedy.

Unfortunately he is a bad and a frustrated artist. He over-estimates his capacities and underestimates the peculiarly intractable nature of his material, which is life itself. He executes a comic parody. But in so far as he is an artist, certain artistic principles may up to a point be applied to his behaviour. Let me say at once that I have not the least idea whether they were in Cervantes's conscious mind in this strange connexion. Probably not; but it is the privilege of books like the *Quixote* to contain far more than the author could ever have been aware of putting in. He was certainly much concerned with those principles on other occasions. Where literary fiction and 'real' experience are so curiously combined it need not surprise us to find unusual applications of literary theory. We shall note them later when they occur.

The *Quixote* is a novel of multiple perspectives. Cervantes observes the world he creates from the viewpoints of characters and reader as well as author. It is as though he were playing a game with mirrors, or prisms. By a kind of process of refraction he adds—or creates the illusion of adding—an extra dimension to the novel. He foreshadows the technique of modern novelists whereby the action is seen through the eyes of one or more of the personages involved, although Cervantes does not identify himself with his own characters in the usual sense.

What is fiction from one standpoint is 'historical fact' or 'life' from another. Cervantes pretends through his invented chronicler Benengeli that his fiction is history (though dubious history, as we shall see later). Into this history fictions of various kinds are inserted. The *novela* of the *Curioso impertinente* is one example. Another, of a different sort, is the story of Princess Micomicona, a nonsensical tale attached to the 'historical' episode of Dorotea which is part of Benengeli's 'history' of Don Quixote, contained in Cervantes's novelistic fiction *Don Quixote*. There is no need to make ourselves dizzy with more examples. Tales and histories, of course, are only the more overtly literary parts of an immense spectrum in the novel, that includes hallucinations, dreams, legends, deceptions, and misapprehensions. The presence of chimerical chivalresque figures in the book has the effect of making Quixote and Sancho and the physical world in which these two move seem more real by comparison. At one stroke Cervantes enlarged infinitely the scope of prose fiction by including in it

with the world of external appearances the world of the imagination—which exists in books, as well as in minds.

If the reader adopts the point of view of any sane travelling
companion of the Knight and Squire, he can see the problem of
the unity of the *Quixote* in another light. The literary episodes or
'digressions' of Cardenio, Leandra, Claudia Jerónima, and others
then appear as true adventures, as opposed to the fantastic ones
imagined by the Knight or concocted for him by other people.
To the characters they are true; to the reader outside they are
things that could have happened; to both they are unusual events,
adventures. On examination it becomes clear that Don Quixote's
reactions to them and the degree to which he intervenes, if he
does, are dictated by the nature of the episode and his state of
mind together. A subtle but essential link is apparent between
himself and these external events. There is a clear exception to this
in the case of the *Curioso*, and another possible one in that of the
Captive's tale; about both of these Cervantes himself expressed
doubts.[1]

The episodes are complicated by the introduction of pastoral
incidents, which, precisely because they are by their nature more
bookish than the others, have a special attraction for Don Quixote,
although he is never able to enter the pastoral world effectively.
Cervantes rings the changes on pastoral in the stories of Grisóstomo and Marcela, the fair Leandra, Camacho's wedding, and
the incident of the simulated Arcadia. They have a special place in
the life-literature theme, because they represent different levels
of an intermediate region which is not impossibly fabulous fiction
in the way the novel of chivalry is, or part of the everyday world
of innkeepers, barbers, and friars—which is a world that also
includes runaway Moorish ladies, seducers, and dukes and duch-
esses, who are no less real, only less commonly encountered.

Cervantes's ironic vision enables him to put within the pages of
Don Quixote things that are normally outside books automatically;
and also to manipulate the story so that the principal characters
are actually conscious of the world outside the covers of the book.
He includes within its pages an author (supposedly *the* author),
Benengeli. He brings his real self in incidentally as the man who
presents Benengeli's fiction to the public. On occasion he mentions
himself just as if he were a personage who existed cheek by jowl

[1] See E. C. Riley, 'Episodio, novela y aventura en *Don Quijote*', *ACerv* v (1955–6).

with his characters: as the author of the *Galatea* and friend of the Priest; as the soldier 'something Saavedra' whom the Captive knew in Algiers; and we are also indirectly reminded of him as the author of the *Curioso impertinente*, *Rinconete y Cortadillo*, and the *Numancia*. Not only this, he brings his public into the fiction. Part II is full of characters who have read Part I and know all about the earlier adventures of Quixote and Sancho. He even introduces into Part II the sequel by his rival Avellaneda: the book itself and one of the characters who belonged to it. He makes Quixote and Sancho conscious of themselves as the literary heroes of a published work and therefore conscious of the world outside their story. The claims to reality of Avellaneda's spurious *Quixote* become in Part II an issue of some moment to the protagonists. We shall examine these aspects of the theme of life and literature in Chapter VI.

Cervantes handles his work in such a way as to show his complete control over the creation he tries so hard to make seem independent. A curious instance of this occurs at the end of chapter 8 in the First Part. He abruptly stops the action as one might cut off a cinematograph projector. Everything is arrested at a dramatic moment when Don Quixote and the Biscayan are engaged in mortal combat. They are left frozen, with their swords raised, while Cervantes interposes an account, several pages long, of how he discovered Benengeli's manuscript. He often uses the device of interruption as a way of procuring suspense and variety, just as Ercilla and other writers had done, but nowhere so graphically as here.[1] This destruction of the illusion is another typical piece of irony. It is also a piece of artistic exhibitionism displaying the power of the writer.

Nevertheless, he sometimes has difficulty in containing his novels and stories within the bounds prescribed by art and the capacities of his readers. The trouble is the vastness of his imaginative vision of life. The problem faces every fertile novelist, but life and literature are so intricately geared for Cervantes that sometimes they seem actually to interfere with each other. A couple of passages are revealing in this respect. The convict Ginés de Pasamonte has his picaresque autobiography fully planned, but even he cannot say how long it is going to be. When asked

---

[1] It will be remembered that this particular scene is also reproduced as a picture, 'muy al natural', on the first page of Cide Hamete's manuscript (*DQ* I. 9; i. 285)

whether it is finished, he replies, 'How can it be, when my life is not finished yet?' (*DQ* I. 22). The other is from the *Persiles*. When Periandro says to Arnaldo:

Do not be concerned for the time being. We arrived in Rome only yesterday and it is not possible that in so short a time procedures can have been devised, schemes drafted and inventions set up that will bring our actions to the happy conclusions we desire (*Persiles* IV. 4),

it is hard to avoid the suspicion that what he really means is 'Give the author time to work out the plot!' The length of Ginés's book is adjusted to the length of his life; Periandro leaves it to the author to bring his travails to their happy conclusion whenever the exigencies of the novel permit. These curious suggestions illustrate the way in which life and literary composition run *pari passu* in Cervantes.

There is artistic point to the whimsical tricks in *Don Quixote*. Those alluded to (with the exception of the interrupted combat, which is the same trick in reverse) all contribute to two major effects. They give the novel an appearance of receding depths, by comparison with which most other prose fiction is two-dimensional. They also give solidity and vividness to the figures of Quixote and Sancho and make them appear to exist independently of the book that was written about them. The comments of other characters sometimes help in this. Cardenio agrees that Don Quixote's madness is so extraordinary that he doubts whether anyone could have managed to invent the idea (I. 30). Sansón Carrasco finds Sancho in the flesh even more amusing than he had suspected from reading Part I (II. 7).

The author stands well back from his own work, seeming not to be responsible for his own manipulations. They are conjuring tricks that enhance the general artistic illusion of reality. One might consider them 'improper' aesthetic procedures, if one could possibly call anything that furthers the end of art unaesthetic. They are certainly unconventional, but the illusion to which they contribute is an important constituent of the 'poetic truth' of the literary fiction. The word 'contribute' must be stressed: the effect owes more to art than to artifice in the end. But it is impossible to doubt Cervantes's single-minded purposefulness behind these tricks. He practically succeeds in making the reader say of Don Quixote what Don Quixote said of the hero who was so vividly real to him: 'I can almost say that I have seen Amadis of Gaul with my own two eyes' (II. 1). And he was successful enough to deceive Unamuno and those who have judged the creation to be, in some freakish way, bigger than the mental capacity of the creator. Like conjuring tricks, however, they should not be resorted to too often. As Corneille said in the *Examen* of his *Illusion comique*: 'Les caprices de cette nature ne se hasardent qu'une fois.' Cervantes used similar devices in a few other writings, but he never again attempted feats of literary legerdemain on the same scale in a single work.

Two problems of importance to Cervantes's theory of the novel underlie these intricate manipulations of his invention. The first is the nature and limits of a work of art. The Knight's confusion of fiction and fact is an extreme case, but the author clearly shows that there is some justification for it. Not only the boundaries between what is imaginary and what is real, but those between art and life, are indeterminable. Life and art are continually interfering with each other. Inherent in this problem is that of the nature of artistic truth. What truth is to history, verisimilitude is to fiction. But can you by pretending fiction is history turn verisimilitude into something as potent as historical truth? The question is insistent throughout the *Quixote* and the *Persiles*.

The second problem concerns the effects of imaginative literature on people. Here again Don Quixote is an extreme case. But the matter was one of considerable importance in the Counter-Reformation, especially in Spain. In the century or more since the invention of printing the size of the reading public had enormously increased. The Church was naturally sensitive to the effects of literature on men's minds, and there was a wide awareness, not confined to the Church, of the power of literature and art to influence men's lives. The impact of the printed book in the sixteenth century has some analogy with that of television today, and produced some perhaps not wholly dissimilar reactions.

In Cervantes's novel, imaginative literature has affected the behaviour of many people beside the hero. What sort of a hold, for instance, has fiction on the minds of the Duke and Duchess and all those who concoct for their own amusement fantastic and elaborate situations involving Quixote and Sancho? Or on the Inn-keeper, of whom Dorotea, with a significant confusion of ideas, says, 'Our host is not far from making a second Don Quixote

[or *Don Quixote*]' (I. 32)? Or on the people who devise imitation
Arcadias? Books affect people's lives; literature is a part of their
experience; Cervantes's novel is, among other things, about books
in life.

Precedents of a sort can be found for the way in which Cervantes
treats *Don Quixote*.[1] Many of the more obvious forms of critical
detachment in writing were formalized early in rhetoric as topics
of apology, topics for use in the exordium, the conclusion, and
so on.[2] Moral reflections and asides and even the conventional
formula 'the history relates', common in the novels of chivalry,
implied a measure of detachment. In Renaissance prose and poetry
comments on the progress of the narrative and announcements
of new developments or scenes were common, a relic, probably,
of oral poetic techniques. Ariosto and Ercilla regularly remind
one of their presence in this way at the end of cantos. Ariosto
especially takes up positions alongside his creation from time to
time, in the poem yet not of it. This, and his ironical way of
suggesting that the story is really controlling him, begin to remind
one strongly of Cervantes's methods.[3]

The effect of literary fiction on literary characters makes itself
felt in some degree in the *novelle* written after Boccaccio. The
influence of the *Decameron* was so powerful that it often occurs to
later *novellieri* to make their ladies and gentlemen consciously
imitate those in Boccaccio's 'framework' by telling tales.[4] A
member of the company may even have the *Decameron* with him,
when they decide to entertain themselves in this manner.[5] The
examples are slight, but to make an invented character aware of
literary fiction as such is an advance in sophistication over the
mere appropriation of another author's fictional characters for
one's own use, as was quite commonly done.

But it was still a long way from making a character aware that

---

[1] For observations on developments before and after Cervantes, see J. E. Gillet,
'The Autonomous Character in Spanish and European Literature', *HR* xxiv (1956).
For later developments, see A. Lebois, 'La Révolte des personnages, de Cervantes et
Calderón à Raymond Schwab', *RLC* xxiii (1949).

[2] E. R. Curtius, *European Literature and the Latin Middle Ages* (London, 1953),
pp. 410 ff.; also 85–91.

[3] Ariosto, *Orlando furioso* (ed. Naples–Milan, 1954), e.g. xxxii. ii; xxxv. ii.

[4] e.g. in Firenzuola's *Ragionamenti*. See L. Di Francia, *Novellistica* (Milan, 1924–5),
i. 601–2.

[5] Thus in 'Il Lasca's' *Cene* (Di Francia, op. cit. i. 622).

he or she had a literary existence. Glimmerings of this Pirandellian idea, however, appear in one of the earliest of all novels, Heliodorus's *Ethiopic History*. 'It's just like a play!' exclaim the characters of the events in which they are participating, thus recognizing the resemblance to fiction, if not the identity with it.[1] Heliodorus's little trick of making his figures themselves draw attention to the exceptional nature of the story is strongly reminiscent of Cervantes. Another striking procedure for its time is that used in the remarkable Renaissance novel *La Lozana andaluza*, by Francisco Delicado. The author introduces himself into the work, not as a character of any importance, nor yet as a mere vehicle for conveying the story, but as a sort of sixteenth-century Isherwood (an exceedingly candid camera), actively engaged in observing and recording everything the prostitute Lozana says and does. He does not exploit the possibilities of this, however, for Lozana's conduct is not influenced by knowing herself (as she does) to be the subject of Delicado's 'portrait'.[2]

The writer's personal relationship with his narrative was often very complex and its clear expression important to the understanding of the work. The distinction between Dante the author and Dante the pilgrim has been described as 'fundamental to the whole structure' of his poem.[3] In the sixteenth century, one may observe a good deal of confusion give way to a clarifying of the author's position *vis-à-vis* his own work. The *Arcadia* suffers from Sannazaro's failure to define his role within the work, and his position outside it as writer, with any clarity. The confusion over who's who in Garcilaso's *Eclogues* arises from the medley made by the poet of personal matters from his own experience, details from the lives and personalities of his intimates, and pure fiction. The chivalresque novelists, feeling the need for some sort of detachment, formally dissociated themselves from the fiction but only confused the issues. Bandello, much more clear-sighted, nevertheless raised other questions when he sought to use detachment

[1] *Historia etiópica de los amores de Teágenes y Cariclea*, Fernando de Mena's translation of 1587 (ed. Madrid, 1954): cf. pp. 183–4; also pp. 91, 388, 424. Cervantes may have read this translation or the anonymous one of Antwerp, 1554, based on Amyot's French version.

[2] A. Vilanova, whose edition of the book I have used (Barcelona, 1952), suggests that Delicado's work inspired Cervantes in this respect—'Cervantes y *La Lozana andaluza*', *Insula*, no. 77 (May 1952). It is an extremely doubtful supposition.

[3] Francis Fergusson, quoted by R. H. Green, 'Dante's "Allegory of Poets" and the mediaeval theory of Poetic Fiction', *CL* ix (1957), 124.

as a moral alibi, disclaiming responsibility for the crimes and vices of his characters. A richer and less dubious complication of moral attitudes was contrived by Mateo Alemán, who used the autobiographical form habitual to picaresque novelists. He was remarkably successful in combining objectivity with autobiographical method in *Guzmán de Alfarache*. The picaroon's conversion made this possible: the reformed character could look back and write about himself as 'a different man'.

Though Alemán's method was not that of Cervantes (who for one thing never presented a prose story as happening to himself), the peculiar achievements of both novelists demanded a highly developed sense of the difference between poetic fiction and historical fact—a development which followed the diffusion of the Aristotelian poetic doctrines, which justified poetic fiction by the universal truth it contained. A heightened awareness of the relationship between life and literature made possible the unparalleled degree of autonomy enjoyed by Don Quixote and Sancho, and also permitted the author to achieve a simultaneous detachment from and involvement with his work, a highly complex operation but one that no longer brooked confusion. Confident in his freedom and power to control his work completely, he might then, like God, be both in and outside his handiwork. Cervantes, at the very end of his novel, draws away from his creation when he makes Cide Hamete—or rather, makes his pen—say: 'For me alone Don Quixote was born, and I for him; he knew how to act, and I how to write . . .', only to reaffirm their identity with the words 'we two are one'.[1]

In the critical thought of the sixteenth century, life and literature, though distinguished with a preciseness unknown since Antiquity, came closer together. This is exemplified in Scaliger's doctrines. He ultimately makes the matter of poetry and the matter of reality indistinguishable.[2] The poet imitates nature; Virgil alone did this perfectly; so the modern poet should imitate Virgil (thereby imitating nature) for the edification of his public. If the argument in this simplified form is hardly persuasive, the narrowing of the gap, of which this is but one illustration from the complex corpus of his theory, can be seen in this fusion of nature

---

[1] 'Para mí sola nació don Quijote, y yo para él: él supo obrar, y yo escribir; solos los dos somos para en uno' (*DQ* II. 74; viii. 267).

[2] See B. Weinberg, 'Scaliger versus Aristotle on Poetics', *MPh* xxxix (1942), 348–9.

with a literary model. The levels of fiction were also explored. Piccolomini we find speculating upon imitations of imitations, which recall the stories within stories of *Don Quixote*:

So being therefore inclined to think that a double imitation of this sort could well be done, I continued to reason how much further one could proceed with this reflection and multiplication [of what is imitated]: that is to say, whether one could not only duplicate, but triplicate and quadruplicate it, and go as far as one liked, finally, as it were one imitator imitating another imitator, and so on and so on. . . .

And in truth, when imitating an imitator, one also in a certain fashion imitates what is true, since it is true that that imitated imitator imitates.[1]

By the early 1600's art had become thoroughly introverted. Some curious optical tricks resulted. Artists turned their glass on the working of art and made works of art out of what they saw. Lope de Vega wrote a well-known *Soneto de repente*, the subject of which is simply the writing of that very sonnet. The ironic vision made possible the 'play within the play' in *Hamlet*, Corneille's *Illusion comique*, and the incident of the puppet-show in *Don Quixote*, to mention no more. It also produced the possibilities so brilliantly exploited by Calderón in *El gran teatro del mundo* and *No hay más fortuna que Dios*.

Some of the juggling with fiction which is an integral part of *Don Quixote* continued to be popular with authors and readers. Such is the case of all that apparatus of fictitious documents and supposedly second-hand stories dear to European novelists from the seventeenth century on; it owes much to Cervantes although he did not invent it. And some of the more tricksy devices had to wait from the seventeenth century until the nineteenth before becoming again a significant part of works by major writers. In fact, of course, the autonomous characters of Pérez Galdós, Unamuno, and above all Pirandello are anticipated by Quixote and Sancho by some three centuries. So are some of the notions of such disparate writers as André Gide and Lewis Carroll. Long

---

[1] 'Inclinando io adunque allora a credere che così fatta doppia imitazione si potesse con ragion fare; andai discorrendo quanto oltra con questa reflessione e moltiplicazione si potesse procedere: cioè se non solo doppia si potesse fare, ma tripla, e quadrupla, e quanto si voglia finalmente com' a dire uno che imiti uno altro imitante, e così di mano in mano . . .' 'Ed in vero in imitar un imitante, s'imita ancora in un certo modo il vero; essendo vero che quel tal' imitato imitante imita' (op. cit., pp. 37, 39).

before Édouard in *Les Faux-Monnayeurs*, Cervantes wrote a book about 'the struggle between facts as proposed by reality, and the ideal reality'.[1] In *Through the Looking-Glass* Alice's distressed and angry reaction to Tweedledum's provoking suggestion that she is only one of the things in the Red King's dream recalls that of Quixote and Sancho when their reality is challenged by Avellaneda's rival heroes.

But the closest analogy with the 'looking-glass game' Cervantes plays in *Don Quixote* is not in a book at all but a painting. It is roughly contemporary, a masterpiece of comparable magnitude, and the effect is similar. I mean Velasquez's *Las Meninas*.[2] It is full of tricks. There in the picture is the painter at work on his own painting, the largest figure in the scene, but dark and unobtrusive. There too is the back of the very canvas we are looking at. Arrested, half in half out of the room, and, as it were, of the picture, is the figure in the doorway. The King and Queen are seen reflected in a mirror on the far wall, which is hung with dim paintings. And the viewer realizes with a shock that he is looking at the picture from the spot, close to the watchful monarch and his wife, from which the picture was painted in effect. One all but glances over one's shoulder. Did a mirror stand there (there is some doubt), or did Velasquez, projecting himself mentally right outside his subject, paint from that spot as though he had been someone else altogether, painting—himself—at work? In either case, he has contrived to be simultaneously outside and inside his subject, and what is more, to draw the outside spectator into it too. 'But where is the frame?' exclaimed Gautier when he saw the picture. Picasso's comment was, 'There you have the true painter of reality.' 'His aim', Sir Kenneth Clark has written, 'was simply to tell the whole truth about a complete visual impression . . . maintaining, unobserved, a measureless impartiality.'[3]

They might all, no less aptly, have been speaking of Cervantes and *Don Quixote*.

[1] Quoted through E. M. Forster's *Aspects of the Novel* (London, 1927). Like so many contemporary writers on the subject, he quite forgets the first modern novel and describes the attempt to combine the two truths as 'new' (p. 135).

[2] I believe the analogy extends further and is much more fundamental than is suggested either by Ortega, op. cit., p. 169, or H. Hatzfeld, 'Artistic Parallels in Cervantes and Velázquez', *Estudios dedicados a Menéndez Pidal* (Madrid, 1950–7), iii. 289, who touch on the point I am making.

[3] Sir Kenneth Clark, *The Sunday Times* (2 June 1957).

II

FIRST PRINCIPLES

1. *From the Epic to the Novel*

It is not rhyming and versing that maketh a poet—no
more than a long gown maketh an advocate.

SIR PHILIP SIDNEY

THE Canon of Toledo follows up his adverse criticism of the
novels of chivalry in *Don Quixote* I. 47 with a sort of blue-
print for the ideal romance, which reads remarkably like
a description of *Persiles y Sigismunda*. This well-known passage is
central to Cervantes's theory of the novel. It is the most compact
and concrete expression of his views on what such a novel ought
to be and, more especially, ought to contain. It ends with the
statement which is the point of departure of his whole novelistic
theory: that the epic may be written in prose as well as in verse.

What we have here is not so much a theory of The Novel as a
theory of a certain type of novel—a type, however, which specially
appealed to Cervantes. It is certainly not the sum of his theory
and still less a description of his own achievements. It accounts
well enough for the *Persiles*, but only very partially for the *Quixote*,
and not at all for such things as the psychological exploration of
character in *novelas* like the *Curioso impertinente* and the *Celoso
extremeño*, or the comic 'realism' of *novelas* in the low style like
Rinconete y Cortadillo and the *Coloquio de los perros*. It does nothing
to explain the complex creative processes of *Don Quixote*. This is
not to say that Cervantes excludes such accomplishments from
his ideal romance, for he expressly allows the writer room to
include many varieties of fiction. But the emphasis on adventure
and idealization in effect weigh against them. Apart from its
significance as a point of departure, the chief importance of
the passage lies in the attempt to raise the novel to the level
of the most esteemed form of poetry.

It has been suggested more than once that the idea of writing the model romance may have come to Cervantes before the idea of the *Quixote* occurred to him. In any case, it is certain that the genesis of both *Don Quixote* and *Persiles y Sigismunda* owes much to speculation on chivalresque literature. The Canon is probably speaking with the author's voice when he says that he had been tempted to write an ideal romance (*DQ* I. 48). However, unlike Cervantes in the case of the *Persiles*, he was discouraged by the philistinism of the general public and gave up after the first hundred pages or so.

His recommendations for the ideal novel are not a collection of random remarks but a set of ideas arranged in a reasonably ordered fashion, as may be seen when they are rendered schematically:

The ideal romance offers:

1. a wide field for an intelligent author to describe:
    (*a*) a variety of exceptional happenings,
    (*b*) an exemplary hero,
    (*c*) tragic and happy events (changes of fortune),
    (*d*) a variety of characters,
    (*e*) a variety of subject-matter representing different branches of knowledge,
    (*f*) a variety of exemplary human qualities and situations,
2. with:
    (*a*) a pleasing style,
    (*b*) ingenious invention,
    (*c*) verisimilitude,
3. so as to:
    (*a*) attain aesthetic perfection in a unified, variegated work,
    (*b*) give pleasure and instruction.
4. It offers the possibility of including:
    (*a*) features of the four main literary genres,
    (*b*) all the best qualities of poetry and oratory.
5. For the epic may be written in prose as well as in verse.

The passage, as we shall see in more detail later, is not only reminiscent of El Pinciano, but redolent of certain Italian theorists. The whole argument derives from epic theory.[1] The

---

[1] The reference to assigning sometimes to one man alone, sometimes to many, all the actions that can make a man illustrious (I. 47; iii. 351) stems from the unsettled question whether the epic poem should deal with the actions of one man or more than one. Cf. El Pinciano, op. cit. iii. 218–19.

main tenets of Cervantes's theory of the novel are here. There is only one major omission, reference to the arousing of *admiratio*. However, just a few moments before, the Canon had made its importance perfectly clear. Three features of the scheme may be noted: the variety of content possible in the novel, its exemplary nature, and the particular qualities needed to make it a work of art—qualities stressed by Cervantes on other occasions. This is an attempt to allow the novelist the utmost freedom compatible with the claims of art; to encourage him to write dignified, intelligent fiction for a large public; and to reconcile epic and romance in the novel. The final observation, 'for the epic may be written in prose as well as in verse', is no afterthought, but the basis of the argument. Cervantes does not refer again directly to the prose epic, but the idea was already almost a commonplace. In the later seventeenth and the eighteenth century it became the one great justification of the novel, when the novel was considered worth justifying at all.

When El Pinciano exclaims, in the voice of one who has made a discovery, 'I have come to realize that the *Ethiopic History* is a much praised poem, but a poem in prose',[1] he betrays the fact that there had been a growing sense of the separateness of prose and poetry. For obvious reasons there always was a distinction, and writers in Antiquity often referred pointedly to the fact that certain prose works were poetic in character and that verse was not necessarily poetry; but for all that, poetry and prose were not felt to have been essentially and originally distinct. This failure to discriminate continued, with further confusion, in the Middle Ages. Italians in the sixteenth century were more particular, but they held different opinions as to whether or not poetry might be written in prose. Giraldi and Tasso, for instance, evidently accepted the idea without demur, the former including the novels of chivalry with the *romanzi* as poetry, and the latter speaking of the Byzantine novel and *Floire et Blancheflor* as epic.[2] Scaliger, although he seems to have been the first to point to Heliodorus's *Ethiopic History* as a model for epic poets,[3] nevertheless took the opposite view, insisting that poetry must be imitation in verse.

[1] El Pinciano, op. cit. i. 206.
[2] G. B. Giraldi Cinthio, 'Risposta a Messer G. B. Pigna', *Scritti estetici* (ed. Milan, 1864), ii. 161–2; Tasso, *Del poema eroico* ii. 63.
[3] Scaliger, op. cit. iii. 365.

So did Patrizi. Others again, like Robortelli, Maggi, Varchi, Castel-vetro, Piccolomini, and Minturno, while accepting Aristotle's doctrine that poetry depends on imitation not metre, and allow-ing therefore that there might be poetry in prose, considered that the best sort of poetry was written in verse.

Spanish writers accepted the idea more uncritically. The very fact that it led away from the formalist approach to literature and the rigorous delimitation of literary kinds would have appealed to many of them. Cueva, for example, made invention not verse the criterion of poetry.[1] El Pinciano was inclined to think, like Scaliger, though a little hesitantly, that perfect poetry required verse, but he was clearly charmed with the idea of the prose epic and referred to Heliodorus's model work on numerous occasions. He said emphatically:

the loves of Theagenes and Chariclea, by Heliodorus, and those of Leucippe and Clitophon, by Achilles Tatius, are as epic as the *Iliad* and the *Aeneid*; and all those books of chivalry, like the four poems mentioned above, have, I say, no essential difference that distinguishes them, nor do the individual conditions of one differ essentially from those of another.[2]

Vives, Soto de Rojas, Lugo y Dávila, Cascales, Lope de Vega, and González de Salas are a few of the others who referred to works of imaginative prose as poetry. There was nothing unusual or original about Cervantes's observation. What made it significant was, first, that he used it as a basis for a theory of prose fiction and, secondly, that in *Persiles y Sigismunda* he was almost certainly trying to put it into practice.

He chose his moment well. Heliodorus's romance was at the height of its career in Spain. The second edition of Fernando de Mena's translation appeared in Barcelona in 1614, followed by that of Madrid, 1615, and another in Paris, 1616 (the last until the eighteenth century). The year 1617 saw the appearance not only of the *Persiles* but also of Diego de Agreda's version of Achilles Tatius's romance, *Los más fieles amantes Leucipe y Cletifonte*. But it

---

[1] Cueva, op. cit. i, verses 250–2.

[2] '. . . los amores de Teágenes y Cariclea, de Heliodoro, y los de Leucipo y Clito-fonte, de Aquiles Tacio, son tan épica como la *Ilíada* y la *Eneida*; y todos esos libros de caballerías, cual los cuatro dichos poemas, no tienen, digo, diferencia alguna esencial que los distinga, ni tampoco esencialmente se diferencia uno de otro por las condiciones individuales' (op. cit. iii. 165–6). I fail, however, to find in El Pinciano a theory of the novel as well defined as Canavaggio does (op. cit., pp. 25, 70 ff.).

must be recognized that the Byzantine novel was not as universally popular as *Amadis of Gaul* had been. Heliodorus was the darling of the humanists, and it was the cultivated intellectual in the early seventeenth century who entertained himself, or herself, with the *Ethiopic History*. Nise, who explains the nature of the work to Celia in Lope's *La dama boba* (1. iv), is a good illustration. The work was published in Spanish only six, or perhaps seven, times in the sixteenth and early seventeenth centuries, but it had as many as four different translators. In other words, it enjoyed a high prestige, with a limited circulation.

While no Spanish epic poet in the Golden Age reached the level of Camoens, Tasso, or Milton, Spain must be given credit for some notable experiments. For while Cervantes attempted an epic in prose, Góngora was experimenting with lyric poetry on an epic scale. A book like the *Persiles* was right in the current of advanced literary ideas of the time and in the forefront of literary fashion. The age of the heroic romance in Europe was just beginning, and Cervantes showed the way to Gomberville, La Calprenède, and Mlle de Scudéry. As a new novel by a now successful novelist, the *Persiles* had a ready reception; it ran rapidly through eight editions and was soon translated. There was an English version by 1619.

It is not always remembered what an up-to-date novelist Cervantes was in his day, what a tireless experimenter. His first novel was in the extremely fashionable medium of pastoral; his *Novelas* were in fact, as he claimed, the first of their kind in Spain; and the originality of the *Quixote* needs no emphasizing. For his last venture he had high hopes, tempered, it seems clear, with a certain anxiety. The *Persiles* 'dares to compete with Heliodorus, if only its boldness does not prove its undoing' (*Novelas*, prol.). It will be either the worst or the best book of entertainment in the language, he claims in the second dedication of the *Quixote*, and he regrets having said 'the worst', for his friends have assured him of its excellence. He calls it a work of 'entertainment', for though he sought in it to dignify the novel, he still meant his last book to be a work of popular appeal. It is a contemporary Byzantine novel and a romance of chivalry brought up to date.

It is nevertheless a failure, not principally on grounds of inverisimilitude, I believe, but of excess of incident. In the light of the novel, one can see more clearly the strengths and weaknesses of the Canon's theory. The emphasis on exemplariness and variety (qualities advertised by the first translators of the *Persiles*)[1] does not make for great character-creation. The Canon clearly puts the abstracted exemplary qualities of character before character itself. The emphasis on variety, underlining the importance of the action, reflects the priority given to plot over character by Aristotle.

Cervantes clearly understood what too many modern novelists have forgotten, that storytelling for its own sake is the bedrock of fiction, that to know 'what happened next' is a natural desire of most readers; but still he failed where Heliodorus succeeded. The ancient author never loses the main thread of his narrative, the fortunes of his hero and heroine, who incidentally are a much more appealing couple than Persiles and Sigismunda. There is less abuse of coincidence, more skilfully sustained suspense, and a more spectacular and better-prepared climax. The humanists' praises were not unfounded. Both works are in certain respects a refinement of epic. The heroes of each are perfect lovers rather than perfect warriors. Theagenes is of a 'generosity worthy of Achilles', we are told, but cast in a gentler mould.[2] Epic itself had changed. Love, Tasso and other writers agreed, was a fitting subject for a heroic poem.[3]

By a stroke of irony that Cervantes might have appreciated, posterity has judged not *Persiles y Sigismunda* but *Don Quixote* to be his 'epic'. In the eighteenth century the epic nature of the *Quixote* was seriously discussed and there was a good deal of debate over whether Cervantes had imitated Homer or not. In the nineteenth century the German romantic critics divined something of the wider, more elusive poetry of *Don Quixote*. It was seen as a derivation of the chivalresque romance and also as an epic. Meanwhile the concept of literary imitation became disreputable. 'Cervantes is above an imitation', protested Urdaneta;[4] and in the latter half of the century it was something like a critical indecency

---

[1] '. . . the variety thereof may rob some hours from thy untimely sleep; and the seriousness of it divert idleness from bringing forth worse effects' (*The Travels of Persiles and Sigismunda*, London, 1619, 'To the Reader').

[2] Heliodorus, ed. cit., p. 146.

[3] Tasso, *Del poema eroico* II. 62–63. El Pinciano admits this with a slight qualification, op. cit. III. 180–1.

[4] A. Urdaneta, *Cervantes y la crítica* (Caracas, 1877), p. 282.

to suggest that the *Quixote* was not wholly original. 'Epic' came to be little more than a vague superlative. However, Luis Vidart, who paid some attention to Cervantes's literary theories, tried to restore some real meaning to the idea,[1] and this has been done by modern Cervantine criticism also.

For Cervantes the word certainly had a definite meaning. It is unlikely that he consciously thought of *Don Quixote* as a prose epic in the way in which he thought of the *Persiles*, although this does not mean that it does not owe anything to epic. Apart from the parodies and echoes, there is a fundamental connexion with epic through the novel of chivalry. But it is mock-epic at most. It lacks the elevated tone of the real thing, and its high moral seriousness is not heroic but of the sort that belongs, rather, to great comedy. Yet a heroic quality, emanating chiefly from Don Quixote's aspirations, pervades the work, and Cervantes makes us associate the novel with epic in his shrewd, comical, and prophetic conclusion, when he tells us that the name of Don Quixote's village has not been revealed so that all the towns and villages of La Mancha may contend for the honour, as the seven cities of Greece did for Homer (II. 74).

Epic plays another curious role in the *Quixote*. Like the chivalresque novel, it is, in a sense, contained in the book. When the Knight speculates on the history that has indeed, he discovers, been written about him, he attributes to it qualities that were commonly attributed to great epic poetry: 'it must, perforce, be grandiloquent, lofty, distinguished, magnificent and truthful' (II. 3). Contemporary definitions of epic resemble this idealized conception of his own story. 'We can say', said Tasso, 'that the heroic poem is an imitation of a great, illustrious, and perfect action narrated in highly elevated verse.'[2]

Prose epic and novel of chivalry were all one to Don Quixote. But he could only see the basic connexion, and not the aesthetic disparity, between great epic and bad romance. His point of view was essentially medieval. As is well known, there was little distinction in the Middle Ages between the heroes of Antiquity and the heroes of chivalry. They existed on the same plane and were equally 'real'; it made no difference whether they were fabulous

---

[1] L. Vidart, 'Cervantes, poeta épico', *Apuntes críticos* (Madrid, 1877); *El 'Quijote' y la clasificación de las obras literarias* (Madrid, 1882).

[2] Tasso, *Del poema eroico* I. 45.

or historical. This lack of discrimination was something that Cervantes could not countenance, in so far as it implied a failure to distinguish aesthetically. It was a characteristic of the writers he deplored. Feliciano de Silva, for instance, disguised as 'the sage Alquife', said that he could see no difference between the deeds of the first Amadis and those of all the great men who had preceded him, such as Hector and Achilles and the 'doughty Romans'.[1] By the end of the sixteenth century, on the other hand, critics, while still aware of the common ground of epic and romance, made a distinction of values. 'It is one thing', El Pinciano said, 'to seek out the essence of epic; another to seek out perfection in all its qualities.'[2]

Conscious of these differences, poets like Tasso in Italy and Balbuena in Spain sought to reconcile the poetic forms of epic and romance. But Cervantes's attempt to do the same thing for the novel was of much greater significance in the history of European literature. For although in the early seventeenth century epic could hardly be considered moribund, narrative poetry was in fact destined to give way to the novel. We will not credit Cervantes with intuitions about this, but he did see the connexion between the ancient epic, its degenerate progeny the romance of chivalry, and what was to be the offspring of the latter, a type of novel that would combine, he hoped, the charm of the parent with the noble virtues of the grandparent. As it happened, there was another influential relation—a sort of highbrow uncle —that had a hand in the infant's upbringing: the Byzantine novel.

In fact the *Quixote* usurped the role that Cervantes allotted to a novel of the type of *Persiles y Sigismunda*. Menéndez y Pelayo has pinpointed its historical significance, as 'the definitive, the perfect and the last of the novels of chivalry, the one that concentrated its diffuse matter in luminous focus, while it raised the events of everyday life to the dignity of the epic, and provided the first and unsurpassed model of the modern realistic novel'.[3]

With the knowledge that epics might be written in prose Cervantes had a basis for a theory of the novel. But ultimately he

[1] F. de Silva, *Amadís de Grecia* (ed. Seville, 1549), prol. It was first published in 1530.
[2] El Pinciano, op. cit. iii. 166.
[3] M. Menéndez y Pelayo, *Orígenes de la novela* (Madrid, 1905–10), introd., i, pp. ccxcviii–ccxcix.

found it not enough. History made itself felt in the novel in a way with which epic theory was not adequate to deal, a fact that had the most far-reaching consequences.

2. *Art and Nature, Imitation and Invention*

The work of art is a fragment of nature with the mark on it of a finite creative effort. A. N. WHITEHEAD

At the heart of Cervantes's literary theory lies the ancient dichotomy of art and nature. The great problem it embodies is how to make a work of art out of the profuse and disordered matter of life. Unfortunately the basic axiom that art imitates nature, like many others of the time, is not very clear. In the Golden Age in Spain, as elsewhere, it was a commonplace repeated over and over again, and sometimes what was meant was that art represents the phenomena of nature (*Natura naturata*); sometimes that art imitates the creative processes of nature, who is herself another creator (*Natura naturans*); and sometimes the ideas were mixed together. Both occur in Cervantes. Don Quixote remarks on one occasion that 'art, imitating nature, seems to have surpassed it' (I. 50); and Tomás Rodaja, in *El licenciado Vidriera*, 'that good painters imitated nature, but that bad ones vomited it forth'. (Writers did not differ from painters in this, of course. The idea of *ut pictura poesis* inherited from Horace, Plutarch, and Simonides of Ceos, one of the commonest of critical topics, figures more than once in Cervantes.)[1]

Since nature could be 'artistic' and art could be 'natural', the dichotomy was not so simple as it looked, but these are complications we need not pursue. Some of the dangers of the theory of imitation were at any rate mitigated by the complementary notion that art perfected nature. This, it is true, gave rise to further difficulties, but it did mean that art was not just 'copying'. It serves also as a reminder that imitation did not imply what we now understand by 'realism'.

---

[1] *DQ* II. 71; viii. 223. *Persiles* III. 14; ii. 139. Problems common to the painter and the novelist occupy Cervantes in the second half of the *Persiles*, where he several times toys with the notion of his story executed as a painting—and also, incidentally, as a drama.

Cervantes did not say very much about imitation or puzzle over the meaning of this difficult term in his writings. He probably understood by it 'producing' or 'creating according to a true idea', as sixteenth-century theorists, anticipating Butcher, generally seem to have done. He did not ponder the moral implications or other related matters that preoccupied some of the Italians. But the doctrine was as fundamental to his theory as it was to the literary theory of the day in general. The problem of artistic truth, about which he was intensely concerned, depended on it. His 'friend', advising him how to write *Don Quixote*, says: 'You have only to make proper use of imitation in what you are writing, and the more perfect the imitation, the better will your writing be.'[1] Here, and even more when the Canon speaks of 'verisimilitude and . . . imitation, in which is found the perfection of what is written',[2] we are reminded of El Pinciano, who says: 'the poet who looks to imitation and verisimilitude best attains poetic perfection'.[3] El Pinciano describes imitation as the 'form' of poetry, and for Cervantes verisimilitude and formal aesthetic qualities meet and mingle inextricably in imitation, for imitation of the impossible is an aesthetic *disparate*.

The words 'imitation' and 'invention' sound almost incompatible. In fact, there is no really clear distinction between them in sixteenth-century theory. Tasso, who examines them minutely, finds that 'imitation and invention are one and the same thing as far as the plot is concerned'.[4] The rhetorical word *inventio* is often used with little or no discrimination from *imitatio*, *fictio*, and *fabula*. It means primarily the finding of material for the work; *dispositio* meaning primarily its selection and arrangement, though the distinction between the two is far from clear. Cervantes uses the terms in this rhetorical sense at the end of the prologue to the *Galatea*. Vives says invention is principally a task for the author's *prudentia*, which is a combination of his *ingenium, memoria, judicium,*

---

[1] 'Sólo tiene que aprovecharse de la imitación en lo que fuere escribiendo; que cuanto ella fuere más perfecta, tanto mejor será lo que se escribiere' (*DQ* I, prol.; i. 39).

[2] '. . . la verisimilitud y . . . la imitación, en quien consiste la perfección de lo que se escribe' (*DQ* I. 47; iii. 349).

[3] '. . . el poeta que guarda la imitación y verisimilitud guarda más la perfección poética' (op. cit. ii. 95).

[4] T. Tasso, *Apologia in difesa della sua 'Gerusalemme'*, *Opere* iv. 185.

and *usus rerum*.[1] The main emphasis is generally placed on the first of these combined faculties, innate talent. Since, however, invention does not mean indulging in unbridled fantasy, but rather the 'devising of matter, true or plausible',[2] some exercise of intellectual discrimination is clearly called for. Ideally, the material chosen should be such as will make a credible and unified work. But this did not always happen in practice, even if classical theorists believed it ought to. Invention and verisimilitude are not identical. At the end of the *Coloquio de los perros* Peralta admits that the story shows good invention, but he has strong doubts about its truth. This amounts to casting doubt on the verisimilitude of the tale as fiction. So although verisimilitude is a very important quality of invention for Cervantes, they are not inevitably united.

Cervantes is particularly proud of his own powers of invention, to which indeed even his contemporaries paid tribute, and on more than one occasion he congratulates himself on this score. In the *Parnaso* he recognizes invention as a natural gift, or 'superhuman instinct' as he calls it, and he underlines its importance for the work of any writer who wishes to be remembered.[3] Among the two or three requisites of good books mentioned by Don Diego de Miranda is the requirement that they should surprise us and hold our interest by their inventiveness (*DQ* II. 16). 'Let the judicious reader be astonished at the invention', says the author's friend (*DQ* I, prol.). 'Ingenious invention', in intimate association with verisimilitude, is also demanded by the Canon of Toledo in his prescription for the ideal novel of chivalry (I. 47).

Cervantes's concern for invention, and the patent pleasure he takes both in his own and in that of other writers, reflects something of the spirit in which many of the theorists of the time treated it. Some could have scarcely been more emphatic about its importance. Castelvetro sees it at once as the poet's most difficult task and as constituting the essence of poetry—without

---

[1] J. L. Vives, *De conscribendis epistolis, Opera* i. 60.
[2] *Rhetorica ad Herennium*, trans. Caplan, Loeb Cl. Lib. I. ii. 3.
[3]   'Y sé que aquel instinto sobrehumano,
            que de raro inventor tu pecho encierra,
            no te ha dado el padre Apolo en vano.' (*Parnaso* I. 20)

            'Yo soy aquél que en la invención excede
            a muchos, y, al que falta en esta parte,
            es fuerza que su fama falta quede.' (ibid. IV. 55)

invention one simply is not a poet.[1] Huarte goes so far as to say that those who lack inventive ability should be forbidden by the state to write or publish books.[2] Emphasis on invention effectively highlights the creative aspect of poetry, which Plato had stressed. For El Pinciano among others it is precisely the measure of the poet's superiority over the historian: 'the poet writes what he invents and the historian finds it already dished up'.[3] This exaltation of creativity, which was basically inseparable from the imitation of nature, is the best evidence of how little hampered writers felt themselves to be by the latter doctrine, even theoretically. The exhilaration with which Sir Philip Sidney in England speaks of the poet 'with the force of a divine breath' bringing forth things far surpassing nature's doings is quite common in works of criticism.[4]

The scope of the poet is held to be nothing less than boundless. So he becomes a godlike creator, resembling the Almighty himself, and the poem a world in miniature. Like Scaliger and Tasso, Carvallo sees the poet as making something out of nothing, like God.[5] A few writers intimate that there are some things not amenable to poetic treatment, but the general view is that there is nothing that the poet is not free to describe. It is appropriate that he should be informative, and a few words about the arrangement of the universe in an epic poem would certainly not come amiss.

For there is nothing either above the heavens or below them, or in the very depths of the abyss, which is not completely within the hands and the discretion of the judicious poet.[6]

This universal comprehensiveness is not restricted to epic, though epic is sometimes held to excel on this account. In the many eulogies, defences, and apologies for poetry of the time, the liberty to deal with any subject under the sun, or beyond it, is one of the great virtues ascribed to the art of poetry in general. The eulogy of poetry in Cervantes's own *Parnaso* IV offers a typical example.

[1] Castelvetro, op. cit., pp. 78, 216.
[2] J. Huarte, *Examen de ingenios* (ed. Leyden, 1591), fol. 60^r.
[3] El Pinciano, op. cit. ii. 11.
[4] Sir Philip Sidney, *An Apology for Poetry*, in *Elizabethan Critical Essays*, ed. G. Smith (Oxford, 1904), i. 157.
[5] Carvallo, op. cit., fol. 213^v.
[6] Giraldi, *Dei romanzi*, p. 26.

The same liberty is available to the novelist. The variegated items enumerated by the Canon in his recipe for the ideal romance reflect something of the idea. Cervantes's claim that he has the 'ability, sufficiency, and wit' to deal with the whole universe is also a probable reminiscence of the vast range permitted to the poet. But merely finding something to say was the least of his problems. It was shaping what nature offered into a work of art which was unified and credible and in other ways in conformity with required standards that was difficult.

3. *The Imitation of Models*

The essence of chivalry is the imitation of the ideal hero.

J. HUIZINGA

In the poetic theory of the Renaissance, as in Antiquity, the imitation of literary models was scarcely less important than the imitation of nature. Obscure in origin, but connected with the imitation of nature and implicit, it has been said, in Aristotle, the doctrine quickly took root in the theory and practice of literature. The principle was laid down for poetry by Horace and amplified by adaptation from Quintilian. Renaissance rhetorics echoed the *ars, imitatio, exercitatio* of the *Rhetorica ad Herennium*. Vida popularized the idea, which then appeared regularly in poetics of the sixteenth century and was much invoked by Ciceronians and Virgil-worshippers. Thanks largely to Scaliger it was harnessed to the imitation of nature, and in the seventeenth century Reason drove the team. This cardinal principle of classical theory was finally rejected in the romantic period and all that was left was a term of abuse—'plagiarism'.

It had uncritical adherents and also some vigorous opponents, like Castelvetro in Italy and Francisco de Barreda in Spain. It was subject at all times to a wide variety of interpretations, rationalized and made flexible. The imitation of models was distinguished from literary robbery and pilfering, and prescribed for general inspiration and the formation of style. The number and sorts of models were debated. Writers were told that they should seek to improve on their models, imitate only what was excellent, choose according to their needs and imitate appropriately. The doctrine undoubtedly sanctified tradition in the worst sense, encouraging the ungifted to extremes of servility. On the other hand, it also sanctified tradition in the best sense, ensuring a fixed high standard, encouraging emulation, and, since it was capable of a liberal interpretation, never standing in the way of original genius. Moreover, as Lope de Vega pointed out, there were original geniuses like Góngora whose most ambitious poetry it was disastrous folly for inferior writers to try to imitate. Imitation properly demanded a corresponding spark of native genius in the imitator. The reproduction of superficialities was not enough.[1] It was no good, as Cervantes intimated, for an ape to try to be a swan.[2] The sensible attitude towards literary imitation that on the whole prevailed in the Spain of Cervantes may be summed up in the words of a sixteenth-century rhetorician as a 'prudent liberty'.[3]

Nothing shows more clearly the complete compatibility of this imitative doctrine with the originality of which Cervantes was so proud than the fact that his boast in the prologue of the *Novelas ejemplares* that he was the first to write *novelas* in Castilian, that they were his own and neither imitated nor stolen, is first preceded by the observation that his *Parnaso* was written in imitation of a work by Caporali, and then followed (in the very next sentence) by the assertion that his *Persiles* dared to compete with the *Ethiopic History*. Liberally interpreting the doctrine, he followed it in practice and admitted as much.

Don Quixote states the basic precept in the Sierra Morena when he is about to undertake a full-scale imitation of a knight errant doing penance:

> Similarly I say that when a painter wishes to become famous in his art, he tries to imitate the original works of the most outstanding painters he knows; and the same rule holds for all notable professions and pursuits that serve as the ornament of states. (I. 25)

But Cervantes, like other intelligent critics, is also alive to the dangers of the doctrine, that it could and did lead to the excesses and abuses of plagiarism. In the mock-serious *Adjunta* to the *Parnaso* Apollo distinguishes legitimate borrowing from theft in poetry:

> Item, be it known that no poet shall be held a thief for stealing someone else's line and inserting it among his own, provided that

---

[1] Lope de Vega, *Respuesta a un papel*, pp. 138–9.
[2] 'Monas que de cisnes tienen talle' (*Parnaso* VIII. 111).
[3] Pedro de Navarra, op. cit., fol. 10ᵛ.

it be not the whole concept and the entire stanza, in which case he is as big a thief as Cacus.[1]

This passage itself looks suspiciously·like a mischievous 'theft' from Carvallo's *Cisne de Apolo*:

Carvallo: Apart from that, is a poet permitted to take a line or a short saying from another poet and insert it in his works as his own? *Lectura:* Yes, because a line or a short saying can easily be said by me as someone else said it, even though I never heard it from him . . .
C.: And could a concept be taken from another poet?
L.: As long as it is put in a different form and a different style from that which it was in before, it is allowed . . .
C.: And should I be allowed to take an entire stanza, or more, or an exordium, or someone else's ballad, and insert it in my works, selling it as my own, and profiting by the work of another? *L.:* Certainly not, because that is stealing.[2]

Cervantes alludes on several occasions to the prevalence of such abuses. There is also implicit criticism of this in his ironical presentation of a few curious and pathetic figures who make fleeting appearances in his works. There is the humanist author of heavily imitative forthcoming masterpieces in *Don Quixote* II. 22. In the *Persiles* we meet a literary hack whose job it is to patch up and renovate old plays (III. 2), and later that very odd character, the 'new and modern author of new and exquisite books', who is compiling a collection of other people's aphorisms, without involving himself in any personal effort (IV. 1).

Cervantes's criticism is directed above all against indiscriminate borrowing. The borrowing must serve the writer's purpose. This is illustrated on the occasion when Don Quixote is discussing

---

[1] 'Ítem, se advierte que no ha de ser tenido por ladrón el poeta que hurtare algún verso ajeno, y le encajare entre los suyos, como no sea todo el concepto y toda la copla entera, que en tal caso tan ladrón es como Caco' (*Adjunta al Parnaso*, p. 133).
[2] *Carvallo :* Dejando eso aparte, ¿será lícito al poeta tomar un verso o sentencia breve de otro poeta y encajarle por suyo en sus obras?
Lectura : Sí, porque un verso o una sentencia breve, fácilmente puedo yo decirla, como la haya dicho otro, aunque yo jamás se la haya oído . . .
C. : Y un concepto, ¿podríase tomar de otro poeta?
L. : Como lo ponga en compostura diferente, y por diferente estilo del que antes tenía, lícito es . . .
C. : Y tomar una copla entera, o más, o un exordio, romance ajeno, y encajarlo en mis obras, vendiéndolo por propio mío, aprovechándome del trabajo ajeno, ¿sería permitido?
L. : En ninguna manera, porque eso es hurtar. (Op. cit., fol. 190[r–v]).

the commemorative verses declaimed at the bogus exequies of Altisidora. He remarks that the stanza borrowed from Garcilaso seems to him rather out of place. To this the musician replies that there is nothing to wonder at in that, for the callow poets of the day write as they please and borrow from whom they will, whether it is to their purpose or not; there is no foolishness that is not attributed to poetic licence (II. 70). Cervantes's view is simply the classical one. It might be summed up in the words used by Agustín de Rojas: 'No small praise is due to the man who knows how to make good use of what he steals and which is to the purpose of his subject.'[1]

It is Don Quixote who states the precept of the imitation of models in I. 25. He has embarked on his career stirred by the example of the fabulous heroes he has read about. There is nothing notably unusual in his seeking to imitate some exemplary hero in life, or, like a courtier, to emulate the best in previous models.[2] But what is noteworthy is that he is also behaving very like an artist. This is because he is trying to live literature and be not only the hero of his own story but also, in so far as he can control events, its author. His efforts might not have been very significant in relation to artistic imitation if Cervantes had not made him consciously aware of the doctrine. But Cervantes does, and the Knight recalls it with direct reference to his intended penance. He recalls it specifically on this occasion and no other, I think, because he never has a better opportunity of carrying out what he imagines will be a really splendid imitation of a knight errant, perfect in every detail. At other times his imitation is inevitably imperfect because he is forced to depend on people and things that will not behave with the comparative docility of the material the conventional artist has at his disposal. Reality rebels when he tries to force it into a fictional shape. His penance, on the other hand, will be an almost exclusively solo performance.

Shaken, we may suspect, by the outcome of the adventure of the galley slaves, Don Quixote has withdrawn into the Sierra Morena and into himself. His confidence is perhaps restored somewhat by the promisingly chivalresque beginning of the Cardenio episode—a mad hermit in the wilderness, like another Roland or

---

[1] A. de Rojas, *El viaje entretenido* (ed. Madrid, 1945), p. 510.
[2] See B. Castiglione, *Il Libro del Cortegiano* (ed. Florence, 1947), pp. 62–63.

Amadis. The new exploit could very plausibly have been suggested to him by the real example of Cardenio (life) as well as the ever-present memory of his chivalresque heroes (literature); the former probably consciously, the latter unconsciously. At any rate, he decides that this is the moment to imitate one of the most admirable episodes in the life of Amadis (or Roland) with a real chance of success. Hence his high hopes for the venture and the importance he attaches to it. Of course, he is destined to execute the usual comic parody, because even when he is on his own the gap between himself and his models cannot be bridged. (The first essential in literary imitation, one sixteenth-century Spanish scholar observed, was some resemblance between the imitator and the author imitated.)[1]

There has to be some official reason for his penance, apart from imitation for its own sake, which Dulcinea, of course, must supply. He cannot very well complain of her disdain for him, so he will lament his absence from her. She is simply part of his plan; she is not the real motive cause. The real motive cause is the desire to carry out a famous exploit in imitation of Amadis of Gaul, who, spurned by his lady Oriana, changed his name to Beltenebros and retired to live the life of a hermit on Peña Pobre. Or shall he perhaps imitate Roland mad? In either case, it is quite clear that Dulcinea, the official reason for the penance, comes a poor second to his desire to do an imitation. How can he imitate Roland in his madness if he does not also imitate him in the occasion of it? he asks himself at quite a late stage in the proceedings (I. 26).

He savours the name 'Beltenebros' like an artist, and he is activated by several considerations that are, among other things, artistic. The project is, for once, suited to his abilities. It will be easier to imitate Amadis in this than in splitting giants in two, beheading serpents, slaying dragons, routing armies, wrecking fleets, and breaking spells, he observes. The setting is just right for the occasion. He deliberates whether Amadis or Roland should be his model. He carefully selects the site of his first formal oration, composes his letter, insists that Sancho witness part of his performance, and, in chapter 26, after further deliberations on the choice of a model, settles finally for Amadis and gets on with

[1] S. Fox Morcillo, *De imitatione* (cited in Menéndez y Pelayo, *Ideas estéticas*, ii. 163).

the business. The whole procedure has rightly been called that of a *littérateur* and almost a 'transposition of art'.[1]

It is Sancho who devastatingly exposes the fundamental weakness of this 'rare, felicitous and unprecedented imitation', as Quixote calls it. He points out the inadequacy of the professed motive. Don Quixote's models had some provocation, but who has disdained him? What reason is there for supposing that Dulcinea has 'been up to some nonsense with either Moor or Christian'? The imitation is irrelevant—a criticism we have met already in a conventional literary context. Don Quixote's reply is a splendid piece of lunacy:

> That is the point of the whole thing and . . . the beautiful part of my plan. What thanks does a knight errant earn for going mad when he has cause? The point is to go out of my mind without any occasion for it, thus letting my lady realize that if I do this for her in cold blood, what would I do in hot? (I. 25)

Only as an evident afterthought does he add that he has ample cause in their long separation. It is no occasion, of course. Even if the penance had been an excellent imitation, it did not arise out of the needs of the imitator and was therefore gratuitous. The criticism is an artistic one inasmuch as its object is art transposed into life.

As it happens, Don Quixote is not the only one to act out living imitations of literature. Not to mention the performers in the chivalresque fantasies, devised by persons whom the aberration of the Knight has in a way infected, it is particularly true in pastoral situations which are quite independent of him. There is a good deal of artistic deliberation about the way in which the lovers of Leandra comport themselves after her loss. Anselmo laments her absence by going about 'singing verses that display his fine abilities as a poet'. Eugenio follows an 'easier' course and one 'more to the point', as it seems to him, which is to rail at the frailty of women (I. 51). More spectacularly, there are the counterfeit shepherds and shepherdesses with their simulated Arcadia in II. 58. The difference between them and Don Quixote, who applauds their game, is only that they do not deceive themselves that it is anything more than an elegant charade. When he himself speculates on a pastoral career in II. 67, he similarly considers it on this altogether less serious level.

[1] M. I. Gerhardt, op. cit., p. 19.

In real life too people were inspired to identify themselves with pastoral characters and imitate their behaviour. Admirers of *L'Astrée* turned the *roman à clef* inside out when, writing to Honoré d'Urfé in 1624, they told him:

we have, not long since, changed our real names (having done the same with our clothes) to those in your works which we judged to be the most appropriate and suitable to the humour, actions, history, supposed resemblance, and parentage of each and every one of us.[1]

As for the chivalresque, there was ancient precedent. The influence of chivalresque literature on chivalric practices in the fifteenth century is well known. Once more we see that Don Quixote is just an extreme case, in whom heroic emulation, courtly perfectionism, and amateur dramatics commingle on an extravagant scale.

The artistic nature of his attempted imitation is but one facet of his penance in the Sierra Morena; I do not want to exaggerate it. This episode in chapter 25, however, holds a unique place among the endeavours of Don Quixote, and occupies a sort of dead-centre in the action of Part I, where thematic echoes reverberate back and forth. Perhaps it is not just coincidence that this central point is also the occasion when Don Quixote makes his most elaborate and desperate attempt to live literary fiction. The imitation of Amadis lacks any rational purpose other than imitation for its own sake, it is inappropriate to the needs of the imitator and could only be comically superficial. This happens to be a misuse, of which Cervantes is critical elsewhere, of an accepted principle of art.

4. *The Making of a Writer* —Natura, studium, exercitatio

> Any book I write starts with a flash but takes a long time
> to shape up.   ROBERT PENN WARREN

The old question asked of the poet in Plato's time, 'Is he born or made, or both?', was still asked of the imaginative writer in the Golden Age. The common tag that the poet is born, the orator made, was obviously an over-simplification, and the standard formula for the orator, *natura, studium, exercitatio,* was also applied

---

[1] H. d'Urfé, *L'Astrée*, Bibl. Romanica (Strasbourg, n.d.), i. 15-16.

to the poet. The usual view was that the poet must be born with a natural ability, but that he will only achieve perfection if he studies and applies the rules of his art.[1] Preceptists were understandably inclined to stress the rules. But in some quarters the supremacy of natural aptitude was insisted upon—by Lope, for instance, in his *Arte nuevo* and by the author of the prologue to the *Romancero general* of 1604, Francisco López.

Cervantes holds the usual view, that a person born with an aptitude for poetry perfects it by art. In a passage where the influence of Juan Huarte has been noted[2] we read that the power may be visited upon anyone, regardless of class or profession:

It is possible for an artisan to be a poet, because poetry lies in the understanding, not in the hands; and the soul of a tailor has as great a capacity for poetry as that of a quartermaster. For all human souls are equal, in their beginnings created and formed of a single substance by their maker; and according to the form and temperament of the body that encloses them, they prove more or less judicious and seek out the knowledge of those arts, sciences and skills to which the stars most incline them. But it is more often and properly said that a poet *nascitur*. So there is nothing to wonder at in Rutilio being a poet, even though he has been a dancing-master. (*Persiles* I. 18)

Cervantes regrets his own lack of the gift of writing verse and tells us that he tries to make good the deficiency by sheer effort (*Parnaso* I). When Quixote remarks that the verses of the knights of old had more 'spirit' than 'nicety' about them (I. 23), he is criticizing their lack of art—and incidentally echoing a complaint commonly made against Spanish poets in the sixteenth century.[3] He expresses himself more fully, and quite rationally, on the whole subject to Don Diego:

for there is a true belief that the poet is born: that is to say, the natural poet issues a poet from his mother's womb; and, with the propensity heaven gave him and without further study or artifice, he composes things which prove the truth of the saying, *Est Deus in nobis*, etc. I will add that the natural poet who is aided by art will greatly excel and surpass the man who, with only a knowledge of the art, wishes to

[1] e.g. F. de Herrera, *Obras de Garcilaso de la Vega con anotaciones de Fernando de Herrera* (Seville, 1580), p. 293.

[2] R. Salillas, *Un gran inspirador de Cervantes* (Madrid, 1905), pp. 157–8.

[3] Thus Francisco de Medina in Herrera's edition of Garcilaso, 'A los lectores', p. 5; D. G. Rengifo, *Arte poética española* (Salamanca, 1592), dedic.

be a poet. The reason is that art does not surpass nature, but perfects it; thus by combining nature with art and art with nature, a most perfect poet is produced. (*DQ* II. 16)

Don Quixote does not linger over the Ovidian quotation, which would be well enough known to Don Diego, but we find it, and the general idea of the poet as prophet, in other passages of Cervantes's writings.[1] From Aristotle onwards the Platonic doctrine of poetic 'possession' was often modified or criticized, but it persisted with great vigour through the Middle Ages and the Renaissance. Vida, for instance, used it to make a sort of demigod out of the poet. Platonists like Luis de León and Carvallo naturally made much of an idea which even Aristotelians like Cascales could not dispense with absolutely. It was even used in defence of the highly unspontaneous language of *culto*, or Gongoristic, poets.[2] El Pinciano preferred to minimize the role of supernatural intervention in poetic creation.[3] In Cervantes it seems to be one of those *idées reçues* which have a place in his theory but are not subjected to much critical examination.

The number of related ideas ranged on each side of the simple dichotomy 'art and nature' in the sixteenth and seventeenth centuries is formidable. The concept is the ideological nucleus of a variety of situations and conflicts in Cervantes's works. One of the less conspicuous of these has a special literary relevance. It concerns Sancho, who is in the medieval tradition, elaborated by Erasmus in his *Encomium moriae*, of the 'wise fool'.[4] Specifically, I refer to his abuse of proverbs and Don Quixote's criticism of this. The subject is intimately linked with the question that makes itself heard with some insistence in Part II: how suitable is he to be a governor? Sancho has the inborn wit and wisdom of the peasant but lacks formal education. A symptom of the former is his remarkable facility in proverbs, while his ill-judged use of them reflects the latter. In other words, he is in this respect well endowed by nature but lacks art. This characteristic of Sancho is only really developed by Cervantes in Part II. There is naturally a good deal of talk about it when his master is telling him how

[1] *Lic. Vidriera*, p. 93. *DQ* II. 1; iv. 62.

[2] By Ángulo y Pulgar, quoted in J. García Soriano's 'Carrillo y los orígenes del culteranismo', *BRAE* xiii (1926), 593.

[3] El Pinciano, op. cit. i. 222 ff.

[4] See Hiram Haydn's important book, *The Counter-Renaissance* (New York, 1950), pp. 92 ff.

to be a good governor (II. 43). Don Quixote on occasion evinces a certain irritated admiration, but he is usually critical. The point of his criticism, which is simply an echo of those writers from Quintilian to Mal Lara who warned against the abuse of *sententiae* and *refranes*, is that they should be used aptly and in moderation.[1] The last reprimand Sancho receives on their account follows hard upon the anecdote of Orbaneja and the criticism of Avellaneda's book and of the badly painted wall-hangings at the inn (II. 71). The conjunction is significant, for the Knight's objections are essentially artistic.

What does this imposition of art upon nature mean? Obviously a great deal, but primarily the application of certain controls and the cultivation of, so to speak, the soil in which the native genius blooms. There are in the course of Cervantes's works a number of passing allusions which are to the point.

In the first place, God-given genius or not, the writer is faced with a great deal of hard work. Effort, the exercise of judgement, and the application of accumulated experience are necessary. Horace and Quintilian, whose treatises were standard textbooks, insisted on the sheer labour of composition. To compose histories and books of any sort, Don Quixote informs the Bachelor Carrasco, a great deal of judgement and ripe understanding are needed (II. 3). One writes with one's understanding, not one's grey hairs, Cervantes reminds the peevish Avellaneda, adding that the understanding tends to improve with age. Does he really think there is little work in writing a book? (*DQ* II, prol.). The first part of the *Quixote* certainly cost the author some labour to compose (I, prol.). He is fond of referring to his writings as the products of his understanding and the children of his brain.[2] Despite the persistence of the Platonic doctrine, there was an increasing emphasis on intellectual effort towards the end of the sixteenth century. Indeed, the mere overcoming of difficulties became in itself an ever more laudable object for the writer to aim at—a notion developed in Castelvetro and reaching its culmination in *culto* and *conceptista* poetics.

[1] Cf. J. de Mal Lara: 'Hemos de mirar también que los refranes tengan orden en el decirlos y escribirlos, porque si toda nuestra habla y escritura es toda de refranes, pierde su gracia con la demasiada lumbre' (*Filosofía vulgar*, Seville, 1568, preámbulo 10). Cf. Quintilian, op. cit. VIII. v. 25 ff.

[2] *Galatea*, prol.; i, p. xlix. *DQ* I, prol.; i. 17. *Novelas*, prol., p. 23, dedic., p. 25.

The writer with a great natural facility is apt to have difficulty in restraining and directing the flow. Cervantes does not refer to this as a literary matter, but he mentions a number of strictly analogous cases which give every indication of personal involvement in the essential problem. He seems keenly aware of the urge to express oneself in words and the frequent difficulty of doing so effectively, especially under the pressure of strong feeling. Analogously, Sancho describes his trouble with proverbs like this:

when I speak they all come rushing into my mouth at once, fighting with one another to get out; and my tongue starts throwing out the first ones it gets hold of, whether they are to the point or not. (*DQ* II. 43)

Clodio in the *Persiles* has a different affliction with the same effect. He suffers from certain malicious impulses that set his tongue dancing in his mouth and cause him to stifle between his teeth more than a few home truths that are trying to get out into the world (I. 18). Yet another case prompts Cervantes's most extensive observation:

When waters are enclosed in a narrow vessel, the more they hasten to escape, the more slowly they spill forth, because the foremost, pressed on by those behind, hold back and each blocks the way of the other, until at last the flow forces a passage and they are discharged. The same thing happens with the words conceived in the mind of a suffering lover: running together all at once to the tongue, they obstruct each other and discourse does not know where to begin to express what is in the mind. (*Persiles* IV. 11)

In *El amante liberal*, however, Mahamut declares as a general principle that what can be felt can also be said, although sometimes feeling stills the tongue. There is, of course, a difference between spontaneous and literary expression, but what may be clearly deduced is that verbal expression requires calm reason and reflection, things which are impaired by haste and the heat of emotion.

There is no need to ask how conscious the creator of Don Quixote was of the powers of the imagination. They are such, he observes in his last novel, that the memory often cannot tell false imaginings from what was true (*Persiles* II. 15). As a writer, it was his business to keep dreams under control. Since he had always observed common decorum, whether waking or sleeping, he said, he could afford to open the doors of his mind to the visions that come in sleep and use them pleasurably and gloriously.[1] Don Quixote, on the other hand, simply surrenders to his dreams. This is a further aspect of the artist *manqué* in him. Most of his imaginative creation remains in his mind, where he enjoys the private freedom of depicting Dulcinea, for instance, exactly as he pleases (I. 25). Sigismunda is Cervantes's own brave but unsuccessful attempt to realize artistically the perfect woman, who, in the *Quixote*, remains for the reader bright but indistinct in the mind of the hero. Cervantes explores, as no imaginative writer had ever done before, the mysterious territory where not only real life and dream, but also art, meet.

The natural ability of an author requires nourishment and favourable conditions in which to flourish, as well as pruning and training. He needs experience of the world as well as of his art. The frequent references in Cervantes to experience as guide, teacher, mistress of the arts, mother of sciences, and the like are not the less important for being everyday literary commonplaces. Wit-sharpening experience is acquired both through life and through books; as one would expect, he recommends both travel and reading.[2] In his old age, however, he expresses a certain preference for reading, arguing somewhat disingenuously that attentive reading has the advantage over inattentive observation (*Persiles* III. 8).

He cannot himself have often enjoyed peaceful conditions for writing, but he holds the age-old belief that the Muses delight in the fountain and the grove and shrink from the crowded haunts of men.[3] If *Don Quixote* was actually engendered in a prison, the argument against this popular notion seems strong; but it is obvious that Cervantes did not regard such conditions as desirable. He yearns for the quiet and tranquillity of the countryside, with 'calm skies, softly murmuring streams and peace of mind'

---

[1]   'Yo, que siempre guardé el común decoro
en las cosas dormidas y despiertas,
pues no soy troglodita, ni soy moro,
de par en par del alma abrí las puertas,
y dejé entrar al sueño por los ojos,
con premisas de gloria y gusto ciertas.' (*Parnaso* VI. 84)

[2] *DQ* II. 25; v. 226. *Persiles* II. 6; i. 194. *Lic. Vidriera*, p. 76. *Coloquio*, p. 202.

[3] Cf., for example, Tacitus, op. cit., § 9; G. Vida, *De arte poetica* I, verses 486 ff., in Batteux's *Les Quatre Poétiques* (Paris, 1771), vol. ii; Rengifo, op. cit., p. 22.

(*DQ* I, prol.).[1] Leisure is needed, for, as Sancho judiciously observes, 'works done in a hurry are never completed with the perfection required' (II. 4). But of course these conditions are secondary. Writing verses with leisurely calm does not save the wretched dramatist in the *Coloquio* from failure. He has no native talent to nurture.

These considerations are scattered at random through Cervantes's works; they are not ordered argument. But when brought together, they show an awareness of certain basic requirements and initial problems of the writer that would not be out of place in an *Ars poetica*. Inspiration, the extra-human afflatus which comes to the man who is born a poet, is necessary. All human souls are equal and the dispensation is not determined by social considerations. Literary composition depends on much more than this, however; it is also a matter of brainwork. The imaginative powers, of whose force Cervantes is especially aware, have to be controlled and canalized to the end of expression. The writer also needs experience of life and of literature. And he is helped in his task when he enjoys leisure and peaceable surroundings.

There remains the question of his general education.

5. *Erudition*

> The possible interests of a poet are unlimited; the more
> intelligent he is the better; the more intelligent he is the
> more likely that he will have interests: our only condition
> is that he turn them into poetry and not merely meditate
> on them poetically.   T. S. ELIOT

To perfect his natural talent with art, the poet was expected not only to know all the rules and tricks of his trade but to be generally well informed on all sorts of subjects. Ideally, he should be a truly learned man; theoretically, there was no limit to what he might desirably know. The prestige and authority enjoyed by the writers of ancient Greece and Rome, together with the doctrine of the imitation of models, made learning necessary to the poet. Poetic erudition was also the corollary of certain other beliefs. Of the belief in the instructional function of poetry. Of the belief—almost passionately held by Cervantes—in the

[1] Cf. *La gitanilla*, pp. 63–64.

inherent nobility of poetry, which meant its withdrawal from the commonplace and vulgar, from the crowd. Of the belief, finally, that poetry was a sort of compendium of the arts and sciences and embodied much of the substance of philosophy and oratory.

This last concept, inherited from Antiquity, was commonly found in the poetic theory of the day, both Spanish[1] and Italian, although there were a few, like the refractory Castelvetro, who contested it. In Antiquity and the Middle Ages it was generally connected with allegoresis. In the Renaissance it found congenial ground in the current aesthetic theory which required apparent beauty to be completed and perfected with moral and intellectual adornments. It was also part of the idea that anything in the universe might be the subject of poetry. Not surprisingly, the notion was seized upon by the authors of those popular panegyrics of poetry and exploited mercilessly.[2]

So the poet had to do his duty by this conception of poetry, and know not only his own subject, but something about all, or most, other subjects too. Lope de Vega, who more than once alluded to the common ground of poetry and philosophy, put the matter well enough:

The poet must not only know all the sciences, or at least the principles of all of them, but he must have very great experience of all that happens on land and sea, so that if the occasion to dispose an army or describe a fleet arises, he will not talk blindly and be censured and taken for an ignoramus by those who have seen such things. No more, no less, he must know the usages, customs, and manner of life of all sorts of people; and finally, all the things that are talked of, dealt with and lived by, because there is nothing in the world so exalted or base that there is not occasion for dealing with it some time, from the Creator himself down to the lowest worm or creature of the earth.[3]

Poetry appears in Cervantes's *Viaje del Parnaso* IV with the liberal arts and sciences all ministering to her and treating her with

---

[1] e.g. Sánchez de Lima, op. cit., fol. 27^v; Carvallo, op. cit., fol. 42^v; P. Soto de Rojas, *Discurso sobre la poética*, *Obras* (ed. Madrid, 1950), pp. 26–27; C. Suárez de Figueroa, *La constante Amarilis* (Valencia, 1609), p. 42; El Pinciano, op. cit. i. 216, iii. 236–7.

[2] Thus Alonso de Valdés, *Prólogo en alabanza de la poesía*, in Vicente Espinel's *Diversas rimas* (Madrid, 1591); *Discurso en loor de la poesía*, a curious work by an excitable anonymous Peruvian lady, prefacing Diego Mexía's *Parnaso antártico de obras amatorias* (Seville, 1608), fol. 11^{r-v}; F. Vera y Mendoza, *Panegírico por la poesía* (Montilla, 1627), fols. 22^r ff.

[3] Lope de Vega, *La Arcadia*, BAE xxxviii. 93.

'loving affection' and 'most holy respect', enhancing thereby their own prestige. This beauteous, blessed maiden Poetry knows all; she locks up and unlocks secrets; she knows the externals and the innermost goodness of all sciences; she lodges with divine and moral philosophy, is herself incomparably the most learned and universal of all sciences, and knows no limits. The whole time-honoured idea obviously appeals to the idealistic imagination of Cervantes. It is repeated by Don Quixote in another eulogy of poetry and again by the Licenciado Vidriera.[1]

Since Cervantes's theory of the novel is based on the theory of poetry, it is no surprise to find that this encyclopaedic doctrine enters the plan for the ideal novel of chivalry. Other authors concur in this. The Portuguese Rodrigues Lobo prescribes for the chivalresque novelist 'knowledge of all sciences and disciplines'.[2] Lope de Vega says that when one penetrates the shell of these romances through to the heart, one finds there all the branches of philosophy, namely natural, rational, and moral.[3] Similarly the Canon of Toledo says that the writer of the ideal romance 'may show himself to be an astrologer, an excellent cosmographer, a musician, informed in matters of state and even, on occasion, a necromancer if he chooses' (*DQ* I. 47). There is a reminiscence of the link between poetry and oratory in the same passage.

Cervantes shows the esteem for the educated man and the contempt for the ignorant mob common to the writers of his day. His polite expressions of respect for the learning of numerous writers whom he praises in the *Parnaso* and in the *Canto de Calíope* may be more conventional than heartfelt, but his regard for it is beyond question. He subscribed in general principle to a theory of poetic—and, by extension, literary—erudition that was to be found in most contemporary critical writing. Don Quixote recalls the precept when he speaks to Don Diego of those poets who have no knowledge of any 'other tongue or discipline with which to awaken, adorn and assist their own natural talent' (II. 16). El Brocense said, rather similarly, that of Spain's thousands of

[1] *DQ* II. 16; v. 28–29. *Lic. Vidriera*, p. 92.
[2] F. Rodrigues Lobo, *Corte en aldea y noches de invierno*, Spanish translation (Montilla, 1622), fol. 6ᵛ.
[3] Quoted by Henry Thomas, *Spanish and Portuguese Romances of Chivalry* (Cambridge, 1920), p. 155.

poets only a few were first-rate because the vast majority lacked 'the disciplines, languages, and learning necessary to be able to imitate'.[1] Herrera perhaps best illustrates the trend of the times when he expresses approval of the obscurity that results from difficult subject-matter (though not from expression) in poetry:

obscurity which emanates from things and from learning is applauded and much esteemed by the knowledgeable.[2]

Poetic erudition was only a natural consequence of the general Renaissance ideal of the scholar gentleman, for whom the humanists in their pedagogies had prescribed a solid foundation of book learning.

Some Italian theorists, such as Vida, Piccolomini, and Tasso, evidently saw the danger of erudition running riot in poetry and, while accepting the principle, sought to ensure that it was kept in check. In Spain Rengifo, Carvallo, and others required the poet to know something of other arts, sciences, and professions without making himself an expert in them. The theorists of the seventeenth century, however, for the most part took their cue from Herrera, and an entire theory of poetry was based upon the doctrine by Carrillo y Sotomayor in his *Libro de la erudición poética*. As the friend of Cervantes remarked in the prologue to *Don Quixote* I: 'There is no small honour and profit in being a grammarian nowadays.'

The tendency was to overvalue erudition. University graduates were two a penny. Accordingly, Cervantes (who was not one of them) is more critical of the abuse of learning than he is of its neglect. He makes frequent fun of pedants—mildly, for instance, in the case of Don Diego's son Don Lorenzo in the *Quixote*; vigorously in that of the young humanist, the cousin of the fencing expert. The Cousin's works are the last word in useless erudition, consisting entirely of 'things that, once ascertained and known, do not matter a jot either to one's understanding or to one's memory' (II. 22).[3] One of his works, the *Suplemento a Virgilio Polidoro*, is probably intended by Cervantes as a skit upon a popular type of informative miscellany indebted to Polydore

---

[1] El Brocense, ed. *Obras del excelente poeta Garcilaso de la Vega* (ed. Salamanca, 1581), 'Al lector', pp. 4–5.   [2] Herrera, *Anotaciones*, p. 127.
[3] A. Farinelli, *Dos excéntricos* (Madrid, 1936), p. 59, recalls Huarte in relation to this passage. On useless information of just the sort favoured by the Cousin, cf. Seneca, *De brevitate vitae* xiii—Curius Dentatus was the first man who had elephants led in his triumph, &c.

Virgil, such as Pedro Mexía's *Silva de varia lección*—miscellanies, it should be added, of which Cervantes nevertheless made use in the *Persiles*.

The theme of pedantry also occurs in the prologue to Part I of the *Quixote* and in the bogus historicity attributed to the whole novel. In the former Cervantes mocks the ostentatious and erudite paraphernalia introduced by his contemporaries even into works of entertainment. With rueful humour and a touch of malice he affects to be concerned that his novel will be

> wholly lacking in learning and letters, and without the marginal notes or annotations at the end of the book which I observe in other books, even fabulous and profane ones, books so full of maxims from Aristotle and Plato and the whole crowd of philosophers that their readers are filled with wonder and regard the authors as well-read, erudite, and eloquent men.

Whether or not Cervantes is making fun of Lope de Vega, as the commentators would have it, is immaterial: it was a common literary practice. For his part, he declares with some relish that he is by nature a lazy wretch when it comes to seeking out authors to say what he knows very well how to say for himself without them. The irony and the detail of the prologue tend to obscure the essential point he makes. This is that the book's purpose (which officially is to discredit the novels of chivalry) must determine its form, and for its purpose there is no need to go bandying aphorisms from the philosophers and Holy Writ and suchlike. What matters is the artistic realization of the book's aim, and the success of this depends on the author's own skill, not on any borrowed props, however imposing.

The ironic advice to the author on how to adorn the novel with impressive and pseudo-scholarly trappings has a certain resemblance to a passage in Lucian. If you commit a solecism, he says, be ready at once with some entirely fictitious poet or historian whom you can use as your authority.[1] In El Brocense's preface to Gómez de Tapia's translation of Camoens, *La Lusíada* (Salamanca, 1580), there is a passage (probably a gibe at Herrera) which also reminds one of Cervantes's prologue:

> But since it has come to his notice that there is a poetic dictionary which deals with who Phaeton was, and his father and mother, and

---

[1] Lucian, *Professor of Public Speaking*, § 17.

who Venus and Hercules were, and their genealogies, he has not wished to pack any fables in here, or etymologies, or definitions of love or anger or gluttony or fortitude or vainglory; nor has he expatiated on death, or life. He brings in no sonnets either of his own or anyone else's; he has not cared to treat of the many figures and tropes that this work offered, being a matter of little importance for navigation to the Indies, and to the readers as much use as the mill-clack to a deaf miller.[1]

Some parody of erudition is also associated with the pseudo-historical nature of *Don Quixote*. To pretend that a work was translated from one or more foreign tongues was a favourite device of the chivalresque novelists, and even of some who, like Ginés Pérez de Hita, pretended to be historians. Cervantes is, of course, primarily parodying this, but he is incidentally mocking pedantic scholarship, the cult of ancient authority and decadent bookish humanism. This applies more to Part I than to Part II, in which the possibilities of Cide Hamete Benengeli are fully exploited.

The history of Don Quixote is supposed to belong initially to the annals of La Mancha, and there is more than one chronicler. When Cervantes says in chapter 2 that according to some authors the first adventure was that of Puerto Lápice, and according to others that of the windmills, he is not necessarily just anticipating rather carelessly in order to whet our appetites (the two adventures do not occur until the second excursion, when Quixote is accompanied by Sancho); he may well be making fun of the muddled chronicling of historians. The account of the discovery of Benengeli's manuscript makes more fun of scholarly anti-quarianism, and Cervantes makes the alleged historicity more ludicrous still by himself drawing attention to the modernity of some of the books in Don Quixote's library (I. 9). The finding of the commemorative verses by the academicians of Argamasilla is a final piece of parody in the same vein. It is also a good imitation of Montalvo's account of the finding of the manuscript of

---

[1] 'Mas porque ha venido a su noticia que hay un diccionario poético, que trata quién fue Faetón, y su padre y madre, y quién fue Venus y Hércules y sus genea-logías, no ha querido embutir aquí fábulas ni orígenes de vocablos ni definiciones de amor, de ira, de gula, de fortaleza, ni vanagloria, ni a propósito de la muerte, o de la vida, no trae sonetos suyos, ni ajenos, ni quiso tratar las muchas figuras y tropos que se le ofrecían en esta obra, por ser cosa que para la navegación de las Indias importaba poco, y para los lectores es como la cítola en el molino.'

Esplandián (which was found in a tomb underneath a hermitage near Constantinople and brought to Spain by a Hungarian merchant).[1]

Between ignorance and pedantry is the mean of true learning, which Cervantes considers necessary to the poet, and by extension the novelist, since poetic fiction makes use of every branch of human knowledge. It must enrich a natural talent, not act as a substitute for it. The cult of authority for its own sake is laughable; so is the vanity of academics. Above all, while learning is a proper and desirable ornament of imaginative writing, it must be subordinate to the artistic purpose of the work.

To know when to keep quiet in Spanish and when to speak Latin discernment is needed, brother Berganza. (*Coloquio*)

The literary principles we have ranged over so far were attributed in Western Europe to the nature, function, and composition of poetry. Many of the ideas we shall survey in succeeding chapters will also pertain to poetry. Nevertheless, certain of them will acquire a prominence when applied to prose fiction that they did not possess before. The theory of the novel, formed out of that of its parent poetry, and still attached to it, begins to assume a shape of its own. The break will eventually occur at that weak point in the body of poetic theory: the relationship with history.

A few features of what I have called 'first principles' in this chapter already offer intimations of new developments. The creative freedom conceded in particular to the epic poet had at least as great an applicability to the novel; and the novelist was not affected by the exigencies of metre which must sometimes impose a restriction on the best poet in the world. This freedom is the first thing Cervantes, who was not too good at writing verse, notes among the possibilities of romance. Then, the imitation of models, though a form of literary callisthenics intended only to strengthen the Muse, could be crippling in the long run, as the eighteenth century discovered. The scarcity of authorized prose-fiction models further contributed to the freedom of the novel and allowed it to grow, in somewhat ungainly fashion at times, but at least in its own way. Inevitably, though, it had already developed habits, perhaps more bad than good ones. These

[1] G. Rodríguez de Montalvo's prologue to *Amadís de Gaula*, in *Libros de caballerías*, p. 311.

Cervantes pilloried in such a way that prose fiction could never be the same again. Most curious of all, he did it in a novel of his own, which as a result of that act of criticism put itself into an unprecedented alignment with the world from which criticism emanates, the world of here and now, the world of the reader.

Not by coincidence, following the track of another major principle brings us to the same point. Cervantes's insistence on purpose and awareness becomes even more important in view of the comparative freedom enjoyed by the novelist. In a sense it is a transference of disciplinary authority from a traditional body of poetic rules to the author himself, or at least a new emphasis on the responsibility of the latter. The chivalresque romancers offered, most of them, a horrid example of the abuse of freedom. Even attributes that the author had some right to be proud of, such as his knowledge and learning, must be kept in their place and not allowed to interfere with the purpose of the work. But to what or to whom was the novelist responsible? Still to a large extent to accepted, abstract, aesthetic canons, but also, in a way he had never before the later sixteenth century felt himself to be, to the reader.

III

AUTHOR AND READER

1. *The Functions of the Novel—Pleasure and Profit*

Poets aim either to benefit or to amuse, or to utter words
at once both pleasing and helpful to life.   HORACE

ONLY a handful of Spanish critics in the Golden Age penetrate as deeply into the problems of literary art as do the
better Italian writers on the subject. But Spanish writers
of the time show an even deeper concern with the effects of
literature on people. Critics of the novel of chivalry in Spain were
more concerned with its effects on people, and less with its formal
artistic qualities, than were Italian critics of the *romanzo*.

The twin functions traditionally ascribed to poetry were instruction and entertainment, and the qualities associated with
them were, respectively, utility and pleasurableness. They were
applied to prose fiction as well as to poetry and drama. In ancient
Greece the relative importance of the two functions was a matter
of much concern. It did not have the same urgency in the sixteenth
century, because poetry no longer occupied the same position in
practical education as it had held in Antiquity. The most common,
indeed commonplace, view was that poetry should perform both
functions. During the Counter-Reformation emphasis was undoubtedly restored to the didactic function, but it is easy to
exaggerate this. Scaliger made it the poet's business to teach de-
lightfully. Castelvetro, on the other hand, required him principally
to give pleasure and recreation to the common people. Piccolomini,
while admitting both functions, stressed the doctrinal one, and
did not permit good poetry to be merely pleasurable. Tasso's
views were somewhat vacillating, but he expected epic to be useful
while it delighted. Many others made both functions proper to
poetry. There was also added a third requirement, borrowed from
rhetoric: namely, that poetry should be moving. Most Spanish

critics allotted the first two functions, and often the third, to poetry without much discussion, although there were differences of emphasis. Despite all the emphatic declarations of edifying, it seems generally true to say that both critics and other authors were paying increased attention to the pleasure-giving function of imaginative literature. And this for its part involved a subtle shift of attention towards the reader's requirements and reactions.

No one who has paid any attention to Cervantes can doubt that he took the functions of literature seriously. However, in the earliest of his prologues there survives a trace of that tendency, inherited from the Middle Ages and still very prevalent in the Renaissance, to treat poetry as a mere pastime, and to excuse oneself for wasting one's time on such juvenile frivolities. Santillana, for example, had spoken apologetically of his *decires* and *canciones* as belonging to the season of youthful pursuits like dressing up, jousting, dancing, and other courtly exercises.[1] In the same essentially depreciatory vein is Luis de León's presentation to Portocarrero of what is some of the finest poetry in the language. And so too is Cervantes's disarming and misleading description of the *Galatea* as a product of that time of his life when he had scarcely emerged from youth, a time when such occupations are permitted (prol.).

There is more than engaging modesty behind these apologies. They are not apologies for writing immature poetry. They are for writing poetry at all. González de Bobadilla goes so far as to begin his pastoral novel by speaking of things as 'mean' as poetry, adding too that he had hardly completed his elementary study of Latin when he wrote it.[2] While such excuses were an accepted matter of form, the fact that they were so often made by avowed lovers of poetry like Luis de León, Cervantes, and even Herrera, reflects an uneasiness prevailing in sixteenth-century attitudes to poetry before Aristotle's *Poetics* became commandingly established in criticism. There were plenty of defences of poetry—all the more impassioned, perhaps, because they lacked the really cogent arguments Aristotle supplied. But exemplariness and allegorical

---

[1] Marqués de Santillana, *Proemio y carta* (ed. Oxford, 1927), p. 69. The opinion is older than the Middle Ages. Plutarch calls poetic compositions 'but a childish pastime' compared with the deeds of men of arms (*On the Fame of the Athenians*, 350. 8, *Moralia*, trans. Babbitt, Loeb Cl. Lib.).

[2] B. González de Bobadilla, *Ninfas y pastores de Henares* (Alcalá de Henares, 1587), fol. 5ᵛ.

meaning, the great medieval justifications of poetic fiction (a ruder name for which was 'lies'), no longer seemed quite enough, as ever more printed entertainment rolled off the presses. The *Poetics* restored seriousness to the conception of fiction. Apologies and defences of poetry did not cease thereafter, but there was a change of tone. Poetry was on solid ground.

We find no more excuses of this sort in Cervantes. His many allusions to the functions of literature may be commonplaces, but they are not heedlessly repeated; he had evidently thought about them. He gives more importance to the function of entertainment, but he takes the business of entertainment very seriously indeed.

On a few occasions Cervantes applies the one absolute standard by which literature could be measured. By this standard only sacred writings and devotional works were absolutely beneficial; in comparison with these the rest must be trivial. The effect was simply to divide all literature between two extremes, according to a quite common formula:

> [Literary] subjects are either divine or profane, and on that account very different from one another; for the first deal with things that are useful to the salvation of the soul, arousing the two principal virtues of hope and charity. . . . The second undertake merely curious subjects, matters that simply give pleasure to the world; these are works that do not nourish the spirit, but rather are set about and decked with vanities, being founded only on mental pleasure and recreation.[1]

This austere view of literature is often reflected in the ideas of writers whom, like Cervantes, one would not call puritanical. He does not waste time on fruitless comparisons, but, like many sixteenth-century moralists, he does occasionally mention the wholly salutary type of literature in antithesis to the novels of chivalry and other frivolous confections. The Canon, seeking to canalize Quixote's interests, advises him to read not only true but sacred history, reading that will redound to the advantage of his conscience and the enhancement of his good name (I. 49). The same literary extremes are brought together in the visit to the printing-house in Barcelona (II. 62). Marasso has ingeniously

---

[1] C. Suárez de Figueroa, *Plaza universal de todas ciencias y artes* (Madrid, 1615), fol. 125^{r-v}. This is the Spanish version of Tommaso Garzoni's *Piazza universale* (Venice, 1587).

suggested that we need not look for a lost Italian book called *Le Bagatelle*, and that the *Luz del alma* is not necessarily the work of that name by Fray Felipe de Meneses: one stands for literary trivia and the other for books of devotion.[1] When the Knight recovers his sanity on his deathbed, he recognizes the novels of chivalry to be foolish and fraudulent, and regrets that he has been left no time to read that other sort of book which is the 'light of the soul' (*luz del alma*) (II. 74).

The simple statement of the aim of writing is made by the Canon of Toledo. It is 'jointly to instruct and to delight' (*DQ* I. 47).[2] But in what way was a story expected to be instructive and useful? Neither Cervantes nor his readers were likely to suppose that the *Galatea* was a handy work for the sheep-farmer, as Virgil had claimed to teach agriculture in the *Georgics*. Certainly, something might be expected of prose fiction in this respect. The writer ought to be learned, or at least well informed, and the reader could hope to profit by that. But the function, at any rate in the eyes of Cervantes, was not narrowly doctrinal. It was chiefly connected with exemplariness, which, despite new ideas about fiction, still influenced literature to an extent that the modern reader can often appreciate only with an effort. The effect of the Aristotelian doctrines on the concept of exemplariness, as we shall note later, was ultimately to broaden it. Cervantes's obsession with truth in literature was so powerful that it is difficult not to believe that the 'utility' of prose fiction depended for him above all on its poetic truth.

Entertainment, however, came first. No one can have failed to notice the readiness of Cervantine characters to tell and to listen to tales. They are an agreeable pastime for the audiences in the novels as well as the reader. They afford mental relaxation, distraction, 'escape'. The pleasure of those who have listened to a story is repeatedly mentioned. Entertainment, Cervantes plainly implies, is the first duty of prose fiction.

The highest form of pleasure in imaginative literature derives from that harmonious beauty which is inseparable from the poetic truth of the work. Fantastic imaginings, charming in appearance, as León Hebreo explained, cannot really be beautiful because they

---

[1] A. Marasso, *Cervantes: la invención del 'Quijote'* (Buenos Aires, 1954), pp. 257-9.
[2] Cf. *Coloquio*, p. 163.

offend the intelligence, which judges them, intellectually, to be ugly.[1] Thus the Canon argues against the novels of chivalry:

And granting that the main intention of such books is to delight, I do not see how they can achieve this when they are so full of outrageous nonsense [*disparates*]. For that pleasure which the soul conceives must come from the beauty and harmony [*concordancia*] it either sees in the things presented to it visually or contemplates in those that occur in the imagination; and nothing that is ugly or disordered can give us any satisfaction.[2]

If literature delights and instructs, it is not just 'doing something'; it is 'doing something to someone'. The effectiveness depends in part on who is at the receiving end. Different sorts of literature please different sorts of people. This produces an important complication, because Cervantes implicitly admits more than one level of operation. At the highest level, only a true work of art pleases a discerning person like the Canon, who looks for that harmonious note to be struck in his mind. At a lower level, the novels of chivalry please an undiscerning person like the Innkeeper, who does not bother his head about 'art'. Those same novels displease the Canon—but (and here the complication arises) even he can enjoy them, on the lower level, when he allows himself to suspend his critical faculty.

For myself, I can say that as long as I do not stop to think, when I read them, that they are all lies and frivolity, they give me a certain pleasure; but when I reflect upon what they really are, I fling the best of them against the wall. (*DQ* I. 49)

From the highest point of view, this pleasure is false, and even when he does read them uncritically he is, like most people in similar circumstances, eventually bored.

Although, carried away by a false and idle pleasure, I have read the beginning of nearly all that have been written, I have never managed to read any of them from beginning to end, because it seems to me that they are all more or less the same and not one has anything more in it than another. (*DQ* I. 47)

---

[1] León Hebreo, op. cit., p. 314.

[2] 'Y puesto que el principal intento de semejantes libros sea el deleitar, no sé yo cómo puedan conseguirle, yendo llenos de tantos y tan desaforados disparates; que el deleite que en el alma se concibe ha de ser de la hermosura y concordancia que ve o contempla en las cosas que la vista o la imaginación le ponen delante; y toda cosa que tiene en sí fealdad y descompostura no nos puede causar contento alguno' (*DQ* I. 47; iii. 346–7).

They fail to please him on account of their artistic defects and because they entirely ignore the function of instruction (though their authors frequently claimed the contrary), just like the ancient Milesian fables, 'which are nonsensical tales designed solely to amuse and not to instruct, unlike apologues which entertain and instruct at the same time'.[1]

The enormous popularity of the romances, though declining fast, was an important factor. They did not perform the function as it should be performed, but they did perform it after a fashion. Cervantes was far from being a literary snob. He wanted a prose fiction that would succeed with both levels of the public. He was intensely aware of the spell cast by romance, the hypnotic element in entertainment, which even art that is defective by the highest standards can possess. Don Quixote, in every other way a *discreto*, is bewitched by romance. This ability of Cervantes to regard the romances of chivalry on two levels (or, more strictly, on as many levels as there are characters in the *Quixote* affected by them) is an instance of his remarkable aptitude for looking at things with a sort of multiple vision. It helps to explain the ambiguity of the sentence passed on the author of *Tirante el Blanco*. The Priest condemns him for artistic ineptitude (on the higher level), having just praised the book (on the lower level) for the entertainment it affords.

The primary function of the pastoral novel is entertainment too. This is clear from the definition given by Berganza in the *Coloquio*, where the novels are described as being 'for the entertainment of the idle'. In the *Quixote* I. 6 they are called 'works of understanding [*entendimiento*]'. Rodríguez Marín and earlier editors have amended this to read *entretenimiento*. It seems more likely that Cervantes would call them 'works of entertainment', but either would make sense. If he did mean *entendimiento*, he would be further distinguishing the pastoral novel from the chivalresque, indirectly stressing the useful, instructional function, which he did not exclude from pastoral, since he could tell the reader that he had mixed some philosophical discourse with amorous shepherds' talk in his *Galatea* (prol.). We may suppose that he thought philosophical discussion no less instructive than entertaining.

What I take to be Cervantes's definitive statement on the func-

---

[1] '. . . que son cuentos disparatados, que atienden solamente a deleitar, y no a enseñar; al contrario de lo que hacen las fábulas apólogas, que deleitan y enseñan juntamente' (ibid., p. 346). Cf. J. L. Vives, *De ratione dicendi* III, *Opera* i. 144.

tion of the novel is in effect an elaboration on a very ancient and common notion: that imaginative literature (the writing as well as the reading of it) is a relief from work and a solace for care.[1] By agreeably occupying the mind, literature for the time being releases it from toils and troubles. It can even give more lasting relief and so has a certain therapeutic value. This is to bring the two functions together: to say that 'delectare' *is* 'prodesse'. A tendency to reconcile the functions in this and other ways may be noted in the literary ideas of the sixteenth and seventeenth centuries. Some of the better theorists seem to have realized that the two mechanisms were really complicated and could not be disengaged absolutely. Bernardo de Balbuena observed that what is useful always has some pleasure in it, although the reverse is not always true.[2] For Cervantes fiction offers recreation, which is beneficial re-creation. The answer to the charge that reading novels is a waste of time, when not actually harmful, is that they are not merely a pastime for the idle but a recreation for the busy, 'for it is not possible for the bow to be always bent,[3] nor can our weak human condition be sustained without some legitimate recreation' (*DQ* I. 48).

Since novels have this beneficial effect on the reader, they are socially useful, like games, or like gardens and other pleasant places designed for refreshment and relaxation. The age, says Cervantes, is in need of merry entertainments (*DQ* I. 28). Even the Priest concedes that there is a place for such books in well-ordered states, just as there is for chess, handball, or billiards (*DQ* I. 32). Much the same idea occurs in Piccolomini, who speaks of the 'advantage of refreshing and restoring the forces of the mind for other activities, in the same way as do games, jokes, pranks and other similar ways of refreshing one's spirits'.[4] Cervantes uses the parallel again for his *Novelas ejemplares*:

My intention has been to set up in the public square of our nation a billiard table where everyone may come and amuse himself without harm. . . .

[1] e.g. Plutarch, *Comparison of Aristophanes and Menander*, 854. 3; Marqués de Santillana, 'Carta a su hijo', *Prose and Verse* (London, 1940), p. 38; Suárez de Figueroa, *Amarilis*, p. 44.
[2] B. de Balbuena, *Siglo de oro en las selvas de Erífile* (Madrid, 1608), 'Al lector', fol. 2ᵛ. Cf. Aristotle, *Poetics*, 1448ʙ. And see El Pinciano, op. cit. i. 212.
[3] Cf. El Pinciano, op. cit. iii. 229–30; J. Ferrer (pseud. 'Bisbe y Vidal'), *Tratado de las comedias* (Barcelona, 1618), fol. 7ᵛ.   [4] Piccolomini, op. cit., p. 371.

A vital condition of such works, as we shall see later, is that they should be morally unexceptionable, but Cervantes's view is not an ascetic one.

For one is not always in church; the oratories are not always busy; one is not always engaged in business matters, however important they may be. There is a time for recreation, when the weary spirit may repose.

It is for this purpose that public walks are laid out, fountains are dug, hills are levelled and gardens are cultivated with care.[1]

In the theory of Cervantes, as in much of that of his time, the traditional functions lose something of the narrowness and rigidity to which they were liable. Entertainment comes first, for plainly the effectiveness of the other depends much on this in fiction. There are standards of pleasure, as there are differences in the intellectual level of different readers; the highest is a response to beauty. Entertainment is beneficial and even necessary. The best novels are works of art which offer pleasure, profit, and recreation. In a passing remark of Don Quixote's he makes the analogy that perhaps best combines the ideas of the beneficial and the enjoyable: 'It only remains for me to give sustenance to my mind, as I shall do by listening to this good man's story' (I. 50). A story is spiritual nourishment.[2]

2. The Functions of the Novel—Admiratio

All things are admired either because they are new or because they are great.   BACON

Something else was expected of literature in Cervantes's time, something which came to acquire a dignity comparable with the traditional functions of instruction and entertainment. This was

---

[1] 'Mi intento ha sido poner en la plaza de nuestra república una mesa de trucos, donde cada uno pueda llegar a entretenerse, sin daño de barras . . . Sí, que no siempre se está en los templos; no siempre se ocupan los oratorios; no siempre se asiste a los negocios, por calificados que sean. Horas hay de recreación donde el afligido espíritu descanse. Para este efecto se plantan las alamedas, se buscan las fuentes, se allanan las cuestas y se cultivan, con curiosidad, los jardines' (Novelas, prol., p. 22).

[2] Cf. Coloquio, pp. 249–50.

that it should arouse *admiratio* in the reader or spectator. It is not easy to fix the variegated meaning of the word. Dryden, like Sidney, could say 'admiration', but the modern English sense of this is misleadingly narrow. It could also mean 'pleasurable surprise', 'astonishment', 'wonder', and 'awe'. Fundamentally it seems to have been a sort of excitement stimulated by whatever was exceptional, whether because of its novelty, its excellence, or other extreme characteristics. Its causes ranged from the crudely sensational to the noble, the beautiful, and the sublime. They may be divided broadly into two types, the surprising and the excellent. The concept in its simplest form is as old as art; the most primitive story-teller knows the value of surprising his listeners. But *admiratio* must be reckoned a fundamental principle of baroque art in particular, as Croce and others have recognized. For Cervantes, as for Tasso, one of the greatest of literary problems was how to reconcile the marvellously 'admirable' and verisimilitude.

The origins of the idea in literary theory are found in Antiquity. It follows from Aristotle's stipulation of the need for the marvellous in tragedy and especially in the epic. In a passage of his *Rhetoric* he also alluded to the 'admirable' quality of unusual language.[1] Either matter or style, then, could be the occasion of *admiratio*. In Cervantes's theory of the novel the first is much the more prominent. An equally important source was the requirement that oratory should stir men's minds.[2] The arousing of *admiratio* cannot be identified with *movere*, but the idea owes much to rhetoric. 'Longinus's' treatise, though published by Robortelli in 1554, seems to have been too little known before the end of the seventeenth century for his notion of poetic 'transport' to be significantly influential.

The Italians of the Renaissance made the concept important. Pontanus seems to have been the first to elaborate it in his *Actius*.[3] Robortelli made significant observations that were followed up by later theorists. He particularly realized the difficulties that arose from the conflicting demands of verisimilitude and the 'admirable'. By the time of Minturno's and Scaliger's poetics the arousing of

[1] Aristotle, *Rhetoric* III. ii. 2.
[2] Thus, for example, Cicero, *De Oratore* ii. 121.
[3] Giovanni Pontano, *Opera omnia* (Florence, 1520). A relevant extract is appended to Girolamo Fracastoro's *Naugerius, sive de poetica dialogus*, with translation by Ruth Kelso, *UISLL* ix (1924).

admiratio was established as a primary function of poetry. In Spain, El Pinciano and Cascales, both of whom examined its types and causes, had no doubt of its importance.

Admiratio is something of the greatest importance in any kind of poetry, but above all in heroic poetry. If the poet does not make us marvel, he can arouse little pleasure in our hearts.[1]

Cervantes refers to it repeatedly as an audience-reaction to events related. These references are usually quite casual, so the theoretical importance of the concept for him must be gauged from numerous passing remarks. Their frequency, however, is an indication that he took the matter for granted. He knew the doctrine, but we may be certain that the function emanated from the very nature of story-telling as far as he was concerned. The human fondness for being surprised by new things lies at the heart of romance, and Cervantes knew the necessity of engaging and holding the reader's attention. The Canon requires of works of fiction that they should 'amaze, grip, exhilarate, and entertain in such a way that *admiratio* and pleasure go hand in hand' (*DQ* I. 47).

Here and on other occasions the function is introduced in association with that of giving pleasure. Rutilio's story left his listeners 'marvelling and contented' (*Persiles* I. 9). At Periandro's account of events in the barbarous isle 'Arnaldo·was astonished, and the company were delighted and marvelled anew' (*Persiles* I. 15). The innkeeper in *La ilustre fregona* promises the magistrate that he will hear things that 'will cause him both pleasure and amazement'.

If Cervantes does not specifically connect *admiratio* with the other, the instructional, function of the novel, they were probably not unconnected in his mind. Spingarn sees *admiratio* as a logical consequence of the Renaissance belief that poetry teaches by example.[2] This is to restrict it unduly, but there is certainly evidence of their association. The learned humanist Alexio Venegas says the principal aim of ancient poetry was to direct men to the precepts of moral philosophy 'by way of *admiratio*';[3] Vera y

[1] Cascales, *Tablas*, p. 146.

[2] J. E. Spingarn, *A History of Literary Criticism in the Renaissance* (New York, 1899), p. 53.

[3] A. Venegas, foreword, dated 1552, to A. Almazán's translation of L. B. Alberti, *El Momo* (ed. Madrid, 1598).

Mendoza in his *Panegírico*, that the aim of the heroic poet is to 'astonish and fire the imagination of his contemporaries and posterity' by singing the sublime deeds of past heroes.[1] Thus it is no accident, I think, that the novel of Cervantes most calculated to astonish the reader, the *Persiles*, is also the most edifying.

Seventeenth-century writers aimed to startle and impress their readers not only because this was pleasant, but in order to engage their attention and put them in a receptive frame of mind in which a moral lesson could be driven home, a universal truth conveyed. Manneristic writing achieved the effect by stylistic and conceptual means, capturing the reader's attention, rousing his wits and challenging his intellect. One prized the truth of the meaning more when one had had to struggle to reach it. The methods used to stimulate one, however, sometimes suggested not so much a concentration on the reader as a positive assault, and they were indeed not unconnected with the militant techniques of the Jesuits.

Admiratio was to a large extent an intellectual principle, for if it could be associated with ignorance, so it could with curiosity, the beginning of knowledge. Lope de Vega scornfully called it 'the daughter of ignorance' on one occasion,[2] but he corrected himself on another, asking, 'How can *admiratio* be ignorance, if the desire to know is only natural, and *admiratio* the beginning of knowledge?'[3] Like the other literary functions, then, especially the pleasure-giving one, it was in part a two-way affair, to some extent governed by the intellectual level of the readers addressed. Surprising the enlightened was not like surprising the ignorant. Cervantes realized this in connexion with the *comedia*, where *admiratio* was all too easily abused. There was no particular virtue in making ignorant groundlings gape (*DQ* I. 48, II. 26). Nor would the truly judicious reader be amazed at cheap displays of erudition which had no place in a work of fiction designed to entertain, as he intimated in the first prologue to *Don Quixote*.

Admiratio is evidently a powerful sensation for Cervantes,

---

[1] Vera y Mendoza, op. cit., fol. 19ᵛ.

[2] Lope de Vega, *La Filomena*, BAE xxxviii. 491. Cf. Erasmus, *Encomium moriae* (ed. Leipzig [1905?]) ii. 300–1: 'qui non intelligunt, hoc ipso magis admirentur, quo minus intelligunt'.

[3] Lope de Vega, *Laurel de Apolo*, BAE xxxviii, prol., 185. Cf. J. L. Vives, *De instrumento probabilitatis*, Opera i. 614: 'Ex admiratione nascitur quaerendi cupiditas.'

something just less intense than *espanto*, or verging on fright.[1] Its principal source is events themselves:

There can be no need to ask if the company were astonished or not by Isabella's story, for the story in itself contained *admiratio* enough to enter the minds of those who heard it. (*Persiles* III. 20)

But he implies too that it may depend on the manner of their narrating:

and if you are not astonished, either I have not known how to tell [the story] or you have hearts of marble. (*Persiles* III. 16)

An observation of Cascales (who treated the subject more systematically, if less imaginatively, than El Pinciano) is apposite here. '*Admiratio*', he said, 'is born of things, words, order and variety.'[2] For the author of the *Persiles* variety evidently has a hand in it too. At any rate, the 'variable history' of Ricla has the appropriate effect on the audience (I. 6).

Since surprise is associated with novelty, literary invention is expected to be 'admirable'. The word 'invention' also frequently implies the ingenious or the elaborate in Spanish writing of the time. Using the word in this sense, the Mayor in *Pedro de Urdemalas* remarks that new inventions 'cause either *admiratio* or laughter'.[3] The distinction suggested here between the 'admirable' and the ridiculous is also present in Cervantes's statement that 'Don Quixote's exploits are to be greeted either with *admiratio* or with laughter'.[4] The explanation of this not altogether obvious distinction is to be sought, I believe, in the idea that the truly 'admirable' must have verisimilitude. When it does not, El Pinciano

---

[1]
        'De espanto, no estoy en mí.
        Mal dije; de admiración,
        que espanto jamás le tuve.'
                    (*Casa de los celos* II, p. 199)
        '. . . o caso nuevo,
        digno de admiración que cause espanto.'
                    (*Parnaso* VIII. 112)
        '. . . de admiración, que llegue a ser espanto.'
                    (ibid. I. 22)

[2] Cascales, *Tablas*, p. 147.

[3]
        '. . . invenciones noveles,
        o admiran, o hacen reír.'
                    (*Pedro de Urdemalas* II, p. 163)

[4] '. . . los sucesos de don Quijote, o se han de celebrar con admiración, o con risa' (*DQ* II. 44; vi. 273).

says, '*admiratio* for the thing is turned to laughter'.[1] The corollary of this is that what is both extraordinary and incredible is a source of the comic, or at least of a certain type of it. But neither El Pinciano, who is talking of unintended comedy, and whose views on *admiratio* are not entirely consistent in this respect, nor Cervantes, who has so disappointingly little to say on the comic, follows up the idea. The creator of Benengeli and the author of the *Viaje del Parnaso*, of course, knew in practice how to exploit the comic possibilities of the unbelievably extraordinary, but the idea does not figure in his theory. His criticism of the inadvertently comic (which he also knew how to enjoy) does, but that was a very different matter.

The importance of this function in Cervantes's theory of the novel stems from his personal fondness for the exceptional—for what in modern journalism would make 'a story', just as it did for him. But the exceptional may be miraculous, marvellous, or simply unusual, and here the trouble begins. For, to quote El Pinciano again, 'there seems to be a contradiction between the "admirable" and what has verisimilitude'.[2] We shall see in Chapter V how Cervantes attempts to reconcile them.

He pinpoints their potential disparity in occasional remarks. The Viceroy exclaims at the assertions of Ana Félix that they are more amazing than credible (*DQ* II. 63). The author describes the astonishing jump by what must be the first lady parachutist in literature, aptly enough, as 'rather to be wondered at than believed' (*Persiles* III. 15). The chapter-heading of *Don Quixote* II. 23 advertises the 'admirable' things which the Knight said he saw in Montesinos' Cave, 'the grandeur and impossibility of which have caused this chapter to be regarded as apocryphal'. The extraordinary events that offered such desirable material set Cervantes a problem so great that he was driven to conclude in his last novel (how far seriously and how far ironically, I do not know):

I maintain that it would be better not to relate them, as is advised by those ancient Spanish verses, which say: 'Do not tell or narrate

---

[1] '. . . la admiración de la cosa se convierte en risa' (op. cit. ii. 104). Herrick notes that Maggi's theory of the 'admirable' as an important source of the comic was unusual ('Comic Theory', pp. 44 ff.). The idea of the absurdly or grotesquely 'admirable' appears in other theorists, however, including El Pinciano, op. cit. ii. 61, 63–64.   [2] El Pinciano, op. cit. ii. 61.

astonishing things, for not everyone understands just how they are.'[1]

But he was unable to heed the advice he recalled. He could no more exorcize the 'admirable' from his idea of the novel than he could stifle the voice of reason in him. The intelligence had to be satisfied, but not at the expense of the imagination. The two must come to some working arrangement.

3. Morality

> But I incline to come to the alarming conclusion that it is just the literature that we read for 'amusement' or 'purely for pleasure' that may have the greatest and least suspected influence upon us.   T. S. ELIOT

The problem of Cervantes's religious and moral opinions has undoubtedly been inflated beyond its real size by critics since the 1920's. Ideological affiliations have lent passion to argument, and we have seen Cervantes depicted, at one extreme, as a battling champion of the Counter-Reformation, as a cunning free-thinker at the other, and assigned to most of the possible positions in between. No exclusive view is satisfying, and something can be said for the most disparate interpretations. To clarify the picture it is necessary to start from the fact that there are lines of thought in his works that run counter to each other. Religion and morals are not the only department of his ideas of which this is so, and he is not the only great European writer of the critical period of history he lived in of which this is true. However, the larger problem is not our concern; our task is simply to determine the role of morality in his theory of prose fiction.

All the same, we cannot ignore the fact that on a very few occasions his novels cannot honestly be said to live up to certain high principles of morality professed, notably, in the *Novelas ejemplares*. There is also the notorious case of *El viejo celoso* (*The*

---

[1] '. . . yo digo que mejor sería no contarlos, según lo aconsejan aquellos antiguos versos castellanos que dicen:
>Las cosas de admiración
>no las digas ni las cuentes:
>que no saben todas gentes
>cómo son.' (*Persiles* III. 16; ii. 154)

jealous old man). How, after 'all that "cutting off his hand" ', in Castro's phrase,[1] could Cervantes have published this dramatic interlude? We can only speculate. The main reason I shall suggest for such lapses as there are in his novels may not be inapplicable here. It is evident too that he was always liable to loosen his grip and surrender to popular custom when writing for the theatre, and the *entremés* was a traditionally bawdy genre. But then again, it has been replied very properly to this that morality is not a matter of genre. What there can be no arguing about is that by Cervantes's professed standards (if not by those of some other writers of his time, or even of the censor who passed it for publication) the piece is indecent. And what is important is not to draw false conclusions from this. It is a false conclusion that Cervantes's lapse from principle is incompatible with belief in that principle. On the contrary, the two not uncommonly go together.

The lapses in his novels are not very spectacular as breaches of rule. Greater gulfs than this yawn between his theory and his practice. Nor should they be exaggerated morally. His own protestations have drawn more attention to these lapses than they could have attracted for themselves. Taking his work as a whole, Cervantes is one of the most profoundly moral of writers.

The strong moral note that sounds in Italian and Spanish literary theory in the later sixteenth century was not so uniquely a product of the Counter-Reformation as some scholars have implied. An ethical preoccupation with literature was not the peculiar gift of the Council of Trent to the world. The difference in moral climate in Spain before and after Trent has also been exaggerated; it was less pronounced there than it was in Italy. The most unbending theologian or puritan of the time was not more stern with poets than Plato had been in the *Republic*, or more severe on the insidious charms of poetry than Boethius and the Church Fathers. The ancient Greeks had laid more emphasis on poetry's doctrinal possibilities. The exemplary was valued more highly in the Middle Ages than ever before or since. Humanists of the Renaissance had little use for anything but the plain lessons in poetic fictions.

What was distinctive in the later sixteenth and earlier seventeenth centuries was a peculiar awareness of the influence and persuasive powers of literature on a public no longer restricted

[1] A. Castro, 'La ejemplaridad de las *Novelas* cervantinas', *Hacia Cervantes*, p. 348.

to the courtly and scholarly few. In return, the influence of the
public on literature grew, and sixteenth-century Italian critics
paid considerable attention to the interplay of forces between
author, work, and audience or readers, as Weinberg has shown.[1]
It is this sense of literature as an active force that gives the note of
urgency to moral considerations in the criticism of the time. 'The
purpose of poetry is to make man perfect and happy', said Bene-
detto Varchi.[2] One could hardly rate its aims, and by implication
its powers, more highly.

The main aspects of the subject as it occurs in Cervantes's
theory of the novel are: sexual morality, the exemplary qualities
of fiction, and the problem of truth and falsehood (which requires
a chapter to itself). They go, I think, in ascending order of importance as far as he is concerned. He does not enter the deeper
waters of problems that exercised some of the Italian theorists
and a few Spaniards, such as whether the portrayal of evil was not
always harmful. But he is, of course, aware of the complexity of
any problem involving good and evil.

Good and evil appear to be so little removed from each other that
they are like two concurrent lines, which, though having distinct and
separate beginnings, end in one point. (*Persiles* IV. 12)

The morality of the novel is not different in kind from the
morality of poetry, and poetry is good in itself, although men may
misuse it. Tyrsi had asked in the *Galatea* IV:

now tell me what praiseworthy thing there is in the world today, the
use of which cannot be turned to evil, however good it may be?
Condemn philosophy because it often lays bare our defects, and because
many philosophers have been bad men. Burn the works of the heroic
poets because they castigate and censure vices with their satires and
verses.

This is an old and much-used argument.[3] Cervantes has an ideal
of Poetry as the 'sum of the useful, the decent, and the delightful',

---

[1] B. Weinberg: 'From Aristotle to Pseudo-Aristotle', *CL* v (1953); 'Robortello
on the *Poetics*' and 'Castelvetro's Theory of Poetics', both in *Critics and Criticism,
Ancient and Modern*, ed. R. S. Crane (Chicago, 1952); also the article cited above on
Scaliger.   [2] Toffanin, op. cit., p. 97.

[3] e.g. in *Rhet. ad Herenn.* II. xxvii. 44; A. de Cartagena, *Libro de Marco Tulio
Cicerón que se llama de la retórica*, prol. and dedic., in Menéndez y Pelayo, *Ideas estéticas*
i, appendix 2, p. 494; J. del Encina, *Arte de poesía castellana*, ibid., appendix 5,
p. 514. The immediate source of the passage in Cervantes is Mario Equicola's *Libro
di natura d'amore*, according to F. López Estrada, 'La influencia italiana en la *Galatea*
de Cervantes', *CL* iv (1952), 165.

the 'glory of virtue and scourge of vice' (*Parnaso* IV) and much
more in the same vein. It seems (he is not too logical on the point)
that this ideal is not essentially harmed, though it is grossly
offended, by scurrilous and trashy versifiers. He comes to distinguish two sorts of poetry on these lines, and there is war
between the followers of each in the *Parnaso*. His views are more
picturesque than consistent, but his sentiments are clear. The
nature of Poetry (like that of Monarchy, say) had nothing to do
with the fact that (like bad kings) there might be bad poets.
Sánchez de Lima expresses the same common idea, accusing mean
and uninspired poets of dishonouring Poetry, trailing her through
the public markets and putting her up to auction.[1] More than just
morality is involved here, but decency is integral to this ideal.
Tasso is speaking for his age when he says, 'Not every pleasure
should be the aim of poetry, but only that which is united with
decency'.[2] Cervantes's ideal of Poetry corresponds closely to his
ideal of feminine beauty, which is imperfect if not completed by
high qualities of mind and soul, and in which any immodesty is
unthinkable.

He speaks roughly enough of poets as a breed, but their profession invests them with a certain dignity. Apollo ordains in the
Adjunta that any poet of whatever quality or condition be accepted
as an *hidalgo* by virtue of his generous profession. The poet therefore owes it to his office to be virtuous, for he reflects his nature
in his work. 'If he is chaste in his habits, so he will be in his
verses', says Quixote (II. 16). This, of course, is the time-honoured
notion that the good orator (or preacher, poet, scholar, painter,
&c.) must be a good man.[3] Tasso makes it clear that the poet who
writes indecencies errs as a man rather than as a poet, but the best
poet is necessarily a good man.[4] From all this we may infer that
Cervantes is not, by and large, sympathetic to Plato's treatment
of poets in the *Republic*, although this treatment is indirectly
recalled with approval in the suggestion that the chivalresque
novels should be banished from the Christian state (*DQ* I. 47),
and again through the Dueña Dolorida (of all unlikely people!).

[1] Sánchez de Lima, op. cit., fol. 20ʳ.
[2] '. . . non ogni piacere sia il fine della poesia, ma quel solamente, il quale è
congiunta coll'onestà' (*Del poema eroico* I. 42).
[3] Thus e.g. Quintilian, op. cit. I, proem., 9, and XII. i. 1; St. Basil, *On Pagan
Literature* vi; Herrera, *Anotaciones*, p. 329.
[4] Tasso, *Del poema eroico* I. 42–43.

She would like the writers of erotic verse expelled from her make-believe country. But significantly, she exonerates them immediately and lays the blame for the harm done by their honeyed poison on 'the ninnies who praise them and the silly girls who believe them' (*DQ* II. 38).

Cervantes, then, believes that poetry is something intrinsically good, although it may be used by poetasters in a manner insulting to its natural dignity and harmful to the public. The poet has a responsibility to his office in the matter of virtue, and, if we can assume that the Duenna's opinion is Cervantes's own, the public is not absolved from all responsibility either, for the foolish and the simple encourage vicious poets. He may have a less exalted ideal of the novel than of his fair maiden Poetry, but since the novel is itself a type of poetry, it is inconceivable that the view we have outlined does not apply to it in all essentials.

Cervantes condemns the novels of chivalry on three main grounds: moral, stylistic, and because they are nonsensically untrue. His most frequent and emphatic criticism is on the third count, as is that of many sixteenth-century writers. If the Niece and the Housekeeper treat the books as heretical and the Priest condemns them to an *auto-da-fé*, it is primarily on account of their falsity. This 'heretical' association supplies an amusing if unwitting riposte to Elizabethan critics in England who branded the romances as typical specimens of monkish bawdry and popish lies. The Council of Trent, of course, condemned literary obscenity,[1] and the correspondence with the types of sentence meted out by the Priest in *Don Quixote* I. 6 has been noted—condemnation, detention, expurgation.[2] There is a sharp distinction to be drawn, however: artistic considerations influence the verdicts of the Priest very much more than they did those of the Holy Office. It should be remembered too that scarcely a novel of chivalry was in fact banned by the Inquisition.

There is no mention of moral improprieties in the novels singled out for comment in the scrutiny of the library, except possibly in the case of *Tirante el Blanco*. However, on a few other

---

[1] 'Libri qui res lascivas sive obscoenas ex professo tractant, narrant aut docent, quum non solum fidei sed et morum qui hujusmodi librorum lectione facile corrumpi solent, ratio habenda sit, omnino prohibentur, et qui eos habuerint severe ab episcopis puniantur' (Regula VII).

[2] H. Hatzfeld, *El 'Quijote' como obra de arte del lenguaje* (Madrid, 1949), p. 187.

occasions the romances are charged with indecency, or, just as often, simply ridiculed for it. The Canon says they are 'lascivious in the love affairs', and he comments on the lack of decorum in their improbable royal amours: 'What are we to say of the readiness with which a hereditary queen or empress falls into the arms of an unknown knight errant?' (*DQ* I. 47). Don Quixote's fears that Cide Hamete may have treated his own chaste love with some indelicacy, redounding to the discredit of his lady Dulcinea, are understandable (II. 3). But after all, Cervantes's ironical humour suggests, the works are so foolish that one can hardly take seriously those damsels

who rode about with their palfreys and riding-whips, carrying all their virginity, from mountain to mountain and valley to valley. There were maidens in those days who (unless some rogue, or some rustic with axe and helmet, or some monstrous giant, ravished them) after eighty years, during all of which time they never once slept indoors, went to their graves as virginal as the mothers who bore them. (*DQ* I. 9)

Cervantes's characters vary, as would real human beings, in their attitude to the novels. The Niece, whose reactions are particularly violent, sees every one as infamous and a corrupter of good morals (II. 6). The level-headed Don Diego, however, says much the same thing. He says they are 'so much to the detriment of good morals and to the prejudice of good histories' (II. 16). Though not original, this is one of the most significant criticisms. Some sixteenth-century writers were very aware of the depressive effect a corruption of taste has on people's values. Don Diego's second objection can be complemented by a passage from Juan de Valdés, whose attitude to the chivalresque novel was not unlike that of Cervantes:

The best ten years of my life, which were spent in courts and palaces, I employed in no more virtuous exercise than in reading these lies, and I took such pleasure in them that I could not have enough of them. See what a thing it is to have your taste corrupted: if I took up one of those Latin books translated into Spanish, and by a truthful historian (or at least held to be truthful), I could not bring myself to finish it.[1]

In *Don Quixote* I. 32 Cervantes reveals something of what it

[1] J. de Valdés, *Diálogo de la lengua*, Clás. cast. (Madrid, 1946), p. 174.

was in the novels that appealed, and to whom. After a description, worthy of Lope, of countryfolk listening to the reading of one of these novels, the Innkeeper says that, for his part, when he hears about the furious and terrible blows the knights deal each other, it makes him want to go out and do the same, and he could go on listening night and day. Maritornes likes to hear about some lady or other lying in the arms of her gentleman under the orange trees, while a duenna, dying of envy and fright, keeps guard. The Innkeeper's daughter, though she is inclined to lose patience with the amorous caprices and *longueurs*, prefers to listen to, and cry over, the lamentations of the knights when they are away from their ladies. Violence, eroticism, and sentimentality—Cervantes has fastened on the perennial worst qualities of literature written for a mass public.

As for other types of prose fiction: the pastoral novels are given a clean bill of health; they do not harm other people (*DQ* I. 6). Cervantes has nothing to say of the picaresque, of which a good deal might have been said; but his single mention of the *Celestina* contains his well-known criticism of this otherwise 'divine' work for its vivid display of the animal side of humanity (*DQ* I, pref. verses). Avellaneda's novel is criticized by Don Quixote, who refuses to read it, 'since we should keep our thoughts, let alone our eyes, away from what is lewd and obscene' (II. 59). The charge is not entirely idle. The book contains passages of greater coarseness and obscenity than anything that can be found in the works of Cervantes, although the author himself made the usual claims of propriety.[1]

We come now to Cervantes's own novels. The harmlessness of the *Galatea* and the *Persiles* (especially the latter, with its wealth of aphorism and the almost perverse innocence of its two matchless lovers) needed no advertisement. But assertions are made of the propriety of *Don Quixote* I and the *Novelas ejemplares*. The Bachelor says Part I contains

the pleasantest and least harmful entertainment that has ever been seen to date; for in the whole of it there is not to be found the semblance of an indecent word or a thought that is anything less than Catholic.[2]

[1] A. F. de Avellaneda, *El Quijote*, Austral (Buenos Aires, 1946), prol., p. 14.

[2] '. . . del más gustoso y menos perjudicial entretenimiento que hasta agora se haya visto, porque en toda ella no se descubre, ni por semejas, una palabra deshonesta ni un pensamiento menos que católico' (*DQ* II. 3; iv. 97).

The author of the *Novelas* maintains that

the amorous gallantries you will find in some of them are so respectable and so compounded with reason and Christian discourse that neither the careful nor the careless reader could be moved to evil thoughts.[1]

His entertainment is

without harm to body or soul, because decent and agreeable exercises do good rather than harm. . . .

There is one thing I will venture to say to you. If I found in some way that the reading of these *Novelas* could induce any evil thought or desire in the reader, I would sooner cut off the hand that wrote them than have them published. At my age one does not trifle with the life to come.[2]

As expressions of novelistic principle there is nothing remarkable about such statements. That imaginative literature should be moral was one of the 'rules'. But to conclude, as has too often been done, that Cervantes quoted the rules just to give a sort of intellectual *cachet* to his work is not justified. His hatred of any debasement of Poetry and all the other evidence of his theory point to a genuine belief in the principle of literary decency. In the passage in the prologue to the *Novelas* there is no sign of the humorous overstatement apparent in the Bachelor's comment on *Don Quixote* I. Irony is highly improbable in view of the remark about his age. He surely meant what he said when he said it.

The discrepancy is not absurd, as it is in the case of some novels of chivalry, nor is it slightly disgusting, as it is in a few picaresque novels, but the fact remains that not all the *Novelas* are as innocent as his declarations would lead one to expect. The *Celoso extremeño*, even in the amended version, certainly is not. It would be surprising if, to mention nothing else, the vividly rendered atmosphere of sensuality pervading the household of Carrizales did not induce an improper thought or two in most readers.

[1] '. . . los requiebros amorosos que en algunas hallarás, son tan honestos y tan medidos con la razón y discurso cristiano, que no podrán mover a mal pensamiento al descuidado o cuidadoso que las leyere' (*Novelas*, prol., p. 22).

[2] '. . . sin daño del alma ni del cuerpo, porque los ejercicios honestos y agradables antes aprovechan que dañan. . . . Una cosa me atreveré a decirte, que si por algún modo alcanzara que la lección de estas *Novelas* pudiera inducir a quien las leyera a algún mal deseo o pensamiento, antes me cortara la mano con que las escribí que sacarlas en público. Mi edad no está 'ya para burlarse con la otra vida' (ibid., pp. 22–23).

The excessive insistence of Cervantes undoubtedly reflects anxiety. There are other indications of this. He submitted the book to the ecclesiastical, before the civil, censor, although the latter alone was strictly necessary. And there are an unusually large number of *aprobaciones* (no less than four). After this he perhaps felt at liberty to tone down the somewhat over-emphatic title, which, to judge from the references of several authorities through whose hands the book passed, seems previously to have been *Novelas ejemplares de honestísimo entretenimiento*.

There are at least two good reasons why Cervantes might have been anxious. He claimed, justifiably, to be the first person in Spain to write *novelas* that were all his own. The word *novela*, as well as being unflatteringly interchangeable with words like *patraña*, or 'deceitful fiction', must have conjured up for the public the names of Boccaccio and Bandello and other *novellieri* well known in Spain, bywords for salaciousness. Cervantes may well have been eager to dissociate himself from precedent in this respect. Secondly, the three stories in the Porras de la Cámara manuscript were evidently read by or to the Cardinal-Archbishop of Seville. He may have raised an ecclesiastical eyebrow high enough to cause the author not only to alter the *Celoso extremeño*, make emendations in *Rinconete y Cortadillo*, and probably suppress the *Tía fingida*, but also to be over-enthusiastic about his good intentions in the prologue (although it should be added that the exemplary idea is clearly present in the Porras versions).

Cervantes's literary ideals included purity as something taken for granted; and things taken for granted are sometimes neglected. The artistic truth or falsity of a work was a matter of greater moment to him, I think, than the presence or absence of a few bedroom scenes. Consequently, I suggest, he was liable on rare occasions to be a little careless over the more limited moral matters that loomed larger in the public and official eye than in his own. It is the eternal difference between the artist's and the social ethic—writ small, however, because in the seventeenth century the artist did not rebel, he conformed. The protestations in the prologue to the *Novelas ejemplares* represent the over-emphatic reactions of the writer to the need to adjust his artistic ethic to the social one. This is not the only instance of Cervantes's showing himself slightly out of key with the trends of the times. The social pressures were extremely powerful because they had the full weight and direction of the Church behind them. But there is no reason to suppose that he made the adjustment reluctantly.

He asserts that the *Novelas* have a positive virtue: that they are actively exemplary as the title promises.

I have given them the title of 'Exemplary'; and if you look well, there is not one of them in which some useful example cannot be found. If it were not that I do not wish to enlarge upon this subject, I might show you the savoury and wholesome fruit that is to be had alike from each one separately and from all of them together. (Prol.)

The last sentence perhaps means that he also looks on exemplariness as a common attribute of the stories, binding them into a sort of unity, which in the collections of Boccaccio and most later *novellieri* had been provided by the background or frame of the story-telling. The title of Cervantes's promised *Semanas del jardín* suggests that he intended to use a similar background device there. The mysteriousness of the hint in the prologue may disguise a suspicion that his brand of exemplariness was not a very cohesive agent.

Assertions of exemplariness were a very old tradition among writers of prose fiction, who claimed this virtue for the most dissimilar works. Applied to works as various as Apuleius's *The Golden Ass* and Gil Polo's *Diana enamorada*, its range was obviously very wide, although the assertions often did not amount to much. Some force was restored to the commonplace claim in the latter half of the sixteenth century, when Giraldi Cinthio, according to Di Francia, first invested *novelle* with a genuine edifying intent.[1]

In Cervantes's time, as in the Middle Ages, the immediate meaning of the word 'exemplary' was 'containing examples and moral lessons'. In this sense it was particularly associated with the short story. Girolamo Bargagli, who deals interestingly with the *novella* in his *Dialogo de' Giuochi*, stresses exemplariness.[2] Suárez de Figueroa, always a good deal preoccupied with literary morality, defined the *novela* as 'a most ingenious composition, the example

---

[1] *Novellistica* ii. 63. The Spanish translation of Giraldi's *I...catommithi* was Gaitán de Vozmediano's *Primera parte de las cien novelas de M. Juan Bautista Giraldo Cinthio* (Toledo, 1590).
[2] G. Bargagli, *Dialogo de' Giuochi* (Siena, 1572), p. 214.

in which is to prompt imitation or act as a warning'.[1] Definitions by Lope de Vega and others will be found along the same lines. Cervantes, of course, understood exemplariness in the same sense. In five of his *Novelas* he specifically draws attention to the moral or some notable example in the tale, just as he does in some of his stories elsewhere.

Exemplariness also distinguishes the Canon of Toledo's recipe for the ideal novel. The exemplary figures and qualities he enumerates recall some of those to be found in Italian treatises on the epic and romance, such as

a valiant captain with all the requisite qualities, showing himself prudent in anticipating the cunning of his enemies, an eloquent orator in persuading or dissuading his soldiers, a mature counsellor, prompt in resolution and as bold in awaiting as in making an attack.[2]

One is reminded of Giraldi's 'captains of great discernment and great boldness'.[3] The Canon goes on to say that the writer

can demonstrate the astuteness of Ulysses, the piety of Aeneas, the courage of Achilles, the misfortunes of Hector, the treachery of Sinon, the friendship of Euryalus, the liberality of Alexander, the valour of Caesar, the clemency and truthfulness of Trajan, the fidelity of Zopyrus, the prudence of Cato;[4]

recalling Tasso:

The excellence of piety is found in Aeneas, of military fortitude in Achilles, of prudence in Ulysses and, to come down to our own [heroes], of loyalty in Amadis and constancy in Bradamante.[5]

---

[1] C. Suárez de Figueroa, *El pasajero* (ed. Madrid, 1913), p. 55. In the *Plaza universal*, fol. 276ᵛ, he speaks of the evil effect of the 'lascivious' novels of Boccaccio, Giraldi, and Cervantes on feminine morals. But he is merely 'improving' on his model Garzoni by substituting the name of Cervantes for that of Straparola.

[2] '... un capitán valeroso con todas las partes que para ser tal se requieren, mostrándose prudente previniendo las astucias de sus enemigos, y elocuente orador persuadiendo o disuadiendo a sus soldados, maduro en el consejo, presto en lo determinado, tan valiente en el esperar como en el acometer' (*DQ* I. 47; iii. 350).

[3] '... capitani di molto avvedimento e di molta prodezza' (*Dei romanzi*, pp. 65–66).

[4] 'Puede mostrar las astucias de Ulises, la piedad de Eneas, la valentía de Aquiles, las desgracias de Héctor, las traiciones de Sinón, la amistad de Euríalo, la liberalidad de Alejandro, el valor de César, la clemencia y verdad de Trajano, la fidelidad de Zópiro, la prudencia de Catón' (*DQ* I. 47; iii. 351).

[5] 'Si ritrova in Enea l'eccellenza della pietà, della fortezza militare in Achille, della prudenza in Ulisse, e per venire ai nostri, della lealtà in Amadigi, della costanza in Bradamante' (*Dell'Arte poetica* i. 16). Tasso stops at Ulysses in *Del poema eroico* II. 60. Cf. also Minturno, op. cit., pp. 46 ff.

The narrow interpretation of exemplariness may serve for some of the *Novelas* and even the *Persiles*, but it will scarcely do for such works as the *Coloquio*; something more diffuse or more subtle is needed. I shall not add to the many interpretations of the *Novelas* made by modern critics but shall confine myself to the theory. If Cervantes believed a work had poetic truth, how could he not believe it was in the widest sense and at the highest level exemplary? In accordance with the anti-realistic criteria of the day, characters were said to be depicted as they ought or ought not to be, as better or worse than normal, for exemplary reasons. Quixote says Homer and Virgil portrayed Ulysses and Aeneas not as they were 'but as they ought to have been, so that they might remain as an example of their virtues to men in the future' (I. 25). But poetic truth could also reside in less idealized representations, in the actions of fictitious characters who were not necessarily all that they should have been. Over and above edifying examples and warnings there was a region where the poetically true and the exemplary were at one, and this must have been the generous sense of exemplariness that Cervantes understood. In the long run, imaginative literature was exemplary simply as a representation of life. The ideas are combined in the quasi-Ciceronian definition of comedy as 'a mirror of human life, an example of manners and an image of the truth' (*DQ* I. 48). So they are again later when Lugo y Dávila describes the purpose of *novelas* as

to put before the mind's eye a mirror in which human actions are reflected, so that, just as a man composes himself before a glass, he may compose his actions, observing himself in the variety of represented events which the *novelas* contain, imitating the good and shunning the bad.[1]

Chivalresque novelists had no hesitation about commending their works for the good that there was (they said) to be derived from them. For Cervantes, a book that was to be really effective morally had to be acceptable intellectually and satisfy aesthetically. The novels of chivalry generally spoiled the effect by the incredible nonsense of their stories. But Cervantes was too given to looking at things from different angles not to offer another point of view. Don Quixote may not be a very reliable witness on the subject of books of chivalry, but he puts up a defence not wholly to be

---

[1] Lugo y Dávila, *Teatro popular*, introd., p. 26.

despised. Mixed up with the nonsense and the unconscious irony there is an element of truth. Are there no inspiring examples in the novels? He at any rate thinks so:

Who was more chaste or more valiant than the famous Amadis of Gaul? Who was more prudent than Palmerin of England? Who more practical and skilful than Tirant the White? Who more gallant than Lisuarte of Greece? . . . (II. 1)

and so on. Of course, there is something in this. And we cannot ignore his claim to have been, since he became a knight errant, 'brave, polite, liberal, well-bred, generous, courteous, bold, gentle, patient and long-suffering' (I. 50).

Sixteenth-century moralists and theologians did not hold this Quixotic view of the romances. But there were writers who did. Rodrigues Lobo recalls a valiant Portuguese captain, the best man of his time, who imitated fruitfully the virtues of a fictitious hero, and many damsels similarly and admirably influenced by the books.[1] Sidney knew men who had been moved to courtesy, liberality, and especially courage by reading *Amadis of Gaul*— 'which God knoweth wanteth much of a perfect poesy'.[2] The author of the *Quixote* obviously felt the force of the exemplary virtues in the novels of chivalry. More was the pity that their influence was so crippled by their absurdity. By way of compensation, however, so was their influence for bad. Their most serious menace lay in the perversion of truth they concealed behind their charms.

It is the charming illusion that Don Quixote first succumbs to, and then to their exemplary influence. When he sets out to imitate his incredible heroes he is behaving in a manner beyond the wildest dreams of their inventors, but his reaction is only an exaggerated instance of that which heroic literature was supposed to provoke. He is only responding to example more dramatically than Castiglione would have expected when he wrote:

What soul is there so lowly, timid and humble that, when reading the great deeds of Caesar, Alexander, Scipio, Hannibal, and so many others, it is not fired with a most ardent desire to resemble them?[3]

Don Quixote expects to be in his turn 'an example and a model for centuries to come' (I. 47). But what becomes ironically clear

[1] Rodrigues Lobo, *Corte en aldea*, fol. 11ʳ.   [2] Sidney, op. cit., p. 173.
[3] *Il Cortegiano*, p. 108.

in Part II is that it is his madness, rather than his heroic qualities, which is catching.

For Cervantes fiction offers examples to follow and to shun. It tells us something true about life while it entertains us. Ultimately poetic truth and morality were inseparable for him. His basic attitude, I believe, is that of the most exemplary of his heroes, Persiles, to the story of the adulterous wench Luisa:

> Let her be as free and flighty as a kestrel; the touchstone is not her flightiness but what happens to her, or so I see it by my astrology.[1]

But from the public point of view such an attitude might be held a trifle careless. Not every reader could be expected to meet the author on his own level. Cervantes recognized this when he rewrote the *Celoso extremeño* for the ninnies and the silly girls who would not see the tragic lesson through the charms of the seduction. For, when they might harm someone, 'not all truths should be publicly displayed before the eyes of all' (*Persiles* I. 14). Authorities were quite unambiguous on the point:

> The poet is bound to deal with everything and say everything, for he is the painter of what happens in the world . . .

wrote Carvallo. He added, however:

> but he is obliged to treat what is evil as evil, so that it may be avoided, and what is good as good, so that it may be followed.[2]

4. *Author and Public*

> To speak generally, you should consider that to be truly
> beautiful and sublime which pleases all people at all times.
>   'LONGINUS'

Cervantes hinted that his *Novelas ejemplares* had an esoteric content when he told the reader at the end of his prologue that he would not have been so bold as to dedicate them to the Count of Lemos

---

[1] '. . . séase ella libre y desenvuelta como un cernícalo, que el toque no está en sus desenvolturas, sino en sus sucesos, según lo hallo yo en mi astrología' (*Persiles* III. 7; ii. 72). He does not say *deshonesta*, of course. Preciosa is 'algo desenvuelta; pero no de modo que descubriese algún género de deshonestidad' (*Gitanilla*, p. 32).

[2] 'El poeta, forzoso ha de tratar de todo, y decirlo todo, pues es pintor de lo que en el mundo pasa, pero obligación tiene a tratar lo malo como malo, para que se evite, y lo bueno como bueno, para que se siga' (op. cit., fols. 210ᵛ–211ʳ).

if they were not enhanced by some hidden mystery. Whether this mystery is to be identified with the 'savoury and wholesome fruit' of the stories, or whether it even means anything very serious at all, need not concern us. This venerable idea went back to the most ancient Greek commentators of Homer, besides being in the Pythagorean tradition of philosophical mysteries, which many Renaissance scholars continued to cultivate assiduously and not unfruitfully; even as a diluted literary commonplace which might or might not mean much it had extraordinary tenacity in the sixteenth and seventeenth centuries. The assumption that concerns us in Cervantes's claim, however, is that there would be among his readers a privileged body of initiates and others, the majority, outside the secret.

Now, roughly speaking, this corresponds to the usual division Golden-Age writers made between the two classes of the public, the *discretos* and the *vulgo*. The words were seldom used with any exactness, but they stood for the accepted if artificial division between enlightened and discerning, and unenlightened and foolish, readers.[1] The peculiar defect of the vulgar, as far as authors were concerned, was its utter inability to discriminate. Its habit, Tasso said, was 'to fix its attention on the accidents, not the substance of things'.[2] So it could not appreciate true art. The vulgar was the natural whipping-boy whose stupidity and malice could be blamed by any author who felt that he was not, or might not be, appreciated. Abuse was safe since the individual could be relied upon always to dissociate himself from the crowd. It was a many-headed convenience, an abstraction of almost allegorical stature, but it had a basis of reality. Allusions to the *vulgo* are normally so contemptuous that one is almost surprised to find how often it appears to have gone to the same plays and read the same books as the *discretos*. In fact, although their standards were so different, they together comprised the writer's public.

For Cervantes the *vulgo* is the conventional anonymous enemy, to which he rarely refers without dislike and contempt. It is the power behind the scurrilous hordes of poetasters in the *Parnaso*, and encourages the production of bad plays and novels.

[1] 'Discernment' is a primary connotation of the complex concept of *discreción*, which is studied by A. A. Parker in the appendix to his edition of Calderón, *No hay más fortuna que Dios* (Manchester, 1949), and by M. J. Bates in '*Discreción' in the Works of Cervantes* (Washington, 1945).

[2] Tasso, *Del poema eroico* iii. 77.

It is a collective monster not as a rule individualized, although there are some characters in Cervantes's works who can be considered representative. The Innkeeper Juan Palomeque in the *Quixote* is one; the 'ignorant onlooker who passes judgement on what he knows nothing of, and detests what he does not understand', of whom the Licenciado Vidriera speaks, is another. Barrabás in the *Ilustre fregona*, though not without a certain perspicacity, is a boorish critic too. Also distinguished as a component of the broad public among Cervantes's allusions (though it would not have cared to be identified with the *vulgo*) was the feminine section, which read novels particularly. The musician in the interlude of the *Vizcaíno fingido* mocks presumptuous and *précieuses* ladies who know nothing about anything but pastoral and chivalresque novels and—*Don Quixote*. And the prefatory verses of Urganda the Unknown end with the reminder that the writer has a duty higher than the literary amusement of young girls (*DQ* I).

To the Golden-Age writer the *vulgo* was rather what the *bourgeois* was to that of the nineteenth century: a class distinction went with a general imputation of philistinism. But Cervantes knew that it was only incidentally a matter of class. The Knight says to Don Diego:

> And do not think, sir, that I apply the term 'vulgar' only to humble, plebeian people; for anyone who is ignorant, even if he is a lord and prince, may, and should, be included with the vulgar.[1]

Juan de Valdés had given a very similar opinion:

Pacheco: ... I beg you to tell me whom you call plebeian and vulgar.
Valdés: All those of poor mentality and little judgement.
P.: And what if they are high-born and have large incomes?
V.: They may be as high-born and as rich as they like; in my opinion they are plebeian if they are not mentally superior and rich in judgement.[2]

---

[1] 'Y no penséis, señor, que yo llamo aquí vulgo solamente a la gente plebeya y humilde; que todo aquel que no sabe, aunque sea señor y príncipe, puede y debe entrar en número de vulgo' (*DQ* II. 16; v. 30).

[2] *Pacheco*: ... os suplico me digáis a quién llamáis plebeyos y vulgares.
Valdés: A todos los que son de poco ingenio y poco juicio.
P.: ¿Y si son altos de linaje y ricos de renta?
V.: Aunque sean cuán altos y cuán ricos quisieren, en mi opinión serán plebeyos si no son altos de ingenio y ricos de juicio. (Op. cit., pp. 74–75)

Like most contemporary Spanish writers, however, Cervantes was realistic enough about the influence of the mass of the public in practice. No one who publishes a book, he says, can hope to escape the sentence of that 'ancient legislator' (*DQ* I, prol.). This brings us to the crux of the matter. Dependence on a large public was becoming ever more important to a new and essentially modern type of author, one who was not primarily courtier, scholar, or cleric—the professional writer, who was emerging in the sixteenth century. Of course, there were patrons too, a class whom Cervantes for his part treated in the customary way, generally deploring them collectively while eulogizing the patron of the moment individually. But he treated with the contempt it deserved the polite fiction that patronage would protect a book from adverse criticism,[1] and painful experience taught him that for most writers fame and even fortune were ultimately dispensed by the public at large.

These were the acknowledged rewards in this hazardous profession. 'I well know', said Cervantes,

> what temptations of the devil are, and that one of the greatest of them is to put it into a man's head that he can write a book and have it printed, and thereby earn as much fame as money and as much money as fame. (*DQ* II, prol.)

He habitually presents the two incentives as conflicting. True fame is not simply success, but what is acquired by writing true works of art, and the *vulgo* does not appreciate these. But, as Lope said, it is the *vulgo* that pays, and so to make money one sacrifices one's niche in the temple of Apollo and writes for the masses. The hoary old problem of 'classic or commercial' for the modern writer was a new one in the Golden Age. 'Earn one's bread by the many' or the 'good opinion of the few' (*DQ* I. 48)? 'This business of hunger', he once wrote, 'sometimes drives poets of talent to things that are not on the map.'[2]

The dilemma was most acute in the medium in which the influence of the public was most powerful and demanding, the

---

[1] *Novelas*, dedic., p. 25; *Adjunta*, p. 132. See also ibid., pp. 133–4. Quite a full picture of Cervantes's world of patrons, publishers, printers, booksellers, critics, poetic contests, and theatrical companies can be put together from his work. R. del Arco has something on the subject in *La sociedad española en las obras de Cervantes* (Madrid, 1951), chs. 15, 17, 20.

[2] 'Esto de la hambre tal vez hace arrojar los ingenios a cosas que no están en el mapa' (*Gitanilla*, p. 32).

drama. No one who examines Cervantes's dramatic theories can fail to notice how often he mentions money matters. The commercialization of art was most highly developed in the theatre, for between the playwright and his audience there were such interested parties as actors and theatrical managers. With a flash of perception remarkable even considering his first-hand experience, he puts the blame where a great deal of it certainly belongs— on the middlemen, the purveyors of entertainment, the people who present plays on the stage and have a responsibility to the public more complex than they assume, but who take refuge in the simple plea that they 'must give the public what it wants'. The fault does not lie with the crowd that asks for nonsense, says the Canon, 'but with those who do not know how to put on anything else' (*DQ* I. 48). It is not with the poets, the Priest presently adds, for 'the players would not buy [their plays] if they were not of the usual sort, and so the poet tries to adapt himself to the requirements of the manager who is to pay him for his work'. Cervantes's ideal Poetry, who, as he so often says, does not belong to the market place, can have no part in such base commerce:

she is not to be put up for sale in any manner, unless it is in the form of heroic poems, dolorous tragedies, or pleasing and well-contrived comedies.[1] (*DQ* II. 16).

These are the three major kinds of classical poetry. What can he mean except: 'unless she takes care to remain good art'?

Here is Cervantes characteristically trying to reconcile what he has presented as irreconcilable. But the conclusion toward which chapters 47 and 48 of *Don Quixote* I are directed is precisely that true art in novels and *comedias* need not and should not be incompatible with the tastes of the masses. The case of the novel is less acute and less momentous than that of the drama, but it is substantially the same, for bad works prejudice good ones there too. By a natural association the Canon turns from one genre to the other. The Priest brings the discussion back to the novel of chivalry, and to a close, after advocating an enlightened, and quite impracticable, form of censorship, which would ensure that only good plays and books reached the public (I. 48).

---

[1] Note the cynical last line of the sonnet 'To his Pen', prefacing some copies of the first edition of the *Viaje del Parnaso*: 'yo os le marco por vendible, y basta.'

That is to say, artistically good. His ideas on the subject have sometimes been misunderstood. There is a suggestion of the familiar form of censorship about his views, but the animating principle is quite different. They must be regarded in the light of the preceding discussion on the aesthetic merits and demerits of romances and plays written for a large public. The idea naturally emanates from the Priest, who has already censored Quixote's library in the same way and by the same standards as he is now proposing should be done on a national scale.

It is true that behind the humour of the book there is a violence of sentiment shown towards the chivalresque novels by those who disapprove of them which, with the obvious inquisitional analogies, recalls the passions of religious controversy in the sixteenth and seventeenth centuries. There is a good deal of talk about book-burning. The Priest and the Barber, having done so with Don Quixote's, would not have been sorry to burn the Innkeeper's few romances either (I. 32). The good Canon would have thrown the best of the romances into the fire if there had been one handy, 'as founders of new sects and new ways of life' (I. 49). The Niece and the Housekeeper, who want the Knight's library sprinkled with holy water, repeatedly personalize them as heretics whose souls are damned. But this, of course, is to pay literature the greatest of compliments, to recognize it as a living force with an impact on people's lives, which Unamuno failed to see when he passed over the library scene in his *Vida de Don Quijote y Sancho*.[1]

It is also true that the censorship is designed to prevent the production of *comedias* that give personal offence. But the Priest's 'discriminating [*discreta*] and intelligent person' would not only make sure of this; he would procure 'both the entertainment of the people and the good reputation of Spanish poets',[2] as well as what was in the best interests of the performers. Where the romances were concerned, the censorship would facilitate the publication of such perfect specimens as the one outlined by the Canon, to enrich the language, put the old romances in the shade, and give decent recreation not only to the idle but to the busy.

---

[1] M. de Unamuno, *Vida de Don Quijote y Sancho*, Austral (Buenos Aires, 1946), p. 49.

[2] '. . . la opinión de los ingenios de España' is ambiguous. It could mean 'the good opinion of the best minds in Spain'.

No doubt the Priest's censor would look out for moral and religious delinquencies too, but his conception of the office is really less close to López Pinciano's suggestion for a distinctly inquisitional 'commissary' to scrutinize plays for 'good morals' and 'good politics'[1] than it is to Huarte's pleasant and impracticable notion, that 'those lacking the gift of invention should not be permitted by the state to write books or have them published'.[2]

However, the good writer can count on no such enlightened authority to make his task easy for him. Publishing a book is a risky business, says the Bachelor, for how does a writer compose one that will satisfy everybody (*DQ* II. 3)? Balbuena asked plaintively:

Who would cook for everybody? If I write for the wise and the discriminating, I shall leave unsatisfied the majority of the public, which is not included among these. If I write for the crowd and no more, there is neither pleasure nor profit to be had from what is very trite and common.[3]

Yet 'cooking for everybody' was the summit of Cervantes's literary aspirations, at least with every novel after the *Galatea*, and it would be rash to assert positively that it was not the case there also. The *Novelas* were varied enough to have something for all tastes; the *Quixote* was at once a work of art and a best seller; the *Persiles* patently an attempt to give the novel the intellectual prestige of epic and the popular appeal of romance. He betrays in various ways that he ideally envisages satisfying both the *discretos* and the *vulgo*. The Canon of Toledo submitted his unfinished romance to 'the opinion of both 'learned and discerning men, passionately fond of this sort of reading' and to 'others that were ignorant and intent only upon the pleasure to be had from hearing nonsense' (*DQ* I. 48). Cervantes's friend requires the writing of *Don Quixote* to be such as will satisfy the 'simple' together with the 'discerning', the 'grave', and the 'prudent' (I, prol.). And the author seldom misses the opportunity of advertising the universal popularity of the *Quixote* with all manner of people and, as he justly assumes, at all times.[4]

---

[1] El Pinciano, op. cit. iii. 273.

[2] 'A los . . . que carecen de invención no había de consentir la república que escribiesen libros, ni dejárselos imprimir' (op. cit., fol. 60ʳ).

[3] B. de Balbuena, *Grandeza mexicana* (Mexico, 1604), 'Al lector'.

[4] *Parnaso* IV. 54-55. *DQ* II. 8; iv. 82, 95. *DQ* II. 40; vi. 184.

In that essential passage in the *Parnaso* he sees fiction ideally written in a charming style that will please both extremities of the public, 'the simple and the discreet'. References to this stylistic mean are not uncommon. Quintilian, recommending clarity as the first essential of good style, says: 'Thus our language will be approved by the learned and clear to the uneducated.'[1] Lope speaks of a style neither so grave as to weary those who are ignorant, nor so devoid of all art that the knowledgeable will utterly reject it.[2] Certain writers who, like Cervantes, loved romance and had high artistic standards, spoke of the importance of giving universal pleasure. Giraldi required the writer of the *romanzo* to have a style such that he will 'at all times please not only the learned but all men who speak the language in which he writes'.[3] Finally, another novelist, Lugo y Dávila, required variety in a collection of *novelas*, so 'that not everything should be for the learned, not everything for the vulgar, nor yet everything between these two extremes'.[4]

Literary conditions in the sixteenth century were shaping in a way we can recognize as in many essentials modern. They were the conditions in which modern prose fiction slowly grew. The solid centre of the novelist's market can already be discerned in Carrasco's description of the reception of *Don Quixote* I. It is enjoyed by people of all ages and conditions, he says (*DQ* II. 3), but those most given to reading it are pages (no nobleman's antechamber is without a copy)—in other words, surely, a leisured, literate class, neither scholarly nor ignorant, between the extremes of the *discretos* and the *vulgo*. It is true that this class was the market centre for all imaginative writers, but it was on dramatists and novelists that the existence of a paying public to be specially catered for had a decisive effect.

The case of the drama was much more spectacular, and there the author's problem—Art or Money?—was much more acute. Castelvetro's exaltation of the 'pleasure of the ignorant multitude and the common people' above other considerations was extreme,[5] but eloquent of conditions which, if not absolutely new in the

---

[1] Quintilian, *Institutio oratoria*, trans. Butler, Loeb Cl. Lib. VIII. ii. 22.
[2] Lope de Vega, *El desdichado por la honra*, BAE xxxviii. 14.
[3] Giraldi, *Dei romanzi*, p. 15.
[4] Lugo y Dávila, op. cit., introd., p. 27.
[5] Castelvetro, op. cit., p. 679.

history of literature, differed enough in degree to present a problem that was new in effect. Lope de Vega was as conscious of it as Castelvetro, and returned the same answer. He also explicitly recognized that the situation was basically the same where prose fiction was concerned. *Novelas*, he considered, 'have the same rules as plays, the aim of which, for their author, is the contentment and pleasure of the common people, though art go hang'.[1]

The novel of chivalry, which delighted Western Europe, has the distinction of being the first form of literary entertainment specifically written and produced for a mass public. In this respect there had been nothing quite like it before, because only the invention of printing made literature for the masses possible. Numerically this public was far from being what it is today, but its demands were substantially the same. Two things happened: the professional writer emerged and literature was seen to be a social matter. In Spain, as in England, where conditions were in many ways so very similar, the effects of the theatre on people were a matter of concern to responsible persons. So to a lesser extent were the effects of novels.

For Cervantes, the author was the most responsible person of all. As a novelist he had neither the plurality of the audience nor the commercial interest of the middleman to reckon with in the way that the dramatist did. A novel is a more private affair than a play, and so it was with the individual reader that Cervantes, who was inclined to be touchy in his wider relations with the public, established that sympathetic contact in which he has never been equalled. However remote and abstracted his ideal Poetry may be, his ideas on the novel are humanized by his personal feeling for the reader and grounded in contemporary literary conditions, without being merely relativistic. Their social awareness and his interest in bad books (which would have horrified Boileau and the neo-classical critics) make his views more 'modern' than those of a great many writers who lived a century after him.

His aim in the novel was to communicate with as wide a public as possible without sacrificing his standards to the lowest tastes of its members. The literary work of art in Cervantes's theory did not exist in a void: its formal qualities, which we shall now go on to consider, were really inseparable from the effects it had on people.

[1] Lope de Vega, *El desdichado por la honra*, p. 14.

IV

THE FORM OF THE WORK

1. *Variety and Unity*

> This, gentle lord, is the part that has given rise in our time
> to various lengthy disputes among those 'who are led to
> war by literary fury'. TASSO

ONE of the most important critical questions in sixteenth-century Italy was that of artistic unity. It was crucial in the controversy over the *romanzo* and the epic. How was a heroic poem to charm by its variety of incident, as Boiardo's and Ariosto's undoubtedly did, without breaking the law laid down by reason, let alone authority, that the work must be a single well-proportioned whole? How was it that hardly anybody read Trissino's *Italia liberata*, which obeyed the law, and everybody read and admired the *Orlando furioso*, which broke it? Aristotle, who was so insistent on the importance of good plot-construction, had commended epic for being able to describe a number of simultaneous incidents. These, he said, 'if germane to the subject', prove 'a gain to the epic, tending to give it grandeur, and also variety of interest and room for episodes of diverse kinds'.[1] Cervantes, with a few hesitations, in general accepts this theoretically in the novel. He also recognizes that the central question is: What *is* germane to the subject? One way or another he alludes to it more often than to any critical topic, except, perhaps, literary truth.

Art is an imitation of nature and 'per tal variar natura è bella'. Cervantes recalls the well-known Italian line, and elsewhere expands on it, dwelling on the special virtue of variety, which is to refresh with change.[2] Accordingly, the inclusion of the picaresque story of Luisa in the *Persiles* is justified by Periandro, saying that a dish of fresh green savoury salad is not out of place beside

---

[1] Aristotle, *On the Art of Poetry*, trans. Bywater (ed. Oxford, 1909), 1459B.
[2] *Galatea* V; ii. 110. *Pedro de Urdemalas* III, pp. 210–11.

a well-dressed pheasant on a banquet table (III. 7). Variety was
a 'natural' principle like good invention; everyone agreed that
it refreshed, delighted, beautified, and enriched. It was one of
the two most obvious qualities of the Canon of Toledo's ideal
romance. The one good word he had to say of the novels of
chivalry was on account of

the opportunity they offered for a good intelligence to display itself,
for they afforded a wide and spacious field for the pen to rove in without hindrance, describing shipwrecks, storms, encounters, battles . . .
depicting now some lamentable and tragic event, now some happy
and unexpected occurrence; here a most beautiful lady, virtuous,
discreet and demure; there a valiant, civil, Christian knight; a lawless
barbarian braggart, or a courteous, valiant, considerate prince;
portraying both the goodness and loyalty of vassals and the greatness
and generosity of lords.[1]

Such catalogues are common features of Italian works of poetic
theory, where the 'wide and spacious field' of the heroic poem is
filled by theorists with identical or similar variegated items.[2] This
is not the case in El Pinciano's treatise, but Cascales, who is so
much indebted to the Italians, lists among other things thirty-one
different sorts of character to be found in heroic poetry.[3] Tasso's
list of such items particularly recalls the words of Cervantes. The
epic poet, he says, may describe

tempests, fires, sea voyages, countries and particular places; he may
indulge in descriptions of battles by land and sea, of assaults on cities,
the disposition of an army and the manner of its quartering.[4]

But there was variety in chaos too, never mind nature, and
it was the artist's business to impose a beautiful form on his

---

[1] '. . . el sujeto que ofrecían para que un buen entendimiento pudiese mostrarse
en ellos, porque daban largo y espacioso campo por donde sin empacho alguno
pudiese correr la pluma, describiendo [or descubriendo] naufragios, tormentas,
rencuentros y batallas . . . pintando ora un lamentable y trágico suceso, ahora un
alegre y no pensado acontecimiento; allí una hermosísima dama, honesta, discreta
y recatada; aquí un caballero cristiano, valiente y comedido; acullá un desaforado
bárbaro fanfarrón; acá un príncipe cortés, valeroso y bien mirado; representando
bondad y lealtad de vasallos, grandezas y mercedes de señores' (DQ I. 47; iii. 350).

[2] Giraldi, Dei romanzi, pp. 43, 65–66; Minturno, op. cit., pp. 18—ff.; F. Patrizi,
Della poetica (Ferrara, 1586), 'La deca disputata', p. 135.

[3] Cascales, Tablas, p. 148.

[4] '. . . le tempeste, gl'incendi, le navigazioni, i paesi e i luoghi particolari; si
compiaccia nella descrizione delle battaglie terrestri e marittime, degli assalti delle
città, dell'ordinanza dell'esercito e del modo di alloggiare' (Del poema eroico II. 64).

material. Unity–variety was one of those bipartite concepts uniting antagonistic ideas, beloved of the age. El Pinciano said the plot should be at once 'single and varied',[1] and Tasso that achieving variety was not what was difficult, 'but that that same variety should be found in a single action'.[2] The concept was neat, but not so easy to work out or apply in practice. It was a constant concern of Cervantes, even when, as in the passage just now quoted, all the emphasis seems to be on variety. The Canon envisages the treatment of all this variegated matter by 'a good intelligence', by someone who, having subjected it to the requirements of invention and verisimilitude,

> will without doubt weave a web of beautiful and variegated strands, which, once finished, will be of such perfection and beauty that he will have achieved the highest aim of writing.[3]

'Web' (*tela*) happens to be a word that Cervantes, like other writers, uses elsewhere in connexion with Ariosto's poem,[4] which was admired for its variety rather than for its unity. But the Canon obviously means a *single* fabric of variegated strands, and its 'perfection' and 'beauty' in any case imply organic unity.

The idea of organic unity underlies Cervantes's notion of formal literary beauty. It is the standard one inherited from Antiquity and transmitted by Christian writers, and occurs in the *Galatea* IV, among other works:

> corporeal beauty . . . consists in all parts of the body being beautiful in themselves, and in their forming all together a perfect whole, a body of proportionate members, having also suavity of hue.

A favourite formula of his is appropriately part of this definition, the 'all together and each one in itself' formula, probably borrowed from Boccaccio. Cervantes sometimes describes subtler and more complex harmonic effects—the confused but pleasing harmony of bird-song (*Persiles* IV. 7), the 'disordered order' of an elaborate fountain in which art outdoes nature (*DQ* I. 50). But

---

[1] El Pinciano, op. cit. ii. 39.

[2] Tasso, *Del poema eroico* iii. 79. He gets thoroughly tangled in the problem.

[3] '. . . sin duda compondrá una tela de varios y hermosos lizos [*or* lazos] tejida, que, después de acabada, tal perfección y hermosura muestre, que consiga el fin mejor que se pretende en los escritos' (*DQ* I. 47; iii. 351–2).

[4] *Galatea* VI; ii. 209. *DQ* I. 6; i. 197. It proceeds from Ariosto himself. Cf. op. cit. XIII. lxxxi: 'la gran tela ch'io lavoro'.

whether or not Cervantes applies the current notions of *discordia concors* to the construction of his novels and stories, he does not elaborate these paradoxes theoretically.

The analogy between a living creature and a work of art had been made by Plato and Aristotle, and there was Horace's graphic monstrosity at the beginning of the *Ars poetica* to serve as a warning to writers. Naturally a beautiful unity was normally required in the poetics of the sixteenth and seventeenth centuries too. Nothing is perfect, said Minturno, the parts of which are not put together in an orderly fashion and with excellence of form.[1] The complete failure of the chivalresque novelists to observe this principle is therefore deplored by the Canon:

> I have not seen one book of chivalry of which the plot was a whole body with all its members, so that the middle was adjusted to the beginning, and the end to the beginning and the middle. Rather, they are composed with so many members that you would think the intention was to fashion a chimera or a monster, not a well-proportioned figure.[2]

Shortly before this he had asked what proportion between the parts and the whole and the whole and the parts there could be in their incredible nonsense, of which he went on to give a series of examples. The question looks odd—what has disproportion to do with incredibility? The answer lies in the close association between unity and verisimilitude in contemporary classical theory. The intellectual disharmony of the absurd is frequently equated with formal disproportion, and the chimera so often referred to is monstrous indeterminately because its parts are disproportionate or because it is composed of incredible fictions. Thus Villén de Biedma in his commentary on Horace's *Ars poetica* observes that if verisimilitude is lacking, the result 'would resemble a monster composed of various absurdities'.[3] Unity also depends on verisimilitude in another sense, equally important to Cervantes's theory, as a result of the Aristotelian provision that the

---

[1] Minturno, op. cit., p. 10.

[2] 'No he visto ningún libro de caballerías que haga un cuerpo de fábula entero con todos sus miembros, de manera que el medio corresponda al principio, y el fin al principio y al medio; sino que los componen con tantos miembros, que más parece que llevan intención a formar una quimera o un monstruo que a hacer una figura proporcionada' (*DQ* I. 47; iii. 349).

[3] J. Villén de Biedma, *Q. Horacio Flaco . . . sus obras con la declaración magistral en lengua castellana* (Granada, 1599), introd., fol. 307ʳ.

sequence of episodes should be probable or necessary. We shall return to this.

Artistic proportion involves reference to the norm of human capacities. The over-all size of a work must keep within certain limits. From Antiquity to the Renaissance brevity was traditionally honoured as a stylistic virtue. Rhetorics and poetics in the Golden Age still repeated the standard formula, *brevitas, claritas, probabilitas*. On the other hand, epic had long been admired for its wealth of detail, if not precisely for its prolixity. Neither Antiquity nor the Middle Ages knew a satisfactory way of reconciling the disparate claims of *abbreviatio* and *amplificatio*, and Curtius's comment, 'the absurdity of these excessively generalized precepts seems not to have entered the minds of the theoreticians',[1] can be applied without difficulty to many of their successors in the sixteenth century. But the absurdity was at least mitigated by an increased subordination of the precepts to the nature and purpose of the work.

The importance of being brief is an aphorism with Cervantes. At least half a dozen times he says words to the effect that prolixity engenders tedium.[2] Without attaching too much importance to such an unoriginal observation, we can accept the fact that he regards brevity as a stylistic virtue. Prolixity was an obvious defect of the novels of chivalry (the Canon says their battle descriptions are long-winded—*DQ* I. 47), though many of their authors made a show of avoiding it. It is natural for any good story-teller to be careful not to bore his readers; it was inevitable for an author as aware of his own facility, as liable to self-criticism, and as sensitive to his readers' reactions as Cervantes was. His characters repeatedly allude to the subject (before anyone else has a chance to). They apologize for being prolix or express their intentions of not being so; they applaud each other for telling a tale concisely or criticize failures to do this. They argue politely.[3]

Surprisingly, the story that causes most raising of eyebrows in the *Persiles* for being diffuse is the one told by Periandro in

---

[1] *European Literature*, p. 490.

[2] *DQ* I. 21; ii. 138. II, prol.; iv. 38. II. 26; v. 246. *Persiles* I. 8; i. 57. II. 15; i. 276. II. 21; i. 317.

[3] *Galatea* I; i. 61. III; i. 181. IV; ii. 23. V; ii. 125, 131-2—to mention no more. The *Coloquio de los perros* is said to be presented in dialogue form for brevity's sake (*El casamiento engañoso*, p. 152). The words recall Cicero's in the preface to his *De amicitia*, and are referred to by Carvallo, op. cit., fol. 130ᵛ.

several instalments. Not that all the comments on it are unfavourable; he has his defenders—notably among the ladies. But there are repeated murmurs of complaint, and the reader's attention is naturally caught by any suggestion of imperfection in such a hero. What critical devil prompted Cervantes to make Persiles a bit of a bore to some of his companions? There are grounds for thinking, says the author (though he would not care to swear it), that Mauricio and a few of the others felt a considerable sense of relief when he came to the end of his story (II. 21). Sigismunda is sensitive enough to the atmosphere to put off telling hers, it seems. The criticism of the hero's tale is all the more curious in that brevity in narration is several times taken for a sign of *discreción*—in the case of Dorotea and of Don Gregorio, for instance (*DQ* I. 30, II. 65).

Proportion and size depend on the author's answer to the question: What is relevant? What constitutes a matter worthy of record is a relative matter. 'For two months we sailed the seas without anything of any note whatever happening to us, although we did sweep them clear of sixty privateers or more', says Periandro (*Persiles* II. 16). Ironically, humorously, ambiguously, and even seriously, Cervantes repeatedly poses the question.[1] It is often present in chapter-headings, such as that of *Don Quixote* II. 24.

But he has no single, consistent, and all-inclusive answer, which is not surprising, given the extraordinary difficulty of the problem and his capacity for divided opinions. Three approaches to this immediate and practical matter are successively apparent in *Don Quixote* I, *Don Quixote* II, and the *Persiles*. The variation may be attributed to some change of mind or new definition of principle, as seems to have occurred between Parts I and II of the *Quixote*; to a yet rather uncertain sense of the different natures of different types of novel, which seems to be mainly the case between the *Quixote* and the *Persiles*; and very likely indeed to an inability to come to a complete and final conclusion. Nevertheless, one or two consistent threads run throughout, and in each work he shows a consciousness of the problem's existence.

[1] Cf. Ariosto:
> 'Lasciate questo canto, che senza esso
> può star l'istoria, e non sarà men chiara.
> Mettendolo Turpino, anch'io l'ho messo.'
>   (*Orlando furioso*, xxviii. ii)

The unity even of *Don Quixote* I, most critics nowadays agree, is impressive. But by Cervantes's own admission and criteria it is less complete than that of the second part, where there is a tightening up of principles—to which the objections of some of his first readers may have given the first twist. In I. 28 he comes close to a theoretical justification of variety by pleasure, which is the most powerful argument that can be put up against the demands of artistic unity:

we now enjoy . . . not only the sweetness of this true history, but also its tales and episodes, which, in part, are no less agreeable and well contrived and true than the history itself.

Calling the episodes 'true' amounts, however, to an important qualification, of which there will be more to say.

In *Don Quixote* II he tackles the problem of differentiating between what I shall call an episode and a digression, though he does not clearly distinguish the terms himself. Through his intermediaries in chapter 3 he criticizes the intrusion of *El curioso impertinente* into Part I. Outdoing any possible future critics, Sancho calls the author a 'son of a dog' and Quixote calls him an 'ignorant chatterer'. In chapter 44 the Captive's tale is also labelled a digression, but all the other 'extraneous' stories are specifically excused, in a passage which begins with a piece of wilful and nonsensical obscurity:

They say that in the true original of this history one reads that when Cide Hamete came to write this chapter, his interpreter did not translate it as it had been written, which was a sort of complaint addressed by the Moor to himself for having undertaken to tell a story so dry and limited as this one of Don Quixote. For it seemed to him that he must always be speaking of him and Sancho, without daring to spread himself in other digressions and episodes of a more grave and more entertaining nature. He said that to have his mind, hand and pen restricted always to the writing of a single subject, and to speak through the mouths of a few persons only, was an intolerable labour, in no way fruitful for their author. To avoid this inconvenience in Part I he had employed the artifice of introducing some *novelas*, such as the *Curioso impertinente* and the story of the Captive Captain, tales that are as if separated from the history, although the rest of those related therein are things that happened to Don Quixote himself and such as could not be omitted.[1]

[1] 'Dicen que en el propio original desta historia se lee que llegando Cide Hamete a escribir este capítulo, no le tradujo su intérprete como él le había escrito, que fue

Here is the problem, then, in immediate practical form. A very similar complaint had been made by the epic poet Ercilla:

although this second part of the *Araucana* does not display the labour it has cost me, whoever reads it may yet reflect what must have been endured in writing two books of such rough and scarcely varied matter. For it contains but one thing from beginning to end; and it seems to me that there can be no one whose taste will not be jaded, following me along such a sterile, desert road and rigorously pursuing a single truth. Fearful of this, I would therefore have liked a thousand times to vary it with different things, but I remembered not to change my style.[1]

In *Don Quixote* II. 44 Cervantes goes on presently to make clear what episodes should be:

and so in this second part he did not wish to insert detached or adhesive *novelas*, but only a few episodes which resembled them, arising naturally out of the very events offered by the truth of the story, and even these sparingly and using no more words than necessary to relate them.[2]

In other words, the episodes will spring from the events of the main action, although they will also seem to be separate, and they will be appropriately limited in length.

Authorities of the time, who tend to see the episode as somewhat less essentially a limb of the whole than did Aristotle, offer

un modo de queja que tuvo el moro de sí mismo por haber tomado entre manos una historia tan seca y tan limitada como esta de don Quijote, por parecerle que siempre había de hablar dél y de Sancho, sin osar estenderse a otras digresiones y episodios más graves y más entretenidos; y decía que el ir siempre atenido el entendimiento, la mano y la pluma a escribir de un solo sujeto y hablar por las bocas de pocas personas era un trabajo incomportable, cuyo fruto no redundaba en el de su autor, y que por huir deste inconveniente había usado en la primera parte del artificio de algunas novelas, como fueron la del Curioso impertinente y la del Capitán cautivo, que están como separadas de la historia, puesto que las demás que allí se cuentan son casos sucedidos al mismo don Quijote, que no podían dejar de escribirse' (*DQ* II. 44; vi. 267–8).

[1] '. . . aunque esta segunda parte de la *Araucana* no muestra el trabajo que me cuesta, todavía quien la leyere podrá considerar el que se habrá pasado en escribir dos libros de materia tan áspera y de poca variedad, pues desde el principio hasta el fin no contiene sino una misma cosa; y haber de caminar siempre por el rigor de una verdad y camino tan desierto y estéril, paréceme que no habrá gusto que no se canse en seguirme. Así, temeroso de esto, quisiera mil veces mezclar algunas cosas diferentes; pero acordé de no mudar estilo' (A. de Ercilla, *La Araucana* ii, ed. Madrid, 1866, ii, 'Al lector', 7).

[2] '. . . y así en esta segunda parte no quiso ingerir novelas sueltas ni pegadizas, sino algunos episodios que lo pareciesen, nacidos de los mesmos sucesos que la verdad ofrece, y aun éstos, limitadamente y con solas las palabras que bastan a declararlos' (*DQ* II. 44; vi. 268).

similar solutions to this delicate problem, even if they do not agree on all the details. Giraldi comments on the pleasure that episodes (he calls them 'digressioni') give when they seem to be born out of the subject itself.[1] Minturno sees the episode as 'outside the plot but not so much outside that it is foreign to it'.[2] El Pinciano imposes on epic the difficult condition that 'its episodes must be attached to the main argument as though they had been joined to it at birth and as detachable as though they had never been so connected'.[3]

And yet when Cervantes wrote those words in the *Quixote* he must also have been writing the *Persiles*. It could conceivably be argued that the principle is observed in that novel in a very watered-down form, since every subsidiary tale involves at least one character who enters the experience of—who therefore 'happens to'—Periandro and Auristela. But it is more likely that Cervantes saw his travel romance as a different type of novel, one with a very loose weave. The Canon speaks of the 'loose-woven writing' of the ideal novel of chivalry (*DQ* I. 47), and the author says of the *Persiles*:

Long journeys are always accompanied by a diversity of incidents, and since diversity is comprised of different things, it is inevitable that the events should be so. This story well demonstrates the fact; its incidents break the main thread, leaving us uncertain where best to take it up again.[4]

One is strongly reminded of Tasso on the *Odyssey* here:

Wherefore, owing to the diversity of countries described in three journeys and the multitude and novelty of things seen, the variety is necessarily very great;[5]

or, less forcibly, of El Pinciano's words, 'the matter is a lengthy one for the poet, for in a journey of so many years many very long episodes can be inserted'.[6]

---

[1] Giraldi, *Dei romanzi*, p. 25. [2] Minturno, op. cit., p. 18.
[3] El Pinciano, op. cit. iii. 173.
[4] 'Las peregrinaciones largas siempre traen consigo diversos acontecimientos; y como la diversidad se compone de cosas diferentes, es forzoso que los casos lo sean. Bien nos lo muestra esta historia, cuyos acontecimientos nos cortan su hilo, poniéndonos en duda dónde será bien anudarle' (*Persiles* III. 10; ii. 100).
[5] 'Laonde per la diversità de' paesi descritti in tre peregrinazioni, e per la moltitudine e novità delle cose vedute, grandissima conviene che sia la varietà' (*Del poema eroico* III. 82).
[6] '. . . la materia es larga para el poeta, porque en tantos años de peregrinación se pueden ingerir muchos y muy largos episodios' (op. cit. ii. 357).

But Cervantes is clearly not happy with his own explanation. Nagging doubts still prompt gratuitous allusions to the question of relevance, notably in the case of Periandro's tale, and he is forced back to the justification by pleasure. Mauricio and Ladislao on one occasion judge the instalment somewhat long and not very pertinent, but for all that have had pleasure from it (II. 11). Later Mauricio criticizes the narrative, remarking that the episodes put in to adorn a story should not be as lengthy as the story itself. The concession immediately follows: no doubt Periandro wished to show his wit and elegant style. Any possible hint of irony in this, however, passes over Transila, who repeats the old justification (II. 14).

Cervantes's experiment is not a success. Making every allowance for special intention, and even supposing every incident to have some thematic or symbolic relevance, dreamt of or undreamt of by the author, the organism has not been made flexible; its multiplicity of parts has rendered it helpless. The book is a welter of incident. Story crowds on story. Like Sancho's proverbs they jostle each other for expression. The temptation, successfully resisted in the *Quixote*, to hang a story on almost every character overcomes him in his last novel. To give life and body to the work by suggesting stories behind characters is another matter—as in the case of the Biscayan lady on her way to Seville to join her husband, about to set sail for America with an important commission (*DQ* I. 8). Cervantes seems to have sensed the primitive connexion between prose fiction and gossip.

Digressions are made worse by prolixity, but they need not be lengthy excursuses. The use of mere details is integral to the problem of relevance too. A certain richness and amplitude of treatment was regarded as one of the admirable features of epic. But as we shall see, Cervantes regarded the novel as imitated history as much as prose epic, and for history brevity was commonly prescribed, for obvious reasons.[1] Should details be used abundantly or economically then in prose fiction? Not unexpectedly we find contradictions. Periandro allows one storyteller latitude in this respect, since details often add 'gravity' to the work (a reminiscence of epic theory) (*Persiles* III. 7). On another occasion in the same novel the author declares, 'Details neither demand nor admit lengthy narration' (II. 18).

---

[1] Lucian, *The Way to Write History*, § 56; L. Cabrera de Córdoba, who calls brevity 'divina' in his *De historia, para entenderla y escribirla* (Madrid, 1611); see fols. 48ʳ, 84ʳ.

Nevertheless, Cervantes, while retaining his equivocal manner, makes an important point about the use of detail. The chivalresque romancers for the most part quite failed to cope with the problem, and Cervantes, pretending that Benengeli is an exact historian who imitates them with his scrupulousness (*puntualidades*), makes fun of the profusion of minute detail in their books:

Cide Hamete Benengeli was a very careful and scrupulous historian in all things, as can be seen from the fact that he did not care to pass over in silence those which have just been mentioned, mean and trifling though they were. His example in this might well be followed by those grave historians who give us such short and succinct accounts that we scarcely get a taste of them; they leave the substance of the work in the inkpot, either out of carelessness or malice or ignorance. A thousand blessings then on the authors of the *Tablante de Ricamonte* and that other book recounting the deeds of Count Tomillas: with what exactness they describe everything! (*DQ* I. 16)

Behind the irony the attitude of Cervantes to the over-stuffed novels of chivalry is very like that of the Renaissance to medieval art. Art does not make its effect by overwhelming with sheer weight of detail. Mere abundance is no substitute for harmonious form. So, in prose fiction, the accumulation of detail does not do duty for verisimilitude. It is the appropriate and significant use of every sort of detail, subordinated to the form and purpose of the work, which convinces. Don Quixote, who quite lacks a sense of verisimilitude where the romances are concerned, is taken in precisely by the spurious historicity of all their circumstantial detail:

could they be lies, having, moreover, so great an appearance of truth? For they tell us the father, the mother, the country, the relatives, the age, the place, and the deeds, point by point and day by day, of the particular knight or knights who performed them. (I. 50)

Full, exact, and minute description is inappropriate for a writer of fiction. The poet, says Giraldi, should not describe buildings with all the detail of an architect, for by so doing he sacrifices what is proper to poetry.[1] There is something like an echo of this in *Don Quixote* II. 18:

Here the author describes all the details of Don Diego's house, depicting in them all that a rich gentleman farmer's house contains. But it seemed best to the translator of this story to pass over these and

[1] Giraldi, *Dei romanzi*, p. 62.

other similar details in silence, since they did not suit the principal intention of the story, which has more force in its truth than in frigid digressions.[1]

The universal truth, which is proper to the novel as it is to poetry, must not be obscured by particulars. As has been observed, the single evocative mention of the 'marvellous silence' that reigns over Don Diego's house makes a far more powerful impression than any amount of circumstantial description of its interior.[2]

A decorative description of Don Diego's house was treated as a frigid divergence from the truth. In *Don Quixote* I. 28 Cervantes, clearly referring to the interlinked tales of Cardenio and Dorotea, called the tales and episodes in the book 'true'. In II. 44 he spoke of 'the very events offered by the truth of the story'. In II. 8 Don Quixote fears Cide Hamete may have strayed off to narrate events outside the requirements of 'the sequence of a true story'. Now why should a digression be less true than the main action? For this is the odd but obvious implication. There seem to be two explanations. One is that probability or necessity—that is to say, verisimilitude—is required in the sequence of episodes.[3] A digression, as distinct from a proper episode, cannot by definition have this probable or necessary connexion. The legitimate episode is thus linked with the essential truth of the story contained in the main action.

The other reason is a little more involved. Mauricio's phrase 'the episodes put in to adorn a story' may be recalled in the passage from the *Persiles* II. 14, referred to earlier. It was commonly recognized in poetics, rhetorics, and arts of history that episodes had a certain ornamental function: that they amplified, enhanced, and gave grandeur to a work.[4] But the ornamental principle, as we shall have ample opportunity to observe later in this chapter, clearly disturbs Cervantes on occasion inasmuch as

[1] 'Aquí pinta el autor todas las circunstancias de la casa de don Diego, pintándonos en ellas lo que contiene una casa de un caballero labrador y rico; pero al traductor desta historia le pareció pasar estas y otras semejantes menudencias en silencio, porque no venían bien con el propósito principal de la historia, la cual tiene más fuerza en la verdad que en las frías digresiones' (*DQ* II. 18; v. 59-60).

[2] A. S. Trueblood, 'Sobre la selección artística en el *Quijote*: ". . . lo que ha dejado de escribir" (II. 44)', *NRFH* x (1956), 48-49.

[3] Giraldi, *Dei romanzi*, p. 54; Minturno, op. cit., p. 10; Tasso, *Del poema eroico* III. 72.

[4] Cf. Minturno, op. cit., p. 36; El Pinciano, op. cit. ii. 22; Cascales, *Tablas*, p. 38.

it involves a kind of inflation, distortion, or obscuration of sober fact. Without for a moment rejecting the idea of embellishing the novel by means of brilliant descriptions, the element of artifice in art worries him from time to time. He seems to feel that the author is apt to be diverted from the main purpose of his work by minor artistic divagations. His scruples are those of a historian, whose right to digress from the strict truth was debated by many theorists.[1] As such they are irrelevant, one might think, to the novel. But one of the more original implications of Cervantes's theory is that history does in fact intervene in the novel in a way it does not in poetry.

There are twin examples of ostentatious digression in Cardenio's story. Cervantes typically envelops his own critical interference here in ironical ambivalence, but the scruples still show through. Cardenio had earlier posed the whole problem of selection when he promised to recount briefly the immensity of his misfortunes and, without lingering over his tribulations, to leave out nothing of importance (*DQ* I. 24). A highly rhetorical outburst in I. 27 ('Oh, ambitious Mario, oh, cruel Catalina . . .!', &c.) is followed by a reminder to himself to get on with the story. And another one presently ('Oh, memory, mortal enemy of my peace of mind . . .!', &c.) by an apology to his listeners for digressing. Ignoring the polite protestation of the Priest in reply, what may be noted is that each brief digression is a piece of pompous rhetoric, an artistic inflation, and so to some extent a falsification, of the sentiments of the protagonist. The all-pervasive claims of 'truth' penetrate every main compartment of Cervantes's theory of the novel. We shall see increasingly how inseparable form and content therefore are. In this particular sphere too he seeks a reconciliation, since neither truth nor ornament is to be rejected. Ultimately, I think, he wants to include in his novels 'events that adorn *and* lend credence', as he puts it (without italicizing) in the title of chapter 73 of *Don Quixote* II.

Again and again he simultaneously invites and evades criticism for irrelevance through the objections, apologies, and explanations of his characters. Don Quixote, backed up by Maese Pedro, calls the youthful narrator of the puppet play to order when he wanders off on the subject of Moorish customs (II. 26). The Dueña

---

[1] e.g. Castelvetro, op. cit., p. 5; Piccolomini, op. cit., pp. 138–9; Carvallo, op. cit., fol. 134ʳ.

Dolorida pulls herself up after her untimely divagation on poetic theory (II. 38). Periandro apologizes for being led astray by his delightful dream (*Persiles* II. 15). Ambrosio, as the intimate friend of the dead Grisóstomo, is called upon to explain away the inclusion in the *Quixote* of a not wholly appropriate poem, composed by the author on another occasion (I. 14). Cervantes also uses the trick of making the fault seem less by comparison. Mauricio slyly wagers to Transila that Periandro will presently start describing the whole celestial sphere, as though the motion of the heavens mattered to his story (*Persiles* II. 14). He reminds the reader of the things he has refrained from narrating (often marvellously enriching the work by mere suggestion). In the *Persiles* he advises us that the author had wasted nearly all the first chapter of the second book on a definition of jealousy, but that it had been removed as prolix and banal, and so, he adds significantly, 'we come to the truth of the matter'. He takes his evasive technique to a fine art in the *Quixote*, where the author 'begs that his labours should not be looked upon contemptuously and asks to be given credit for what he has refrained from writing rather than for what he has written' (II. 44).

The struggle between the temptation to let his pen run on and the restraints of artistic conscience is most evident in the *Coloquio de los perros*, where narrative and criticism openly keep parallel courses. Cipión has repeatedly to remind Berganza to keep to the point:[1]

C.: . . . upon your life, be quiet and get on with your story.
B.: How can I get on with it if I keep quiet?
C.: I mean go straight ahead with it, without tacking on so many appendages that you make it look like an octopus.

Some may be tempted to see in this the adumbration of a new novelistic form—the *novela-pulpo*. But it can never have entered Cervantes's conscious theory. The organic unity of a cephalopod cannot conceivably have corresponded to his notion of novelistic beauty.

It is not easy to sum up his diverse, veiled, and shifting views on the unity of the novel. But it may be said that he sees it generally as the novelist's duty to mould the variety of experience into a

[1] Cf. also *Coloquio*, pp. 166, 186, 205, 242.

coherent artistic form that satisfies the intelligence without sacrificing the pleasures that variety produces. Because his interpretation of unity is dubious at times, to say the least, it has been argued that as long as his work pleases, he is not personally exercised by scruples about form. But, susceptible as he is to the charm of variety, the evidence does not show that he is intellectually convinced that pleasure in it alone is an adequate substitute for the aesthetic satisfaction of structural coherence. Why otherwise should he repeatedly draw attention, as a rule quite gratuitously, to the relevance or irrelevance of portions of his work? Simply to silence critics? Undoubtedly this is so in part, but if this were all, it is very odd that he never uses the stock method of self-justification in this connexion, that of pointing to famous precedents. He could have recalled any number from Apuleius to Ariosto and Alemán.

Only in the second part of *Don Quixote* does he arrive at a real theoretical and practical solution of the problem of relevance. Here he defines the major unit, the episode. The episode is separable from the main action in so far as it is complete in itself, but it must be born naturally and convincingly out of the main action, and must not be disproportionately long (which the *Curioso* and the Captive's story were). In both parts of the *Quixote* and the *Persiles* he tends to assimilate unity to verisimilitude. Even small details have a bearing on the poetic truth of prose fiction. The *Persiles*, I think, is a practical attempt to come to terms with variety by means of a more flexible form, but not a very confident attempt. It is unsuccessful mainly because he overloads the structure. The attempt to come to terms is in the end little less than a capitulation.

His literary theory gives no hint of concern with the more recondite species of unity—thematic and symbolic, as opposed to mere formal unity[1]—which it has been fashionable to find throughout his works, or ascribe to them. Important correspondences of this sort can be shown to be there, of course, but many such demonstrations are critical artefacts rather than real illuminations of Cervantine composition. In his greatest work his expressed ideas on the unity of the novel are based on current ideas of epic unity. In execution, more especially in Part II, he

[1] The bond of exemplariness possibly intended in the *Novelas ejemplares* would be a marginal exception.

goes deeper than the mere formal observance of these, achieving a unity that is neither skin-deep nor buried beneath layers of symbol and abstraction, one that is neither superficial nor occult, but vital. It is sustained by those strong and slender threads which link external events with the innermost depths of human personality.

2. *Style and Decorum*

> When the subject is great and the sentiment, then, of
> necessity, great grows the word;
> When heroes give range to their hearts, is it strange if the
> speech of them over us towers?
> Nay, the garb of them too must be gorgeous to view, and
> majestical, nothing like ours.
>
> ARISTOPHANES, *The Frogs*
> (translated by Gilbert Murray)

It is a pity that Cervantes does not say enough about the classical division of styles to make his attitude to it clear. But the fact probably is that, like nine out of ten Spanish writers in his time, he had no very clear opinions on the matter. It is a pity, because the odd way in which he both observes and disregards the doctrine is of great consequence to his writings. The subject has received strangely little attention. Anyone can see how unsatisfactory and even absurd a rigid hierarchy of literary styles is, but how much it has to be reckoned with in literature before the nineteenth century a suggestive study by Erich Auerbach has shown.[1]

Like other ancient literary doctrines which became artificial and impracticable because people tried to attach an absolute validity to them, the division of styles had a rational origin. This was the assumption that there must be a proper correspondence between style and subject-matter. A clear division into three styles (the high or grand, the intermediate or mixed, and the low or plain) did not emerge from the so-called Theophrastean division until Roman times, when it appeared in the *Rhetorica ad Herennium*. There were some subsequent attempts to distinguish other styles (Demetrius, for instance, added a fourth), but in rhetorics and poetics from Antiquity to the Renaissance the threefold division

[1] E. Auerbach, *Mimesis: the Representation of Reality in Western Literature* (London, 1953).

was the most common, although it was often understood in different ways and the terminology varied. Thanks to the close association ancient theorists established between the type of language to be used and the dignity of the subject-matter and (in oratory) the occasion, stylistic distinctions became connected with distinctions of rank.[1] The stylistic hierarchy was heavily undermined in the Middle Ages for a reason we shall mention presently, but it remained ineluctably a part of all critical thinking as long as the hierarchical organization of Creation itself, with its 'Great Chain of Being', continued to exert a poetic fascination over men's minds, as it did even while it was becoming increasingly apparent that the arrangement bore no resemblance to reality—right into the eighteenth century, in fact.

Renaissance theorists sought to adjust the classical levels of style to the carefully graded scale of values still applied to people and things in life. Tragedy and comedy were as completely separated by questions of rank as they were by the fact that one made you cry and the other made you laugh. Suárez de Figueroa, quoting a certain 'grammarian' who is probably Cascales, explains precisely why it is an error to put the affairs of the great into comedies. One cannot play jokes or tricks on princes. They are offended; vengeance is demanded; this leads to tumults and disastrous conclusions; and one is in the domain of tragedy.[2]

This 'socialized' theory of styles was governed by the sense of decorum that was so strong in life. Literary characters had to speak, act, and be written about as befitted their station. (Parody and burlesque, of course, were calculated exceptions.) Scaliger— 'soul-blind Scaliger', who, according to Chapman, never had anything but 'place, time and terms to paint his own deficiency in learning'[3]—devised an exhaustive system, arranging persons and everything associated with them according to their importance, and adjusting to them even details of expression.[4] Castelvetro emphasized rank as a distinguishing mark.[5] The *novella*, for

---

[1] Demetrius says, 'Elevation resides also in the nature of the subject matter' (*On Style*, trans. Roberts, Loeb Cl. Lib. ii. 75). Cf. Quintilian, op. cit. v. xiv. 34; 'Longinus', *On the Sublime*, xliii. 5. The fully social criterion is a medieval development, but Edmond Faral, citing only the *Ad Herennium*, fails to allow for the ancient germ of the idea, in *Les Arts poétiques du XIIe et du XIIIe siècle* (Paris, 1924), p. 86.

[2] Suárez de Figueroa, *El pasajero*, p. 78. See Cascales, *Tablas*, p. 180.

[3] George Chapman, preface to the *Seven Books of the 'Iliad' of Homer*, in *Eliz. Crit. Essays*, ii. 301.   [4] Scaliger, op. cit. iii.

[5] Castelvetro, op. cit., pp. 35 ff.

Bargagli, was either about persons of the lower, or the middle, or else the upper classes.[1] For Robortelli and later commentators, Aristotle's 'better' men meant socially as well as morally better. With supreme lack of realism virtue, wisdom, manners, and beauty were required to assemble in persons of rank and fortune, while corresponding deficiencies marked their social inferiors. If tragedy had to leave room for a flaw of character in the protagonist, the epic hero at least was the perfect pattern, the man who 'had everything'. The exceeding rarity of such individuals in everyday life made no difference to literature. It was, rather, the writer's duty to blow the great, but less godlike, men of the day up to size.

This literary stratification inevitably produced hopeless difficulties. Except in the most approximate way, one could no more keep gradations of style distinct than prevent good people meeting bad. Horace had admitted that comedy sometimes raises its tone and that tragedy on occasion descends to a prosaic level; and Quintilian, while accepting the three principal styles, acknowledged that there were also many gradations. Epic produced a certain problem for Renaissance theorists because its universal comprehensiveness officially allowed some mingling of styles. But there was a far greater complication, for (as Auerbach has pointed out) these literary-social values were quite upset by Christianity, which taught nothing less than that the humblest was the highest and that all human souls were equal regardless of worldly distinctions. The mixing of styles and genres which persisted in the Middle Ages, despite rhetoricians, owed not a little to this.

Theorists in the sixteenth and seventeenth centuries had to qualify their precepts and make all sorts of exceptions. Vives, following on Quintilian, approved the basic accommodation of style to subject-matter, but said that there were really as many possible degrees of style as there were shades between black and white or nuances of taste between bitter and sweet.[2] Muzio, on the social model, allowed stylistic descents but not ascents.[3] El Pinciano began by specifically associating the three styles with

---

[1] Bargagli, op. cit., p. 209.

[2] J. L. Vives, *De causis corruptarum artium* IV, *Opera* i. 397. See Quintilian, op. cit. XII. x. 66–69.

[3] G. Muzio, *Tre libri di arte poetica*, in his *Rime diverse* (Venice, 1551), fol. 80r.

the three estates as an inevitable consequence of the fact that
poetry is an imitation of life. But presently he remembered that
kings do not actually use the high style in address, and that
humble things might be raised by the use of elevated language.
What is more, he rather thought that there might exist but a single
poetic language, above the level of common speech, to which
these stylistic divisions would not apply.[1] Cascales found himself
obliged to suggest such expedients as restricting the main action
to humble folk and episodes to illustrious people, or vice versa.[2]
Attempts were made to subdivide the main styles, which only
added to the confusion.

With their habitual attitude of mingled deference and contempt
for the rules, it is not surprising that most Spanish writers observed
the awkward doctrine of styles in practice very partially, when
they observed it at all. There was little disposition to abandon the
medieval mixing of styles and genres. Nevertheless, every writer
must have known the doctrine. It loomed in the general literary
consciousness like a presence, ineffective perhaps, but real.

It barely figures in Cervantes's stated theory, but a full study of
its effects on his fiction would show that its practical importance
was very considerable—as much for his deliberate breach of rule
as for any observance of it. He shows up the inadequacy of the
doctrine in Don Quixote not by ignoring but by manipulating it.
His allusions to the subject, however, amount to little more than
an acknowledgement of its existence, although he unexpectedly
goes to the heart of the matter in a humorous context in the
Parnaso VII when he says: 'Give me a voice in keeping with the
case.' He says that the verse of his plays is in the style which
comedies demand: namely, the lowest of the three (Comedias,
prol.), a remark which is true to such a limited extent as to be
virtually nonsense. There is one allusion concerning the novel.
When Periandro and his party arrive at an inn, the author writes
that what happened to them there demands 'a new style and a new
chapter' (Persiles III. 15). The observation would not seem to be
called for, were it not that the chapter does include the arrival
of the adulterous Luisa, who is involved in the most picaresque
incident in the book.

The pastoral novel posed a special problem, because its characters were 'discreet courtiers' disguised as 'rustic shepherds'.

[1] El Pinciano, op. cit. ii. 166 ff.   [2] Cascales, Tablas, p. 180.

The style appropriate to shepherds was originally held to be low. This was the style Servius had ascribed to Virgil's *Eclogues* (the *Georgics* and the *Aeneid* being allotted the intermediate and the high). So it was customary for sixteenth-century novelists to ask indulgence for the 'humble style' of their works, as much in deference to rusticity as out of authorial modesty.[1] But Sannazaro had both justified the 'humble' style of the *Arcadia* and excused himself for departing from it on occasion.[2] It thus became quite common to apologize also for not writing in the low style.[3] Cervantes's comment in the prologue to the *Galatea* is conventional:

> I well know how anyone whose style goes beyond that which he ought to maintain in his subject-matter is condemned, since the prince of Latin poetry was maligned for having elevated that of some of his eclogues above the others. And so I shall not be much afraid if anyone condemns me for having mingled philosophical argument with the amorous parley of shepherds. Seldom does it rise above the discussion of rural matters, and then with the customary simplicity. Moreover, when it is pointed out (as is occasionally done in the course of the work) that many of the disguised shepherds were shepherds only in dress, the objection falls through.

Pastoral style became in effect mixed or intermediate. It was in theory more simple than magnificent, but elegant and decorated, not crude, corresponding to the lyrical style in poetry. The levelling upward continued till it achieved its apotheosis in the two major poems of Góngora.

The intermediate style must theoretically have commended itself to Cervantes for use in serious prose fiction, because, while simple, it was elegant and allowed room for decoration; it was also considered the most suitable for history and the one most calculated to give pleasure. But his most original and effective achievement was his use of contrasting styles in the *Quixote*. There he blew the doctrine to pieces and reassembled them in a new artistic form. At the same time, this must be considered an

---

[1] Thus Montemayor, op. cit., dedic., p. 3; Lofrasso, op. cit. 'A los lectores'; González de Bobadilla, op. cit. 'Quintillas a su libro'; B. López de Enciso, *Desengaño de celos* (Madrid, 1586), prol.

[2] Sannazàro, op. cit., pp. 163, 165.

[3] In the learned and interesting essay prefacing his *Siglo de oro* Balbuena explains his style by the fact that pastoral is written for the learned, not the ignorant, and that this is poetry in prose, not history ('Al lector', fol. 3ʳ).

exploitation of the stylistic possibilities of epic, which not only had room for both tragedy and comedy but—being, as Muzio said, a picture of the universe—'comprises in itself every style, every form, every sort of portrait: for often, leaving high endeavours, it descends to humble works'.[1] Cervantes applied the notion to the ideal novel of chivalry, which might contain both the tragic and the happy event, and allowed the author to

> show his talents in the epic, the lyric, tragedy and comedy, together with all that is contained in those most sweet and pleasing sciences, poetry and oratory. (*DQ* I. 47)

Essential to the theory of styles, but having a more positive influence on Cervantes, was decorum. It had figured in Plato and Aristotle; Horace had insisted on it in the *Ars poetica*; and it was still being insisted on in the eighteenth century. It was especially associated with dramatic theory and rhetoric, but also applied in poetry and the novel. Like the three unities, it was essentially meant to ensure a reasonable verisimilitude, but, when prescribed dogmatically and interpreted narrowly, its effect was the very opposite. A doctrine of appropriateness, decorum would have been the death of character-creation, rigidly observed. Juan de Valdés defines it clearly:

> When we wish to say that someone conducts himself in his way of living according to his estate and condition, we say that he observes decorum. This word is applied to actors of plays, of whom it is said that they have observed decorum well when they have acted as was suitable to the persons they were representing.[2]

El Pinciano and Cueva present decorum as one of the parts of verisimilitude,[3] and Cascales recalls the rhetorical precept that the narrative will have verisimilitude if the things narrated correspond to person, time, place, and occasion[4]—a precept which Cervantes remembers to observe even in dreams (*Parnaso* VI). Cervantes's concern for decorum as a part of verisimilitude explains the comments he so often makes on the exceptional

---

[1]
             . . . in sè comprende
      ogni stilo, ogni forma, ogni ritratto:
      perchè spesso lasciando l'alte imprese
      discende a l'opre umili . . .' (op. cit., fol. 80^r)

[2] Valdés, op. cit., p. 137.

[3] El Pinciano, op. cit. ii. 75 ff.; Cueva, op. cit. ɪ, verses 178–80.

[4] Cascales, *Tablas*, p. 126.

discreción, for their years, shown by some of his youthful heroes and heroines. Leocadia of *La fuerza de la sangre* speculates in this curious fashion:

I do not know how I am telling you these truths, which normally spring from much experience and the passing of many years, whereas I am not yet seventeen.

In the same way attention is drawn to the surprisingly ripe judgement of Galatea, Preciosa, Periandro, and Auristela.[1] Such precocity raises the problem of how far natural wisdom, education, and experience each shape a character. It particularly arises in the case of Sancho, whose wit and eloquence surprise everyone from time to time. The 'translator' of the *Quixote* judges his conversation with his wife Teresa, in II. 5, to be apocryphal on this account—because of the 'quixotification' of his speech, that is to say. Whatever the issues and explanations, however, all the cases above involve a question of decorum.

Valdés's definition shows that, apart from general verbal appositeness, there are two aspects of decorum. Cervantes betrays concern with them both. One is strictly literary and has to do with the attributes an author gives his characters to make them lifelike in an accepted way. An important part of this is the language he puts into their mouths. The Priest praises the romance of *Palmerín de Inglaterra* for the right use of decorum in this respect (*DQ* I. 6). The other aspect, which often combines with the previous one, is a literary application of that highly developed instinct for what was proper in life. There frequently results from this a curious sort of dual responsibility. The author is responsible for the artistic handling of his subject, his characters for conducting themselves as real people ought to conduct themselves in life. If they behave too outrageously, the author is blamed, but it is quite possible for them to behave indecorously in a way that is artistically acceptable.

One commonly deplored breach of the rule, for which the author could normally expect to be held responsible, was to mix the sacred and the profane. 'Mixing paganism and Christianity in divine matters', said Giraldi, 'is something alien to all decorum.'[2]

---

[1] *Galatea* V; ii. 149. *La gitanilla*, p. 56. *Persiles* III. 7; ii. 77 and IV. 9; ii. 268. Cf. *Esplandián*, p. 406: 'Pues siendo tan mozo, no cabía en él dar consejo de anciano.'

[2] Giraldi, *Dei romanzi*, p. 71.

Cervantes refers ironically in the prologue to *Don Quixote* I to
those who maintain 'a decorum so ingenious that they will follow
the description of a distracted lover in one line with a little
Christian sermon, which is a treat to listen to, in the next'. This
sort of thing, he adds presently, is 'a form of motley in which no
Christian intelligence should clothe itself'. Naturally, considerations of religious, no less than artistic, prudence were operative
here. Injunctions against such mixtures were very old.[1]

The vice corresponding to the virtue of appropriateness was
the stereotyping of characters, which plagued classical drama with
its 'typical' old men, young men, servants, and the rest. Aristotle
described them in the *Rhetoric* and Horace in the *Ars poetica*.
Cervantes paid his respects to this ossified concept in the indictment of contemporary *comedias* in *Don Quixote* I. 48. The principle
also operated in the cult of archetypal figures and exemplars, like
those the Canon spoke of in his outline of the ideal romance.
Fortunately, life had a way of breaking through the literary con-
vention. When Homer had so often disregarded decorum and
Terence shown his dissatisfaction with the stock characters of
ancient comedy, it was difficult for Golden-Age theorists not to
make concessions. Cueva allowed a departure from the norm for
some express exemplary reason;[2] El Pinciano for the sake of
admiratio and also because the exceptions found in life might be
imitated in comedy, which was permitted a certain licence.[3] For
there are such exceptions outside the natural order of things,
said Carvallo, in which case it is not an error to depict them as
they actually are.[4] Cascales summed up the situation best of all
perhaps. 'Aristotle made the general rule', he said, 'and nature the
exception.'[5]

Decorum was in fact one of the qualities in Cervantes's work
praised by his contemporaries. But even if he had been a slavish
observer of the precepts, which he was not, he need have had no
qualms about occasional departures from the norm. Indeed, it is
apparent that we have often to reckon with what C. S. Lewis has
called the 'calculated breach of decorum'. But it is even more
complicated than that. Like Velasquez again, Cervantes often

---

[1] Thus St. Isidore, *Etymologiarum sive originum libri XX*, ii. xvi.
[2] Cueva, op. cit. iii, verses 634–6.
[3] El Pinciano, op. cit. ii. 361, 81.
[4] Carvallo, op. cit., fols. 166ᵛ–167ʳ.
[5] Cascales, *Tablas*, p. 61.

simultaneously violated and yet did not violate the law of decorum. The effect was a similarly inscrutable presentation of character.

Like most Spaniards, he shows a strong sense of decorum as applied to conduct in life, but this is sometimes combined with literary decorum in his novels. Barrabás's criticism of the pretentious poem in the *Ilustre fregona* is largely based on the assumption that to use such language to a kitchen-maid is unbecoming and absurd. The effort, he considers (and, of course, he turns out to be wrong in the end), is unsuited to the occasion. For the seventeenth-century reader the title of this *novela* would have been even more paradoxical than it looks now. It would have been eye-catching and calculated to set one reading to find out how it could possibly be that a kitchen wench was illustrious. In this and in the similar story of the illustrious gipsy girl, the paradox is resolved with no breach of decorum. Costanza's duties at the inn, it may be added, were significantly confined to doing the silver.

The nature of *Don Quixote* often makes it hard to tell the difference between literary and 'real-life' decorum. The Knight, who repeatedly looks to chivalresque precedent, tries to make a decorum which is in large measure literary operative in his own life, and to impose it on his excessively talkative squire. Forgetting an important rule of the Courtier, that one must act one's age,[1] however, it never occurs to him that his imitation of a doughty knight errant is ludicrously unsuited to an impecunious middle-aged gentleman. Worse than that, as Riquer has pointed out, he never was or could have been a knight, because he was mad, poor, and had once been knighted in mockery.[2]

Real-life and literary decorum are combined too in the comment of the Canon on the promiscuity of queens and empresses in chivalresque novels (*DQ* I. 47). The idea is felt to be so improper as to be improbable. Propriety in this sense was an important part of decorum. 'Decorum cannot be separated from decency', said Tasso.[3] Indeed, decorum was an important part of morality. Dorotea's amorous dalliance with Don Fernando showed that she was no princess, Sancho coarsely and maliciously observed (*DQ* I. 46).

---

[1] Castiglione, op. cit., p. 161.
[2] M. de Riquer, 'Don Quijote, caballero por escarnio', *Clav* vii (1956).
[3] Tasso, *Del poema eroico* III. 85.

Such behaviour in a royal lover like Auristela, of course, would have been unthinkable (*Persiles* IV. 11).

'The good and bad of Princes is more exemplary, and thereby of greater moment than the private person's', wrote Puttenham in England.[1] Like exemplariness, the doctrines of style and decorum were integral to the idealistic world-picture, which was beginning to crack beneath scientifically applied pressures around the year 1600. Cervantes, like other writers, could still make such remarks as this, however:

> Great virtues are never, or but rarely, to be found in humble subjects; and bodily beauty is often a sign of beauty of soul. (*Persiles* IV. 4)

These curious but common notions, which experience and Christian teaching must have belied every day, find powerful expression in his ideal heroes and heroines, those patterns of perfection who lack no worldly advantage or spiritual blessing. Nothing is harder for the modern reader to accept than the necessary and explicit connexion between their dazzling endowments,[2] although traces of it linger in what little is left of traditional heroes and heroines in modern fiction. It seems to make nonsense of the repeated insistence of Cervantes on verisimilitude. But we must not make the mistake of confusing verisimilitude with realism. These unlikely characters are, for Cervantes, poetically true. The ideal is a poeticization of reality without being, as fantasy is, essentially untrue. Yet literary idealization caused him uneasiness on account of the eulogistic, hyperbolical procedures involved. What it meant indeed was the subjection of one sort of verisimilitude (what 'could be') to another (what 'ought to be').

It is true that passages expressing an absolutely contrary view to this idealistic one can be quoted. Quixote says, for instance, that beautiful moral qualities can exist in an ugly man (II. 58). Elsewhere Cervantes recognizes that wisdom can exist in a poor man, though fatally overshadowed by his condition in the world's eyes and treated with contempt.[3] And the theme that true nobility

---

[1] George Puttenham, *The Art of English Poesy*, in *Eliz. Crit. Essays*, ii. 45.

[2] For example, the connexion between wealth, birth, and manners, between manners and beauty, and between beauty and birth is presented as self-evident in *Persiles* I. 9; i. 65 and II. 2; i. 163 and *Las dos doncellas*, p. 30, respectively.

[3] *Coloquio*, pp. 247-8.

has nothing to do with station in life is a commonplace in his writing and in that of the Golden Age generally. The striking thing is that these opposing views were not mutually exclusive; they coexisted and overlapped.

The principle of decorous literary selection is stated seriously in the *Persiles*:

not everything that happens is suitable for narration, when it could be passed over without the story suffering as a result. There are actions about which one should keep silent on account of their grandeur, and others which should not be mentioned because of their paltriness.[1]

The *Quixote* is full of humorous allusions to the same idea. There is the discreet suppression by Benengeli of 'particular chapters' on the friendship between Rocinante and Sancho's donkey (II. 12), or the numerous allusions to things 'worthy of record', for instance. Even where hero and heroine are concerned the principle of idealization in each novel is the same, though in one case treated seriously, in the other comically. Periandro and Auristela, those two 'angels in human shape' (IV. 12), are very little different from Don Quixote's shining vision of himself and Dulcinea, without the magical chivalresque trappings. Since the Knight sees himself as an idealized literary hero, his anxieties about the kind of figure he is cutting take a distinctly literary turn. He worries about the decorum of actions in which he is involved and, even more, over whether his chronicler has known how to make the best of things that enhance his prestige and rejected all that is unworthy. In fact, he would like his whole experience and the manner in which the author represents it to be in the grand manner consonant with his heroic aspirations.

The idealizing ethos of epic could not have been better expressed by Don Quixote himself than in these words of Cascales:

Epic actions are based on the exploits of knighthood and heroic virtue, and aim at giving supreme excellence to the knight whom they celebrate.[2]

Don Quixote, of course, is trying to leap the chasm between life and poetry, to be the epic superman, the finished portrait which

---

[1] '... no todas las cosas que suceden son buenas para contadas, y podrían pasar sin serlo y sin quedar menoscabada la historia: acciones hay que, por grandes, deben callarse, y otras que, por bajas, no deben decirse' (*Persiles* III. 10; ii. 100).

[2] Cascales, 'A don Tomas Tamayo y Vargas', *Cartas filológicas*, Clás. cast. (Madrid, 1930–41), ii. 33.

is an improvement on the living model. He wants to be larger than life. It is easy enough for him to impose this pattern on Dulcinea, as she never materializes. It is another matter to achieve this in his own case, when he is tied to his historical existence whether he likes it or not.

Although he aspires towards this wholly poetic existence, not even he can entirely ignore the historical reality. The great discussion on the difference between the two occurs in II. 3. Quixote now knows that there really is a wise enchanter telling his story, and believes it to be his responsibility to tell it so as to reflect all possible credit on the hero.

'I imagine', Don Quixote said, 'that there is no human history in the world without its ups and downs, especially in the case of those dealing with chivalry, which can never be full of favourable events alone.'

'For all that,' replied the Bachelor, 'some of those who have read the story say they would have been glad if the authors had forgotten a few of the infinite cudgellings which Señor Don Quixote received in different encounters.'

'That's where the truth of the story comes in', said Sancho.

'They could also in fairness have kept quiet about them,' said Don Quixote, 'for there is no reason to write about those actions which neither alter nor affect the truth of the story, if they are going to redound to the discredit of its hero. In faith, Aeneas was not so pious as Virgil paints him, nor Ulysses so prudent as Homer describes him.'[1]

'That is so,' replied Sansón, 'but it is one thing to write as a poet and another as a historian.'[2]

[1] Cf. Ariosto:

'Non sì pietoso Enea, nè forte Achille
fu, come è fama, nè sì fiero Ettore.
(op. cit. xxxv. xxv)

Castro, *Pensamiento*, pp. 32–33, n. 2, thinks the passage recalls Robortelli rather than Ariosto.

[2] '— A lo que yo imagino — dijo don Quijote —, no hay historia humana en el mundo que no tenga sus altibajos, especialmente las que tratan de caballerías; las cuales nunca pueden estar llenos de prósperos sucesos. — Con todo eso — respondió el Bachiller —, dicen algunos que han leído la historia que se holgaran se les hubiera olvidado a los autores della algunos de los infinitos palos que en diferentes encuentros dieron al señor don Quijote. — Ahí entra la verdad de la historia — dijo Sancho. — También pudieran callarlos por equidad — dijo don Quijote—, pues las acciones que ni mudan ni alteran la verdad de la historia no hay para qué escribirlas, si han de redundar en menosprecio del señor de la historia. A fee que no fue tan piadoso Eneas como Virgilio le pinta, ni tan prudente Ulises como le describe Homero. — Así es — replicó Sansón —; pero uno es escribir como poeta, y otro como historiador' (*DQ* II. 3; iv. 85–86).

To have slanted the subject in the way Don Quixote would have liked would have been to do what Cascales called *mudar la cosa* (change the matter).[1]

The trivial business of everyday life is not the concern of the writer of heroic literature. He 'should leave out necessary things like eating and the preparation of food, or describe them only briefly', said Tasso.[2] Accordingly, Don Quixote finds himself unprepared to meet certain unheroic but practical needs. At the very outset of his career the first Innkeeper has to assure him that the chivalresque novelists never mentioned that knights errant always travelled with a full purse, a change of linen, and handy first-aid kit only because the matter was too obvious to need mentioning (I. 3). No one knew better than Cervantes what authorial valeting of this sort did to literary heroes in the eyes of the reader. No one knew better the infallible comic principle of bringing the ideal down to earth with a bump by a simple reminder of the animalities of human existence. The comic essence of *Don Quixote* resides in what Harry Levin has observed is the persistent pattern of the book, 'the pattern of art embarrassed by confrontation with nature'.[3]

Just as Don Quixote was forced to concede that every story has its ups and downs, Cervantes jibs at uniform style and absolute decorum.

> History does not always move on the same level; neither does painting always depict things that are grand and magnificent; nor is poetry's voice always sounding through the heavens. History admits lowly things; painting, weeds and thorns in its pictures; and poetry, singing of humble things, sometimes soars.[4]

The passage is at least in part an *ad hoc* justification, so it would be misleading to take it as absolute and final. Cervantes is not so consistent as that. He is as sensitive to the claims of decorum and the division of styles as he is to their limitations. He shows awareness of the inseparability of matter and form, but at the same time plainly believes in the existence of an immutable, irreducible core

[1] Cascales, *Tablas*, p. 137.   [2] Tasso, *Del poema eroico* ii. 65.
[3] Levin, 'Example of Cervantes', p. 79.
[4] 'No siempre va en un mismo peso la historia, ni la pintura pinta cosas grandes y magníficas, ni la poesía conversa siempre por los cielos. Bajezas admite la historia; la pintura, hierbas y retamas en sus cuadros; y la poesía tal vez se realza cantando cosas humildes' (*Persiles* III. 14; ii. 139).

of truth which is not affected by formal variations. One of his most remarkable achievements in the *Quixote* is to convey the sense of its presence by dressing up the same matter in different versions, or styles.

The Knight is only too aware of the variety of possible literary treatments, especially at the beginning of Part II. Although he decides eventually that the chivalresque subject of Cide Hamete's history is sufficient guarantee of a properly grandiose treatment, he has misgivings at first and feels helplessly dependent on the goodwill of the sage, who if friendly will enhance his exploits, if hostile will debase them (II. 3). Not long before this there has been some speculation on a possible satirical treatment of the fair Angelica (II. 1). The book is filled with double versions of a single event. One of the most conspicuous will suffice here. When Don Quixote sets out for the first time, we have on the one hand his depiction of the occasion as he sees it, tricked out in chivalresque rhetoric and the splendours of a mythological dawn; on the other, the scene as the reader sees it, conveyed more by suggestion than by direct description. The parody ends with the famous knight Don Quixote forsaking his slothful couch of down, mounting his famous steed Rocinante, and taking the road across the ancient and celebrated plain of Montiel. The author's single, laconic, minimal comment on all this is, 'And it was the truth that he was riding across it' (I. 2). The comic discrepancy is one of style, in the fullest sense of the word. The issue is the truth of the matter.

The realism of the nineteenth- and twentieth-century novel is essentially a product of its own age. It is a literary concomitant of the modern historical sense which asserted itself when the breakdown of traditional values and beliefs, on which decorum and the doctrine of styles depended, was well advanced. The writer of fiction learnt like the historian and the scientist, and to a large extent from them, that what was important was not necessarily imposing. Generally speaking, down to some time in the eighteenth century, it is more accurate to regard what is usually called 'realism' as writing in the low style, which was customarily associated with the comic. When it transcended the comic, its interest became, as Ortega said, extra-poetic—scientific.[1]

[1] Ortega, *Meditaciones*, p. 184.

Of course contemporary realism has roots in the past. Fascinatingly modern notes are struck in such novels as *Tirante el Blanco*, *La Lozana andaluza*, or the picaresque novel *La vida y hechos de Estebanillo González* (which contains a private soldier's worm's-eye view of the beastliness of war, antedating Stendhal's by a considerable margin). The common pretence that prose fiction was history, and by implication more truthful and exact than poetry, acted as a very slight counterweight to the dogmas. But as long as the beliefs on which decorum and the division of styles were founded remained in large measure intact, the writers who mixed the styles and broke the rules could not altogether escape their influence. There was scarcely any conception of realism in theory. Indeed poetic theory was determinedly anti-realistic. The poet who dealt with things exactly as they were would have been betraying his art. El Pinciano's practical, intelligent, and forthright Hugo says:

I am of the opinion that poets have seldom depicted men just as they were, and this for the sake of better imitation . . . . If, because of their natural deficiency, men (and even historians, for the same reason) never represent anything in speech or writing exactly as it was, but always add something either good or bad, why should not poets, who are their imitators in these things as in the rest, imitate them in this respect? I will add that if the poet did depict men exactly as they were, the representations would be lacking in the power to move and to arouse *admiratio*, which is a most important part of one of the aims of poetry, I mean that of giving delight.[1]

The narrow literary dogmas of decorum and style reflect a now obsolete world-view arranged on hierarchical lines. *Don Quixote* is an ironic vision in which the old world-view is compounded with one that is essentially modern, with the ideally exalted and the basely material coexisting as distinct but inseparable parts of human experience. In that novel Cervantes served up not a 'slice of life', but, more nearly than anyone had ever done in a work of fiction before, the whole cake.

[1] '. . . yo soy de parecer que pocas veces los poetas pintan a los hombres iguales como ellos fueron; y esto por mayor imitación . . . si los hombres por vicio natural que tienen, y aun los históricos, por la causa misma, jamás dicen o escriben alguna cosa igual a lo que ella fue, sino que siempre añaden alguna cosa o de malo o de bueno, ¿ por qué los poetas, que son imitadores de estos tales, como en las demás cosas, no los imitarán en éstas? Añado que, si el poeta pintase iguales como los hombres son, carecerían del mover o admiración, la cual es una parte importantísima para uno de los fines de la poética, digo, para el deleite' (op. cit. i. 248–9).

3. *Diction*

> . . . uttering sweetly and properly the conceits of the mind,
> which is the end of speech.   SIR PHILIP SIDNEY

The passing references writers make to style are apt to be nebulous
and unilluminating, especially in a period when judicial criticism
can often scarcely be separated from compliment on the one hand
or abuse on the other. Allowing for this, it is still possible to
single out certain qualities of prose writing, held common to one,
other, or all of the three main styles, evidently valued by Cervantes.
They need only be treated briefly. He makes three sorts of comment: direct remarks about literary diction; remarks about
language with a stylistic relevance; and comments about the
manner in which the stories in his works are told. There are many
of the third kind, and, while the stories to which they refer are
all literature, it should be remembered that strictly they apply in
the first instance to oral fiction.

Cervantes thought style very important. Not only does Don
Diego require works of entertainment to give pleasure by their
language (*DQ* II. 16), but several novels of chivalry are condemned on no other specified grounds than stylistic ones. The
Canon charges them generally with being harsh in style (*DQ* I. 47)
and the Priest in particular condemns Feliciano de Silva's *Amadís
de Grecia* and Melchor Ortega's *Florismarte* (or *Felixmarte*) *de
Hircania* for stylistic reasons (*DQ* I. 6). Moreover, though we need
not spoil the joke by taking the words of Cervantes too seriously,
he actually says that Don Quixote was driven out of his mind by
trying to understand Feliciano de Silva's remarkable prose!

And of all [the books of chivalry] none seemed to him so good as
those composed by the famous Feliciano de Silva. The clarity of his
prose and the intricate sentences seemed pearls of beauty to him;
especially when he read those lovers' compliments and letters of
challenge, where he would often find written such as this: 'The reason
for the unreason perpetrated on my reason in such wise weakens my
reason that with reason I complain of your beauty.'[1] And when he read:
'The high heavens which divinely fortify your divinity with the stars
and make you deserving of the deserts that your greatness deserves.'

---

[1] 'La razón de la sinrazón que a mi razón se haze, de tal manera mi razón en-
flaqueze, que con razón me quejo de la vuestra fermosura.'

With these reasonings the poor knight lost his wits, and he would lie awake trying to understand and disentangle their meaning, which Aristotle himself would not have understood or disentangled if he had been resurrected for that very purpose. (I. 1)

Unluckily for Silva, it was as an example of repetitiousness to be avoided that the author of the *Rhetorica ad Herennium* had cited 'Nam cuius rationis ratio non extet, ei rationi ratio non est fidem habere admodum'.[1] Silva's puerile word-play, though of a type much admired in the fifteenth century and known to Encina as the *gala 'redoblado'*, earned him the ridicule of Diego Hurtado de Mendoza before that of Cervantes. 'Do you think, my friend,' he asked in his letter to Captain Salazar, 'that I could write half a book of *Don Florisel de Niquea* . . . and that, to praise your book, I should be able to say "the reason for the reason which I so unreasonably hold to be reasonable"?'[2]

Unnecessary intricacy is one of the more frequent objects of Cervantine stylistic criticism. Don Quixote rebukes Sancho for it in II. 71. It is also one of the faults ascribed to a certain novelist in the *Parnaso* VIII—one Pedrosa, who in the battle of the books fired off (the word punningly used is *disparó*) four tasteless, witless *novelas* in ill-composed, intricate prose. The censure is connected in part with another recurrent motif, the censure of affectation, a vice which the humanists had held in peculiar abhorrence. 'Speak plainly, boy!' cries Master Pedro, 'no lofty flights; all affectation is bad' (*DQ* II. 26).[3]

There are a few honourable exceptions among the chivalresque novels, such as *Palmerín de Inglaterra*, which the Priest commends for its clear and courtly language (*DQ* I. 6). Another is *Tirante el Blanco*—that is, if the phrase 'in its style [*por su estilo*] the best book in the world' is not simply equivalent to 'in its own way [*por su camino*] the best book of its kind', used by the Priest of Lofraso's novel. In general for Cervantes, however, the books of chivalry cannot compete stylistically with the pastoral romances, which in the *Coloquio* he describes as 'well written'. The particular

---

[1] *Rhet. ad Herenn.* IV. xii. 18.

[2] '¿Paréceos, amigo, que sabría yo hacer un medio libro de *Don Florisel de Niquea* . . . y que sabría decir "la razón de la razón que tan sin razón por razón tengo", para alabar vuestro libro?' (*Carta al capitán Salazar*, BAE xxxvi. 549).

[3] See also: *DQ* II. 12; iv. 257–8. II. 43; vi. 247–8. *Vizcaíno fingido*, p. 103. *Cueva de Salamanca*, p. 131.

qualities of style he commends are the obvious ones and need not detain us. Just a few of his tenets stand out.

To tell a story well requires *discreción* in the first place.[1] So indeed does the proper use of language in ordinary intercourse, as the pontificating university graduate in *Don Quixote* II. 19 explains to everyone. The product of this is a language which is at once 'pure, appropriate, elegant and clear'. Of these qualities, all of which may be taken as major stylistic virtues in Cervantes's theory, appropriateness or appositeness is perhaps most immediately the result of exercising *discreción*. Authorities regularly included it among the foremost virtues of style.[2] Periandro describes it as the 'sauce' or flavouring of stories (*Persiles* III. 7).

Three terms which are not only obviously applicable to his own writing but prominent in his critical vocabulary are *gracia, donaire*, and *apacibilidad*, words expressive of related concepts of charm, ease, and pleasing form. It is with the first that Cervantes seeks to please both the judicious and the simple reader. The second (like appropriateness) helps to make the literary absurdity acceptable. The third is used to characterize the ideal romance (*DQ* I. 47). The first two also appear frequently among the tributes paid to his characters for their story-telling.[3]

But there are virtues that make for a higher tone and the enrichment of writing as well as those that make for clarity and simplicity. Cervantes specifically recommends one form of periphrasis demanded by good taste. Circumlocution is often necessary for the avoidance of obscenity or coarseness. This was a delicate matter, for, as Herrera pointed out, indecency might lurk in the very sound of words innocent in meaning.[4] Cipión says in the *Coloquio*:

That is the mistake of the person who said it was not coarse or vicious to call things by their proper names. Just as though it were not better, when one is obliged to mention them, to express them by roundabout phrases and circumlocutions which modify the repugnance

[1] Cf. *Las dos doncellas*, p. 34. *DQ* I. 52; iii. 409.

[2] Thus L. Gracián Dantisco: 'También deben ser las palabras lo más apropiadas que se puedan a lo que se quiere mostrar por ellas' (*Galateo español*, ed. Madrid, 1943, p. 122).

[3] *Galatea* I; i. 51. *DQ* I. 12; i. 341. I. 36; iii. 133. *Persiles* II. 11; i. 238. II. 12; i. 244. III. 7; ii. 77.

[4] Herrera, *Anotaciones*, p. 603.

they cause when we hear them called by their real names. Decent words testify to the decency of whoever utters or writes them.[1]

This recalls the *Galateo español*, where it is said that a gentleman telling a story should

use no indecent or filthy words, or words so foul as to cause repugnance in whoever hears him; for roundabout expressions and clean and decent terms can be used, without naming such things clearly.[2]

There are examples of polite and vulgar words in the same book. One is to say 'mouth' (*boca*) or 'lips' (*labio*), not 'snout' (*hocico*); 'abdomen' (*vientre*), not 'belly' (*panza*) or 'stomach' (*barriga*).[3] Don Quixote similarly advises Sancho that fastidious people now say 'eructate' (*erutar*), not 'belch' (*regoldar*) (*DQ* II. 43). And fastidiously for her part, the Dueña Dolorida prefers to say *oídos* rather than *orejas* for 'ears' (*DQ* II. 38).

In the prologue to the *Galatea* Cervantes paid his tribute to the Spanish language for the opportunity it offered for displaying that diversity of *conceptos* that came so naturally to its writers. There was broad agreement on this point both in and out of Spain.[4] Spanish was held to be peculiarly suited to all forms of word-play, equivocation, and conceit. The word *concepto* was not yet charged with all the meaning Gracián was to give it, and, although it will be more convenient here to call it a 'conceit', it was only just developing from what we should now simply call a 'concept'. Contemporaries of Cervantes like El Pinciano still defined it basically, in terms which Nebrija had used a century earlier, as an 'image formed in the mind'.[5] In accordance with these definitions,

[1] 'Ese es el error que tuvo el que dijo que no era torpedad ni vicio nombrar las cosas por sus propios nombres, como si no fuese mejor, ya que sea forzoso nombrarlas, decirlas por circunloquios y rodeos, que templen la asquerosidad que causa el oírlas por sus mismos nombres. Las honestas palabras dan indicio de la honestidad del que las pronuncia o las escribe' (*Coloquio*, p. 183).

[2] '. . . que no tengan palabras deshonestas, ni sucias, ni tan puercas que puedan causar asco a quien le oye; pues se puede decir por rodeos y términos limpios y honestos, sin nombrar claramente cosas semejantes' (op. cit., p. 101).

[3] Ibid., p. 99.

[4] 'Pare ancor che ai Spagnoli sia assai proprio il motteggiare' (Castiglione, op. cit., p. 201). Cf. Cabrera de Córdoba, op. cit., fol. 86ᵛ; Juan de Jáuregui, *Discurso poético* (Madrid, 1624), fol. 23ᵛ.

[5] El Pinciano, op. cit. ii. 204. Cf. Cascales, *Tablas*, p. 205; Suárez de Figueroa, *El pasajero*, p. 159; and A. de Nebrija, *Reglas de la ortografía castellana*, in *Gramática de la lengua castellana* (ed. Oxford, 1926), p. 237. The evolution of the idea of the *concepto* may be seen in Carvallo's 'tomar y concebir un pensamiento delicado y sobre él discurrir y discantar cosas sutiles, de las cuales conciba el que lo oye lo que con ordinario modo no se dice' (op. cit., fols. 120ᵛ–121ʳ).

Don Quixote says, 'the pen is the tongue of the mind; [one's] writings will correspond to whatever conceits are engendered there' (II. 16).

Conceits were proper to love poetry, but not confined to it. The author of the *Quixote* is advised to express them without intricacy or obscurity (*DQ* I, prol.), dangers to which they were especially open. His hero, using a very popular Renaissance analogy, looks back to the mythical Golden Age as a time when, just as maidens were beautiful, modest, unadorned, and quite unlike seventeenth-century courtesans, so were the amorous conceits of the mind simply expressed, just as they had been conceived, and not tricked out with artificial periphrasis (I. 11). It was the artifice, the 'dolling-up', that Cervantes distrusted. The reason for this, which will occupy us in the final section of this chapter, may be found in a remark of Tasso's: 'Conceits produce an inflated style if they go too far beyond the truth.'[1] We may add that exceeding the truth was of more concern to Cervantes than stylistic excess. But a conceit was not recognizable except by special qualities that marked it out from ordinary discourse, and the approbatory adjective Cervantes most often applied to the word, if I am not mistaken, was 'elevated'.[2] How then was a conceit to be at once natural and direct, and outstanding and memorable?

Behind this small, particular problem lay the whole stylistic dilemma of the novel for Cervantes. How did one invest the novel with the beautiful and desirable ornaments of poetry without sacrificing that matter-of-fact credibility so essential to it? Torn between the verbal opulence of the poet and the sobriety of the historian, his stylistic preferences tended to gravitate in theory towards that *gracia*, pleasing to all tastes, which he also achieved in practice. But not even this central and delightful stylistic formula could lessen Cervantes's awareness of a fundamental distinction between two types of story. Cipión states it in an extreme form in the *Coloquio*:

some contain their charm in themselves, others in the manner of their telling. I mean by this that there are some which give pleasure

[1] Tasso, *Dell'arte poetica* iii. 33.

[2] e.g.: 'agudos, graves, sutiles y levantados' (*Galatea*, prol.; i, p. xlviii); 'bien dispuestos y subidos' (ibid. VI; ii. 215); 'altos y extraños' (ibid. VI; ii. 238); 'agradables . . . profundos, altos, discretos' ('Quintillas' for López Maldonado's *Cancionero*, p. 46); 'la alteza de sus conceptos' (*Lic. Vidriera*, p. 94); 'dulcísimos . . . altos, graves y discretos' (*DQ* II. 20; v. 116).

although they are told without preambles and verbal ornaments, while others need to be dressed up in words and accompanied by demonstrations of face and hands and alterations of voice, whereby something is made out of a trifle and what was pale and flabby becomes pointed and pleasurable.

There is a clear echo here of that practical advice on good story-telling which one finds in contemporary miscellanies and manuals (Bargagli, for example, required of the narrator of *novelle* comparable histrionic abilities).[1] But the distinction was also a straightforward literary one, commonly and variously applied in Golden-Age theory. Balbuena reduced it to its simplest terms when he defined two sorts of narrative: one of them 'natural and historical', the other 'artificial and poetical'.[2]

The coupling of these discrepant concepts engendered *Don Quixote*.

4. *Decoration and Hyperbole*

Every hyperbole transcends the possible. DEMETRIUS

Cervantes faced few difficulties in his own novels more formidable than that of conveying to the reader the outstanding and admirable qualities of his idealized characters without seeming to exaggerate. He does not reject literary representation of the ideal as he rejects direct portrayal of the fantastic, but occasionally he betrays dissatisfaction with the conventional means of conveying it. In doing this he makes a criticism of an important principle connected with idealization: the principle of decoration. The connexion between these two may not be immediately apparent, and so requires a word of explanation.

Beauty, says Lenio in the *Galatea* IV, is of two sorts, corporeal and incorporeal. The former may be animate or inanimate; the latter is divided between 'the virtues and sciences of the mind'. Complete beauty is only found in the conjunction of the corporeal and the incorporeal. This aesthetic formula, besides having consequences for Cervantes's general literary theory (formal beauty

[1] '. . . bisogna anche accompagnarlo con la voce, con i gesti e con la pronunzia in modo che la persona si contrafaccia della quale si racconta' (op. cit., p. 216).

[2] Balbuena's prologue, in J. Van Horne, '*El Bernardo* of Bernardo de Balbuena', *UISLL* xii (1927), p. 146.

must be completed by moral and intellectual content in a work of art), is conspicuously evident in his ideal heroes and, especially, heroines—those compounds of beauty, virtue, and intelligence.

Now it would not make sense for Cervantes to describe moral virtues and intellectual accomplishments as 'ornaments' that grace a person (which, like other writers of the day, he often does),[1] if 'ornament' could only stand for a superficial and removable form of beautification. In fact, while the word had this obvious sense, it could also be a token of some deeper quality, from which it derived its true value. It could point to, and in the last resort depend upon, something within. As Herrero García has pointed out, adornment was regarded as a sort of enticement, drawing attention to beauty, but if the latter did not exist it became an imposture, drawing nothing but scorn from the beholder.[2] It does not seem fanciful therefore to describe the personages of idealistic fiction, so generously endowed physically, intellectually, and morally, as 'decorated' characters, whom it was natural and appropriate to describe in ornamental language. There was indeed a stylistic analogy. Literary decoration too was supposed to reflect intrinsic qualities. The 'flowers and figures' that beautify writing, said Herrera, should show up not only the flesh and blood of the work, but its nerves, so that its strength may be judged from its colour.[3] Just as with human beings, the manifest adornment should have links with the content within.

Cervantes like almost everyone else had a taste for decoration. Ornamentation can never offend, he remarks in the *Persiles*. But his obsessive concern with the truth causes him to add that it also serves to cover up many faults (IV. 7). Here is a hint of a danger to which he was always alive: namely, that the truth would be obscured.

He seems to have been struck by the fact that to portray idealized characters—rare and exceptional, if not completely perfect, persons—the author can hardly avoid some form of eulogy. Cervantes does not suggest that such beings do not deserve praise, and even less that they are impossible, but he intimates quite frequently that what is said even of exceptional people in

[1] e.g. *Lic. Vidriera*, p. 92. *La señora Cornelia*, p. 70. *DQ* I, dedic.; i. 14. I. 14; i. 391. II. 6; iv. 151. II. 16; v. 31. II. 42; vi. 241.

[2] M. Herrero García, 'Ideas estéticas del teatro clásico español', *RIEs* v (1944), 90.

[3] Herrera, *Anotaciones*, p. 292. This may well be a reminiscence of Minturno on the ornate style, op. cit., p. 435.

real life is rarely the literal truth; that it ranges anywhere from a slight colouring of the facts to the falsest flattery. To inspire, edify, and arouse *admiratio* as a rule required the portrayal of the exceptional or the ideal, and this as a rule meant recourse to procedures of enhancement and exaggeration. If he resorted to these, could the writer still be certain of convincing? If he failed to convince, his other aims were emasculated. In life, eulogy and all that went with it were suspect because all too often the real truth was left in doubt. Cervantes often associated adulation and falsehood, and he showed them, in the traditional allegorical way, as sisters in the *Viaje del Parnaso* VI.

He put the matter plainly in the prologue to the *Novelas ejemplares*:

to suppose that such eulogies express the truth exactly [*puntualmente*] is nonsense, for neither praise nor blame can be fixed to a precise or determined point.[1]

A quotation from El Pinciano supplies the ideological context to this:

truth resides in a point and falsehood is all that is not this point of truth.[2]

But, one immediately asks, what has all this to do with the novelist, whose business it is to write fiction? The fact is that Cervantes's scruples are those of a conscientious historian, for whom disinterestedness is axiomatic. We begin to see that for Cervantes the problems of the novelist are those of a historian quite as much as they are those of a poet writing an epic in prose.

It was recognized that history and poetry spoke different languages and that the simple truth was inimical to an elaborate style. To caution the historian therefore against the use of decorated and exaggerated language was virtually a critical commonplace. 'The understanding, whose business it is to know the truth fundamentally, cannot couple itself with such a profusion of speech and verbal ornament', said Huarte.[3] El Pinciano said that plainness and simplicity went hand in hand with truth.[4]

---

[1] '. . . pensar que dicen puntualmente la verdad los tales elogios, es disparate, por no tener punto preciso ni determinado las alabanzas ni los vituperios' (*Novelas*, prol., p. 21).
[2] '. . . la verdad está en punto y la mentira es todo lo que no es este punto de verdad' (op. cit. i. 267).   [3] *Examen*, fol. 111ʳ.
[4] *Filosofía antigua poética*, ii. 208.

Cascales gave the name of 'truthful' to spontaneous and unadorned speech.[1] Cervantes himself expressed an idea similar to these as early as the *Galatea* when he wrote: 'The basis and chief substance of the true story is not in its elegance and manner of telling; it lies in the pure truth.'[2]

To put it another way, all this means that Cervantes was uneasy about rhetorical language. The aims of rhetoric were to persuade and to move. The best authorities had insisted that the motives must be unexceptionable, but rhetoric was traditionally associated with the colouring or distortion of truth by means of alluring language. The 'colours' of rhetoric were not designed to illuminate the plain truth of the matter; they were meant to make the matter more attractive. But it was not easy to do without them. Cervantes could neither dispense with them entirely nor altogether trust them.

And we may be sure that he did not want to dispense with the alluring and high-flown language of poetry. There was general agreement, however, that poets spoke a language peculiar to themselves.[3] This language was held to be more elevated than that used for most other purposes—a notion which cut across the division of styles and drove some of the more thoughtful critics into an awkward corner.[4] The problem for Cervantes was how to retain the decorative beauties and noble idealism characteristic of the most esteemed poetry without sacrificing conviction. He did not really succeed in solving it, except in the *Quixote*, and not always there.

But one important ingredient of stylistic 'elevation' (which was not synonymous with 'decoration') he treated with great caution,

[1] Cascales, *Tablas*, p. 106.
[2]   '... que no está en la elegancia
y modo de decir el fundamento
y principal sustancia
del verdadero cuento,
que en la pura verdad tiene su asiento.'
(*Galatea* III; i. 211)
[3] Thus Muzio, op. cit., fol. 89ᵛ; Herrera, *Anotaciones*, p. 575; Cueva, op. cit. III, verses 725–6.
[4] El Pinciano goes into the matter quite searchingly (op. cit. ii. 181 ff.), but even his Don Gabriel can reach no better conclusion than that either the three styles must each move up a step above the quality of their subject-matter, becoming intermediate, high, and very high, or else that poetic style may be always very high (p. 211). Cascales, yet more vaguely, situates all three styles above the common 'human' level, because poetry is something 'divine' (*Tablas*, p. 103).

and even suspicion. This was the pompous mythological or historical allusion. He excised the following specimens of grandiose embellishment from the final version of the *Celoso extremeño*:

not like impious Bireno fleeing from the bed where he had left the deceived and luckless Olympia, but, rather, with the fury of Vulcan in search of his beloved, he left his hateful couch;

and:

I, the phoenix that sought and heaped up the fuel with which to consume myself.[1]

Admittedly, he may have removed the first because it was clumsy and confused and the second because it was very inappropriate. But when Ruperta in the *Persiles* apostrophizes herself like this: 'Did humble Judith quail before the ferocity of Holophernes?...' the reason for the peculiarly Cervantine second thoughts which follow is quite clear. The disparity of the analogy strikes her immediately:

it is true that her cause was very different from mine: she punished an enemy of God, and I wish to punish one whom I know not whether I am to take for an enemy. Love for her country put the blade into her hand, love for my husband into mine.

And she concludes:

But why do I make such foolish comparisons? (III. 17)

Possibly Cervantes had taken the hint of El Pinciano, who observed that lofty and unusual language was less necessary in prose than in metrical poems.[2] However that may be, in the musings of Ruperta Cervantine self-criticism seems to go deeper than mere considerations of appropriateness and beyond the mere apology for digression we noted earlier in the case of Cardenio's rhetorical elaborations. It seems to threaten the poetic ideal of exemplariness itself. If exact correspondence of circumstances were to be insisted upon, there would be a sad depletion of opportunities for exemplary reminiscence.

The basic device of this sort of language was hyperbole, used in metaphors and comparisons. As Luis de León explained,

those who dearly wish to extol something, declaring and praising its qualities, refrain from using fit and simple words and use the names

[1] Porras version in ed. cit. of the *Novelas*, pp. 245 and 259.

[2] El Pinciano, op. cit. ii. 184.

of things in which the property or quality they are praising is most
perfectly to be found, which enhances and gives greater charm to
what is said. Thus the great Italian poet, wishing to praise hair,
calls it gold; lips, roses or berries; teeth, pearls; eyes, lights, fires or
stars.[1]

The lover, above all, uses this language of borrowed hyperboles, Rodrigues Lobo observed, because he can scarcely find
anything in creation sufficient to compare with the attributes of
his lady.[2]

Cervantes feels the need of it in most of his novels, but in none
more so than *Persiles y Sigismunda*. From the moment hero and
heroine appear, we are made to understand that no praise can do
them justice—which, of course, is only another way of praising
them. The fame of Auristela's beauty spreads through Rome,
and not even the most 'judicious wits' can do it justice (IV. 4).
Yet when on her entry into the city a Roman, who, it is thought,
must have been a poet, indulges in a brief though lavish encomium of her beauty, Cervantes calls his praises 'as hyperbolical as they were unnecessary' (IV. 3). Truth, it seems, ought
to be able to make its own effect without such mythological
allusions and comparisons as the Roman used—he had compared
Auristela with Venus and called her a 'movable image'. Auristela's
remark about Sinforosa expresses the same notion: 'I say she has
credible beauty; and I say "credible" because it is such that it has
no need of exaggerations to exalt it or hyperboles to magnify
it' (II. 4).

Excessive eulogy, at least in verifiable cases, defeats its own
ends, one of which is to inspire wonder.[3] Periandro gently cuts
short Antonio's praises of Lisbon, telling him to leave them something to find out and admire for themselves (III. 1). The most significant words on the whole subject are also put into the mouth of
Periandro. They best illustrate the dilemma Cervantes finds himself in when he wants to convey the magnitude of the exceptional
while being suspicious of eulogy:

hyperbolical praises, however extreme they are, should have definite
limits: to say that a woman is an angel is a polite exaggeration, not

---

[1] Luis de León, *Traducción literal y declaración del libro de los Cantares de Salomón*,
BAE xxxvii. 270. Cf. Lucian, *Essays in Portraiture Defended*, § 19.

[2] Rodrigues Lobo, op. cit., fols. 85ᵛ–87ᵛ.

[3] Cf. El Pinciano, op. cit. ii. 142–3.

an obligatory one. Only in you, my sweetest sister, are rules broken and do the exaggerations of your beauty attain the force of truth.[1]

The exceptional, by definition, is not subject to rule. But how is one to convince the reader that the case truly is exceptional?

This ambivalence is at the root of the comic irony which gives coherence to *Don Quixote* but is mostly absent from the *Persiles*. Irony allows Cervantes to make the dilemma part of his great novel of contradictions. Nobody worries about the paradox in Don Quixote's reference to Dulcinea as 'one, all praise of whom is fitting, however hyperbolical it may be' (II. 73). There are all sorts of safeguards: a madman is speaking; Dulcinea is a creature of the imagination; and between Cervantes and his story is Benengeli in any case. Encomium can always be left as a joke to the Moor. This is what happens with Don Quixote's adventure with the lion in II. 17. After some breathless apostrophe and groping for hyperboles, words fail Cide Hamete and he decides to leave the Knight's actions on their 'point of truth' (*en su punto*) to speak for themselves. He then proceeds to relate the incident as it occurred: the lion's lazy and insulting indifference rendering Don Quixote's display of indisputable courage ridiculously irrelevant.

Like Benengeli, Cervantes or his speakers on occasion prefer to leave something exceptional *en su punto* rather than seek words to extol it.[2] The unique position of Benengeli, so often commended as a *puntual* historian, of course allows Cervantes to have it both ways. But sometimes, and not only in the *Persiles*, the irony is lacking and we are left with Cervantes ambivalently criticizing a poetic exaggeration and at the same time wanting the reader to accept it. Rustic singing of remarkable quality, he observes for example, is more likely to be found among the exaggerations of poets than in the real countryside; but Cardenio's singing, which provoked the remark, is of just such exceptional quality, and we are plainly required to accept the fact (*DQ* I. 27).

The common definitions of hyperbole would have put Cervantes on his guard. Quintilian, who made some shrewd

---

[1] '. . . las hipérboles alabanzas, por más que lo sean, han de parar en puntos limitados: decir que una mujer es un ángel es encarecimiento de cortesía, pero no de obligación. Sola en ti, dulcísima hermana mía, se quiebran reglas, y cobran fuerzas de verdad los encarecimientos que se dan a tu hermosura' (*Persiles* II. 2; i. 164).

[2] Thus *Galatea* I; i. 41. *DQ* I. 33; iii. 47. *Persiles* III. 17; ii. 165.

comments on its use, called it an 'elegant straining of the truth'.[1]
Nebrija said it 'is what we say in excess of the truth when we wish
to magnify or belittle something'.[2] Gracián Dantisco remarked
that:

Exaggerations, no less than affectations, tend to be badly received
and serve ill when we wish to be believed; in our common speech
they should be left to poets and tellers of tales.[3]

But Cervantes had come to see the novelist as more than a mere
teller of tales and as something other than a poet. I know of no
writer contemporary with him in whom poetic exaggeration
produced such manifest symptoms of discomfort. Tasso and
Sidney could talk of embellishing truth with new colours and of
beautifying historical material;[4] El Pinciano and Cascales of
ornamenting the truth.[5] But the author of Don Quixote clearly had
doubts whether the truth—even the truth of fiction—could be so
handled without injury.

Nevertheless, he still wanted things both ways. One result of
this was his equivocal treatment of certain subjects conventionally
regarded as set pieces for decorative description—notably, dawn
landscapes and beautiful women.[6] Feminine beauty is the one
most relevant to his literary theory. This was habitually extolled
by means of imagery involving a good deal of expensive jewellery,
celestial orbs, and the like. A hackneyed topic, it lent itself to
parody, caricature, and effects of violent contrast, which Cervantes like other writers made the best of.

Apollo in the Adjunta, with some ironical amusement, permits
poets to bestow on their ladies attributes borrowed from the
heavens, as well as to pretend to be in love and call their mistresses
Amarili, Anarda, Filis, and so on (or even Juana Téllez, for that
matter). Quixote tells Sancho that all the Amarilis, Filis, Silvias,
and the like in literature are not flesh and blood, but creatures of
fiction (I. 25), and the Bachelor later refers to such ladies as
poeticizations of real women (II. 73). But with the exception of

[1] Quintilian, Inst. orat. VIII. vi. 67.
[2] Nebrija, Gramática castellana, p. 136. Giraldi, Dei romanzi, p. 176, and Tasso,
Dell'arte poetica III. 32, similarly describe hyperbole.
[3] Gracián Dantisco, op. cit., p. 77.
[4] Tasso, Del poema eroico II. 55; Sidney, op. cit., p. 169.
[5] El Pinciano, op. cit. ii. 199; Cascales, Tablas, p. 133.
[6] See E. C. Riley, ' "El alba bella que las perlas cría": dawn-description in the
novels of Cervantes', BHS xxxiii (1956).

pastoral Cervantes seems to have been reluctant to regard prose fiction as *mere* fiction. He will rarely view it in isolation from historical reality. This unwillingness to cut the links accounts for his occasionally mocking, ambiguous, or frankly critical treatment of poetically transformed beauties. It is not a denial of their beauty, but a criticism of the way such dazzling imagery obfuscates its accurate apprehension.

Theoretically, the language used should obey the dictates of decorum. Barrabás's criticism of the poem in the *Ilustre fregona* is a comic statement of this principle:

> You should have told her . . . that she was as stiff as asparagus, as haughty as a crest of plumes, as white as milk, as chaste as a novice friar, as finical and headstrong as a hired mule, and harder than a lump of mortar. If you had told her this, she would have understood and been pleased.[1]

Piccolomini had expressed a remarkably similar idea:

> An educated person, for example, will call the flesh of a woman with white skin alabaster or ivory; while a rough countryman or a humble shepherd will call it buttermilk curds, cheese or mortar. Likewise a cultured person will call the lips of a beautiful woman rubies and the teeth pearls; while a peasant who has never seen pearls or rubies will call those lips wine and the teeth little snails.[2]

Cervantes's main concern, however, is not the propriety of these comparisons, but their exactness.

Behind those that figure in his own novels a whole range of attitudes is apparent. There is, on occasion, serious use of the topic. There is also studied detachment, outright mockery, and a disconcerting medley of acceptance and criticism.[3] This last is

---

[1] 'Dijérasla . . . que es tiesa como un espárrago, entonada como un plumaje, blanca como una leche, honesta como un fraile novicio, melindrosa y zahareña como una mula de alquiler, y más dura que un pedazo de argamasa, que, como esto le dijeras, ella lo entendiera y se holgara' (*Ilustre fregona*, p. 310). The Sevillian muleteer had used some rustic images of this sort to describe Costanza earlier (p. 278).

[3] 'Chiamerà (per esempio) una persona civile le carni d'una bianca donna carni d'alabastro o ver d'avorio; dove ch'un rozzo contadino o un vil pastore le chiamerà carni di ricotta o di cacio o di calcina. Chiamerà parimente una persona urbana le labra d'una bella donna rubini e li denti perle; dove ch'un uom di villa, che non vide mai perle o rubini, chiamerà vino quelle labra e quei denti lumachette' (op. cit., p. 323).

[3] Thus, for example, respectively: *Amante liberal*, p. 139; *Lic. Vidriera*, pp. 94–95; *La gran sultana*, I, pp. 135–6.

nowhere more strikingly exemplified than in Don Quixote's rhetorical description of Dulcinea:

in her all the impossible and chimerical attributes of beauty conferred by poets on their ladies come true: such as that her hair is gold, her brow the Elysian fields, her eyebrows rainbows, her cheeks roses, her lips corals, pearls her teeth, alabaster her neck, marble her breast, ivory her hands, her whiteness snow. As for those parts which modesty keeps covered from human sight, they are such, I apprehend and believe, that discreet consideration can only extol them; it cannot compare them. (I. 13)

This is logically an absurdity. How can the 'impossible' and 'chimerical' be 'true'? The answer is, of course: they can only in the mind of a madman. Essentially, though, this is the same contradiction as we found in Periandro's remarks to Auristela.

The fact that Don Quixote's mind is the crucible in which Dulcinea is transformed points to a solution of the problem, towards which Cervantes hesitantly advances. Don Quixote, like Periandro and others, is a lover; and lovers (including poets who pretend to be lovers, and who like them were held to be touched with madness) do not see their ladies with the eyes of the rest of the world. The illustrious kitchen-maid is beautiful, but Avendaño and Carriazo do not react to her in the same way. It is only her lover Avendaño who speaks of her with 'extraordinary eulogies and great hyperboles'. In another place Cervantes demonstrates the uniqueness of the lover's point of view:

The maiden's beauty had deeply impressed itself on the Butler's heart . . . and it seemed to him that it was not tears she was shedding, but seed-pearls or meadow-dew; and he even raised them a point higher and likened them to pearls of the Orient. (DQ II. 49)

Cervantes may poke fun at the lover, but he does not say that what the lover sees is absolutely false. He takes the argument a stage farther than Vives, who said that where the beloved was concerned, the lover was an unreliable witness, all passion being inimical to truth.[1] The following passage in the Curioso impertinente, finally, brings us to something very like a relative view of the truth:

[1] Vives, De instr. prob., p. 615.

'Is all that which enamoured poets say true then?'
'In so far as they are poets, they are not speaking the truth,' replied
Lotario, 'but as lovers they speak it, and fall far short of it.[1]

Characteristically, however, Cervantes fails to draw conclusions.

The selection, arrangement, adaptation, and ornamentation of
the writer's material, which we have considered in this chapter,
were comprehended in the Spanish word *artificio*. This word stood
for the whole process whereby an artificer gave form to a work
of art. Its connexion with the act of 'imitating nature' can be seen
in the definition Covarrubias gives of the word in his dictionary—
'the composition or simulation of a thing'. But something made
to resemble 'the real thing' inevitably contains an element of fake,
and the suggestion of untruth was very much present in the idea
of *artificio*. 'Truth was ever the enemy of *artificio*', said Lope.[2]
Nevertheless, it was necessary, according to Rey de Artieda, for:
'As there is no pleasure in the plain truth, the wise poet is obliged
to contrive and arrange it with *artificio*.'[3]

The discrepancy between *artificio* and the literal truth is evident
in some of Cervantes's comments too. The Captive introduces
his highly (though not wholly) historical story as true, and as one
unmatched perhaps by any fiction composed with 'cunning and
calculated *artificio*' (*DQ* I. 38). At the end of the dogs' colloquy
the Licentiate, who refuses to believe in the truth of the tale,
praises its *artificio* and composition. Here then is yet another case
for reconciliation. It is no doubt the desire to effect just such
a reconciliation which prompts the claim that the stories and
episodes in *Don Quixote* I are both '*artificiosos* and true' (I. 28).
Their poetic truth is not—or should not be—jeopardized by their
artificio.

Rightness of purpose and competence of execution were all the
more important to those who, like Cervantes, were acutely aware
of the element of falsity in art. He knew as well as Tasso did that
'every fiction is a deception';[4] but he took great pains to ensure

---

[1] '— Luego ¿ todo aquello que los poetas enamorados dicen es verdad? — En
cuanto poetas, no la dicen — respondió Lotario —; mas en cuanto enamorados,
siempre quedan tan cortos como verdaderos' (*DQ* I. 34; iii. 71).

[2] Lope de Vega, *Triunfo de la fe*, BAE xxxviii, prol., 160.

[3] A. Rey de Artieda, 'Carta al ilustrísimo marqués de Cuellar sobre la comedia',
Discursos, epístolas y epigramas de Artemidoro (Saragossa, 1605), fol. 90[r].

[4] T. Tasso, *La Cavelletta, ovvero della poesia toscana: Dialogo*. In *Opere* iv. 229.

that his vivid simulacra of reality should be contrived in such a fashion that the reader would knowingly accept them as artistic illusions. This required the reader's willing participation, which was endangered when too great a strain was placed upon his credulity. Cervantes betrayed uneasiness, therefore, when the matter was puffed up and highly coloured, even though the ornamental beauties of prose and the idealization of character were as necessary to him as chivalrous ideals were to Don Quixote. Unlike Don Quixote, however, he felt the need to root them in the imperfect material of human existence. In his great novel he achieved this; in his last novel he tried another approach, unsuccessfully. His doubts and difficulties were expressed in indirect asides, in contradictions, ambiguities, and irony; they were not clearly stated as a literary problem.

These scruples were not usual among contemporary critics or poets. They also distinguish Cervantes from earlier novelists. They recall rather the uncertain, half-humorous attempt of Vives to legislate in his short allegorical dialogue called *Veritas fucata*, where he set out the ten conditions under which Truth might titivate herself for Poetry's sake.[1] But essentially Cervantes's scruples were those of the Baconian and Cartesian thinkers of the seventeenth century, the true heirs of Vives. His novelistic dilemma was an integral part of the ideological crisis of the age in Europe—the crisis which caused poetry and natural philosophy to part company. Which way was the novel to go? Imaginative literature in the Golden Age was in general moving along a road that Cervantes could not travel without hesitations and looking over his shoulder. The crux of the matter was the problem of history and poetry.

[1] *Veritas fucata, sive de Licentia poetica, quantum Poetis liceat a Veritate abscedere.* Published at Louvain in 1522, it is not included in the Basle edition of 1555, but figures in that of Mayans: J. L. Vives, *Opera omnia* (Valencia, 1782–90), vol. ii; also in the admirable Spanish translation of Vives, *Obras completas* (Madrid, 1947–8), vol. i, by L. Riber.

V

THE TRUTH OF THE MATTER

1. *History and Fiction*

. . . please God he's not a little fibber, that would be worst
of all.   CERVANTES, *La gitanilla*

ALTHOUGH in the early sixteenth century the Spaniards and Portuguese were busy charting vast reaches of the globe, the fabulous world of the medieval European's imagination was slow to fade away. It merged in weird confusion with the one that was being discovered. The mass of the people, like their grandfathers, still did not bother to make much distinction between truth and fiction so long as a story could be marvelled at as strange. They were ready to accept anything, and the tales of travellers did nothing at first to dispel credulity. Tough explorers themselves were no less disposed to believe in centaurs, mermaids, headless men, or men with tails than those who stayed at home. As late as the second half of the sixteenth century it was reported that a unicorn had been sighted in Florida.[1] And just at the time when the Portuguese and Spanish explorers were tracing out continents, the vogue for chivalresque fantasy in their two countries was at its height.

Strange new things were indeed discovered in distant parts, and for this among other reasons monsters and prodigies were felt to be not so much 'supernatural' as 'natural', the possible caprices or aberrations of an all-powerful Nature. Even Vives solemnly accepted the story that in places no more exotic than Naples and Flanders women commonly gave birth to animals. But instead of attributing this remarkable fact to magic or any other supernatural agency, he advanced the more humdrum 'natural' explanation that it was due to contracting a concentrated and putrid humour through a diet of cabbage and beer.[2]

[1] Lewis Hanke, *Aristotle and the American Indians* (London, 1959), p. 6.
[2] J. L. Vives, *De anima et vita* 1, *Opera* ii. 501.

The notion that it might be important to seek a distinction between what was and what was not verifiable fact gained ground slowly in the sixteenth century. History still dressed up as fiction and fiction masqueraded as history. Historians insouciantly spiced their histories with legend and fable or even deliberately fictionalized them. Writers of fiction continued the old tradition of asserting that the story they told was true (*adtestatio rei visae*) to impress and move their readers—a device evidently springing from the ancient idea of epic as designed to commemorate the deeds of famous men: the singer claimed that the deeds were true and revealed to him by the Muses.[1] To add to the confusion, there was no Spanish word to distinguish a full-length novel from a history: each was an *historia*.

But a relentless spirit of inquiry was also at work. New worlds of learning were explored and old ones rediscovered by humanist scholars. The necessity of sorting out fact and fiction was imposing itself in one sphere after another, and affected imaginative literature itself. Considerable nervousness about the subject becomes apparent, for a religious crisis had meanwhile split Christendom, and false—or 'wrong'—ideas had bloodily proved themselves dangerous. Printed books speeded up the circulation of ideas and literature moved into closer contact with the lives of the common people. This was not felt to be an unalloyed blessing. 'Since [the vulgar] cannot distinguish the apparent from the true, it thinks that what is said in any printed book has authority for being believed', said Alexio Venegas.[2] There was certainly living precedent for the opinion of the Innkeeper and Don Quixote (I. 32, 50) that a book published by royal licence would not relate untruths. Was it right that such people should be exposed to the alluring lies of literary fiction, even in uncontroversial matters? Was, in fact, the literature of entertainment justified? Few questions have done as much to stimulate the growth of modern criticism as this one.

With the diffusion of Aristotle's *Poetics*, from the mid-sixteenth century in Italy, came the most authoritative of voices to justify poetic fiction and tell people what the difference between it and

---

[1] On the regularity with which the authors of medieval prose romances claimed that their works were true, taking care to call the authors of metrical romances liars, see J. C. Dunlop, *History of Prose Fiction*, revised Wilson (London, 1888), i. 146.

[2] A. Venegas, *Primera parte de las diferencias de libros* (ed. Valladolid, 1583), prol.

history was—although the explanation was by no means so clear that it did not lead to endless debate. In the words of Cervantes's Sansón Carrasco,

the poet can relate or sing of things not as they were, but as they ought to have been; and the historian must write of them not as they ought to have been, but as they were, without adding to the truth or taking away from it anything whatever.[1]

This particular definition omits 'what could be', the alternative to 'what ought to be', in poetry. As Herrera, for example, puts it: poetry represents things 'as they can be, or should be'.[2] The dual interpretation is most important to Cervantes's theory, as we shall see later on. The brief Cervantine elaboration on the business of the historian may also be noted: it is a peculiar preoccupation of his.

The intellectual climate of the age in which *Don Quixote* was created was one where the old credulity and capacity for wonder coexisted with a nascent empiricism. The impulse behind the strenuous efforts of Vives to establish the truth (or at least come closer to it) in history and philosophy, behind his censure of the muddling of fact and fable in early Greek history and his condemnation of the falsehoods in the *Legenda aurea*, was essentially the same as the impulse behind Cervantes's criticism of the novels of chivalry. Don Quixote typifies an attitude of mind moribund enough to be comic, about the year 1600, and alive enough for criticism of it to have point. It is epitomized in his superbly inconsequential rejoinder to the Canon's objection that the chivalresque novels are untrue—'Read them, and see what pleasure you will derive from this reading' (I. 50).

Cervantes criticizes the novels of chivalry from an Aristotelian point of view. Their lack of poetic truth is his biggest objection to them. But this is accompanied by a deep humanistic distrust of their witlessly prejudicial effect on historical truth. Don Quixote's indiscriminate credulity is an extreme case, but there had been real precedent for it. His gradual progress towards sanity might even be described as a slow self-education in the development of ideas in the sixteenth century, complete with the austere lesson of

[1] '... el poeta puede contar o cantar las cosas, no como fueron, sino como debían ser; y el historiador las ha de escribir, no como debían ser, sino como fueron, sin añadir ni quitar a la verdad cosa alguna' (*DQ* II. 3; iv. 86).

[2] Herrera, *Anotaciones*, p. 329.

disillusionment. It is symptomatic of his improving condition that when he gives Sancho examples of famous exploits in II. 8, he takes them entirely from ancient and modern history and no longer from fabulous romances.

Cervantes could not fail to have been struck by the hopelessly ambiguous attitude displayed by many of the chivalresque authors to their own novels and poems. Writing what were strictly works of entertainment in public demand, they felt the need of some weightier justification than this for their products. Naturally, they claimed exemplariness or allegorical meaning; but not only were such claims dubious in their case, they had lost some of their power over an age that was beginning to care whether a thing had actually happened, whether or not it was in reality so. When Sir Philip Sidney said that 'a feigned example hath as much force to teach as a true example',[1] he was saying something that had been taken for granted in the Middle Ages and of which the operative word is 'example'. The notion had not ceased to be held valid, but the very distinction he makes bespeaks a new and more critical era. Unlike him, the romancers of the late fifteenth and early sixteenth centuries did not know the Aristotelian justification of poetic fiction; they had only the unhappy awareness that they could put up no good defence to the charge— contemptuously hurled at them by learned men of their day— that they wrote a lot of foolish lies. They relapsed at best into awkward comic irony, at worst into confusion. Here are just a few examples.

Montalvo writes with equivocal humour of the reliability of the supposed author of *Esplandián*:

> Although there might be some justifiable doubt about the affairs of Amadis, more credence should be placed in those of this knight [Esplandián], because [Master Elisabat] would only write down what he himself saw or had from trustworthy persons.[2]

The author of the *Caballero Platir* (Valladolid, 1533), anticipating reproach for indulging in 'vain tales and fables' and unable to distinguish literarily between remarkable fact and incredible fiction, defends himself in his prologue by saying that just because stories are so unusual as to arouse wonder, there is no reason to take them as lies. We can believe in the great feats of the Spaniards,

[1] Sidney, op. cit., p. 169.   [2] Montalvo, *Esplandián*, p. 427.

past and present, in Italy and the Indies, on land and sea, he goes on, so why should those in his book be hard to believe? *Oliveros de Castilla* concludes with no less confusion than piety:

And seeing that nothing is impossible for God, no one need be surprised at what is contained in the present book, for God permits many marvellous things, and for our instruction performs many miracles to confirm us in our faith and set us on the true road of salvation . . . Amen.[1]

The miserable poet Jerónimo de Arbolanche, who seems understandably to have suffered from a chronic sense of inferiority, and whom Cervantes puts at the head of the poetaster hordes in the *Parnaso* VII, ludicrously reiterates that he does not know how to compose doubtful tales or poems, that he is no lying Menander, that he does not relate as true a thousand idiotic dreams, that he is disinclined to *disparates* like those of Juan del Encina—not one of which statements is true.[2] Did these chivalresque authors actually deceive themselves? One sometimes wonders.

The irony in Antonio de Torquemada's presentation of his *Don Olivante de Laura* (Barcelona, 1564) is more patent but little less disconcerting. He retails a fantasy by way of prologue, where he describes meeting a medley of ancient Greek, Roman, and chivalresque heroes. He 'wakes' from the experience as from a dream (the episode has a slight resemblance to that of Montesinos Cave), holding the book of *Don Olivante* which the Lady Hipermea had given to him, and so concludes: 'I saw that it was all true and something deserving of complete belief and credit.' We are a long way here from the irony of the mature Cervantes, which may mystify but does not mislead. The deliberate absurdity with which he invests, for instance, Sancho's comment on the story of La Torralba is a measure of how far he has advanced from the naïve ambiguities of the chivalresque authors: 'The person who told me this story assured me it was so true and certain that when I told it to someone else I could affirm and swear that I had seen the whole thing' (I. 20). At its best, Cervantes's irony (though less

---

[1] *Oliveros de Castilla*, NBAE xi. 522.

[2] J. de Arbolanche, *Los nueve libros de las Habidas* (Saragossa, 1566), 'Respuesta del autor'. Cervantes says:

'De verso y prosa el puro desatino
nos dio a entender que de Arbolanches eran
las *Habidas* pesadas de contino.' (*Parnaso* VII, p. 98)

caustic) is as unerring as Lucian's in the *True History*, that parody of extravagant romance which the Renaissance found so hugely congenial.

Though few other writers reacted as absurdly and bewilderingly as the chivalresque romancers, many sixteenth-century authors writing before the divulgation of Aristotle's *Poetics* betray an uneasy feeling that poetic fiction was at a disadvantage compared with historical fact. A growing sense of responsibility among epic poets is apparent, but the thinking of many writers remained distinctly ingenuous. Characteristic were the painful efforts of Luis Zapata to sort out history from fiction in the dedication of his *Carlo famoso* (Valencia, 1566), and, lest the reader be misled, asterisks were employed to mark the fictions in the text.[1]

After the divulgation of the *Poetics* the novels of chivalry were held to be doubly false : historically, because they never happened; poetically, because they never could or ought to have happened. The desirable alternative put forward was either good prose epic, like the *Ethiopic History*, or true history—profane and, better still, sacred history—such as the Priest and the Canon recommend in *Don Quixote* I. 32 and 49. For all Cervantes's love of epic and his appreciation of the universal truth contained in good fiction, history retained for him one powerful advantage over poetry : it was, if not beyond dispute, by comparison certain.

The muddling together of what could not possibly be true with what might be and what was true in the poor deluded brain of Don Quixote thus reflects the muddled thinking of a passing era. When he defends his favourite reading to the Canon he plunges into a sea of legend where fact and fable are confounded. The Lady Floripes, Fierabras, Hector, Achilles, the Twelve Peers, King Arthur, Tristan and Isolde, and others are all as true to him as the Cid, Fernando de Guevara, Pedro Barba, or Suero de Quiñones. Do not tangible proofs of Pierre and Maguelonne, the Cid and Roland, survive? he asks. The Canon is left 'amazed . . . to hear the muddle made of truth and lies by Don Quixote' (I. 49). But although he is right and Quixote wrong, he does not come too well out of this argument. He tries to sort things out, accepting this, rejecting that, and casting doubt on the other; but his doubts

---

[1] On the interesting case of Bandello in Italy, see T. G. Griffith, *Bandello's Fiction* (Oxford, 1955).

and denials, objections and concessions, make a poor showing in the face of Don Quixote's splendid certainty. One sees the force of Unamuno's romanticization of the Knight. In his confused, impassioned defence there is a tough grain of sense. His defence manages to suggest that the Canon's principles are not altogether infallible. So his heroes are unhistorical, are they? Well, what does it matter to later generations whether a celebrated figure actually existed or not? As Unamuno asked, how, when a man dies, is his memory any different eventually from a poetic fiction?[1] Furthermore, as Eugenio d'Ors observed, if you condemn fairy-tale heroes, why should you stop there? What is to save Ulysses?[2] Is pure fantasy—the sort written for its own sake, and not as apologue or to symbolize something—to be expelled from the ranks of good literature just because it represents what could never have occurred? The implications of Quixote's defence (as so often, they are only implications) are that in this respect the current conception of verisimilitude was too narrow. So indeed it was, and the fact gave Cervantes not a little trouble.

Cervantine criticism of the pastoral novels is different. Although the Priest condemns four out of the nine identified in the Knight's library and disapproves of the magic in the *Diana*, and although Mercury accuses Lofrasso of lying and Berganza himself says he had formerly been deceived by these books, their offence is much less serious than that of the novels of chivalry. The Priest, whose judgements are progressively less severe as he moves from chivalresque to pastoral to epic and lyric poetry proper, pronounces them less harmful (*DQ* I. 6). This is because they are patently poetic fictions and do not try to disguise themselves as anything else. No one is really likely to be deceived by them for long, as Berganza's definition makes quite clear:

I came to realize what I think everyone else must believe: that all those books are things that have been dreamed up and well written, for the entertainment of the idle, and without any truth at all.[3]

---

[1] Unamuno, op. cit., p. 113.

[2] E. d'Ors, 'Fenomenología de los libros de caballerías', *BRAE* xxvii (1947–8), 92–93.

[3] '... vine a entender lo que pienso que deben de creer todos, que todos aquellos libros son cosas soñadas y bien escritas, para entretenimiento de los ociosos, y no verdad alguna' (*Coloquio*, p. 166).

Pastoral has nothing to do with history, and 'historical truth' is what Berganza means by 'truth' here. The distance of pastoral from real life, though variable, is more clearly defined than is that of the chivalresque, for its fantasy is less outlandish and it does not seek at the same time to temporize confusedly with historical reality. Pastoral and the chivalresque have an affinity, of course, as Don Quixote is quick to note. He comments on the goatherd's preamble to the story of Leandra, 'This affair has something of a suspicion of an adventure of chivalry about it' (I. 50). But pastoral is the closest thing in contemporary fiction to the ideal world of poetic universals, a quintessence of, in the main, amorous experience. It is a poeticization that lifts love and its attendant emotions out of contingent historical circumstances and resituates them (since some sort of *cadre* is necessary) in idyllic surroundings. As such, and because, after all, its cult of simplicity is the ultimate affectation, the pastoral novel asks to be parodied and laughed at. Cervantes's criticism, which is humorous and indulgent, may be described as essentially the intrusion of a sense of historical reality into this world of pure poetry. The best-known example is in the contrast Berganza draws in the *Coloquio* between the typical employment of literary Amarilises, Lisardos, and the like and that of real shepherds, who spend 'most of the day picking fleas out of themselves or mending their sandals'.

The repeated allusions to the truth of the *Quixote* humorously recall the traditional protestations of chivalresque and other authors, but they are something more than parody. Although the context may be comic, statements like 'no [history] is bad as long as it is true' (I. 9) are not in themselves meant to be funny. There are two sorts of truth in literature and so 'truth' can have a double meaning. Pretending to claim a literal truth for his book, Cervantes makes the claim in such a way that no one can possibly believe it, but at the same time he is often asserting the truth of his work in the only sense in which it could possibly mean any-thing—its poetic sense. The two truths are not confused: they are conjunct. If anyone should be so simple as to be taken in despite Cervantes's precautions, the pretence of historicity is demolished in the first prologue with the words 'nor have its fabulous absurdities anything to do with the fine points [*puntuali-dades*] of truth'. He means, of course, historical truth—or rather, as he makes clear immediately after in the warning not to expect scientific and mathematical precision or logical rigour—the truth of science.[1]

When Cervantes contrasts the truth of the *Quixote* with the pseudo-historicity and the nonsensical lies of the novels of chivalry, he is also in his way behaving like the epic poets of the sixteenth century, who took pains to point out the difference between their poems and chivalresque or other fabulous inventions. But there is an additional subtlety. Within Cervantes's fiction Don Quixote's exploits really—'historically'—occurred, while those of the chivalresque heroes did not. The historical certitude of the former within the fiction is equivalent to their poetic truth, when viewed as part of that fiction, from outside it. The chivalresque romances, on the other hand, lack poetic truth from any point of view. So when Don Diego in II. 16, and the author in the closing words of the novel, contrast the 'true' Don Quixote and his deeds with the 'false' heroes of the romances and theirs, the artistic superiority of Cervantes's creation is being asserted, because poetic truth is not achieved except by good art. His hero's fame will thus eclipse that of the chivalresque heroes. The historical reality of Don Quixote and Sancho within the novel is identified with their artistic superiority to the rival protagonists of Avellaneda's work in just the same way. We shall examine this in Chapter VI.

Cervantes knew that the highest obligations of the novelist were not to the truth of history, or science. Indeed, no one knew better that 'to bring a truth to light much proof and counter-proof are needed'.[2] Thus the importance of the particular detail for him was its artistic relevance rather than its factual accuracy. He lavishes a good deal of ironical humour on accuracy of detail. Behind the joke, however, lies the well-known Aristotelian contention that an error of fact in poetry is of less consequence

[1] '. . . ni caen debajo de la cuenta de sus fabulosos disparates las puntualidades de la verdad, ni las observaciones de la astrología; ni le son de importancia las medidas geométricas, ni la confutación de los argumentos de quien se sirve la retórica' (*DQ* I, prol.; i. 39).

[2] '. . . para sacar una verdad en limpio menester son muchas pruebas y repruebas' (*DQ* II. 26; v. 244). This recalls Cabrera de Córdoba: 'Antes porque es ordinario y cierto el variar, habrá de argumentar sobre probables en la diversidad de los hechos que le refieren, para sacar en limpio la fineza de la verdad, y establecer lo que más verdadero o verisímil le pareciere' (*De historia*, fol. 10ᵛ).

than an error of art.[1] Errors of fact turn out to be of two sorts. There is the error of common or historical fact which exists outside the fiction (the sort Aristotle meant) and the error within the fiction. The first arises mainly in other connexions than with the novel in Cervantes's theory. The second, which crops up quite frequently in *Don Quixote*, may be either a simple matter of inconsistency or a failure, noted with mock-gravity in passing, to elucidate some essentially unimportant detail—such as whether the three country girls came riding on he-asses or she-asses (II. 10).[2] His whimsy reminds one of a peculiarly pedantic and futile form of literary criticism that flourished in his day, and some oblique parody of this may well be intended. Common sense would have told Cervantes that in respect of both sorts of error or omission poetic licence must not be abused, and that internal accuracy and consistency were part of verisimilitude (a part that came to weigh heavily with seventeenth-century novelists, incidentally). But he also knew that verisimilitude was not destroyed by the trivial inaccuracy any more than it was created by the multiplication of minutiae.

Another way in which he showed his sense of obligation to the higher truth of poetry was in his frequent vagueness about exact particulars such as names ('a village in La Mancha'), dates, ages, and numbers. Evidently, up to a point at least, a calculated technique, it was probably by reaction too against the ineffectively documentary manner of the chivalresque novelists, whose profusion of particulars did not constitute verisimilitude. Sancho's ridiculous story in I. 20 is among other things a *reductio ad absurdum* of the misuse of detail. In a maze of unnecessary particulars he loses not only whatever poetic truth there might conceivably have been in the story, but the story itself.

Nevertheless, despite Cervantes's awareness of which truth had novelistic priority, his literary theory is distinguished by his inclination to treat the pole of historical truth as more fixed than that of poetry. In practice he always measures his distance from the former, as it were, while he directs his course towards the latter. His respect for the ascertainable truth of history is quite

---

[1] Thus Herrera, *Anotaciones*, pp. 682–3; El Pinciano, who makes some qualifications, op. cit. ii. 78–81.

[2] And e.g. *DQ* II. 3; iv. 84–85. II. 27; v. 267. II. 60; viii. 32.

evident, and a number of his observations come straight from the theory of history:

it being the duty and obligation of historians to be exact, truthful, and dispassionate; . . . neither interest nor fear nor rancour nor bias should ? lect them from the path of truth, whose mother is history— that rival of time, repository of deeds, witness of the past, exemplar and counsellor to the present, admonisher to the future.[1]

The Ciceronian formula (*testis temporum*, &c.) is commonly found in the writing of the time, as are references to the importance of truthfulness and impartiality.[2] When Cervantes invokes the Muse at the opening of the *Parnaso* VII, the words are ironical and the occasion supremely fictitious, but the sentiment is that of the historian. He asks for 'a fine and well-cut quill, free of bias and passion', with which to write clearly and honestly.[3] Again ironically enough, it is Don Quixote who, now knowing that a book has been written about him, utters the most impassioned words of all on the subject of historians who lie:

historians who make use of falsehoods should be burned at the stake like those who make counterfeit money. . . . History is like something sacred; for it must be true, and where truth is, inasmuch as it is the truth, there God is. Yet despite this, there are some who compose and toss off books like fritters.[4]

The Canon attributes to history all the functions of good literature: instruction, delight, and the arousing of *admiratio*. He commends the uses of history, in the manner of Vives,[5] assuring

[1] '. . . habiendo y debiendo ser los historiadores puntuales, verdaderos y no nada apasionados, . . . ni el interés ni el miedo, el rancor ni la afición, no les hagan torcer del camino de la verdad, cuya madre es la historia, émula del tiempo, depósito de las acciones, testigo de lo pasado, ejemplo y aviso de lo presente, advertencia de lo por venir' (*DQ* I. 9; i. 286).

[2] Thus Vives, *De rat. dic.* III. 139; F. Patrizi, *Della historia* (Venice, 1560), fol. 26ʳ; Carvallo, op. cit., fol. 135ʳ.

[3] He sets out the literary virtues of the perfect historian in one of the sonnets to B. Ruffino de Chiambery as 'verdad, orden, estilo claro y llano' (p. 19). Cf. Juan Costa: 'Es narración verdadera, clara y con orden distinta de algunas cosas pasadas o presentes' (cited by Cabrera de Córdoba, op. cit., fol. 11ʳ).

[4] '. . . los historiadores que de mentiras se valen habían de ser quemados, como los que hacen moneda falsa . . . La historia es como cosa sagrada; porque ha de ser verdadera, y donde está la verdad, está Dios, en cuanto a verdad; pero, no obstante esto, hay algunos que así componen y arrojan libros de sí como si fuesen buñuelos' (*DQ* II. 3; iv. 97–98). Cf. Lucian, *The Way to Write History*, § 39.

[5] '. . . ex qua tantum utilitatis potest colligi, nempe usus rerum, et prudentiae, tum formationis morum ex alienis exemplis ut optima factu sequamur, sicuti Livius inquit, prava devitemus' (*De rat. dic.* III. 139).

the Knight that it will afford him reading worthy of his intelligence and render him learned in the subject, enamoured of virtue, instructed in goodness, improved in manners, and valiant and brave in just measure (I. 49). And in the *Parnaso* VII it is to a scrupulous historian that Cervantes gives the task of sorting out the sheep from the goats in the confusion of the battle of the books. He gives it to Pedro Mantuano, that 'great scrutinizer of all histories', who criticized Fr. Mariana for introducing fable into his history of Spain. (Mariana, incidentally, is not honoured in the poem.)

The whole excellence of history consists in the fact that it carries the stamp of truth (*Persiles* III. 10), and the historian's task is easier than the novelist's because he has only to tell the truth 'whether it looks like it or not' (*Persiles* III. 18). In his own two major works, the *Quixote* and the *Persiles*, Cervantes simply *pretends* that his fiction *is* history. What distinguishes this pretence from the clumsy efforts of earlier romancers to do the same thing is his awareness that the novelist's task is distinct from the historian's. But the mere pretence that his novels are historical fact is a major constituent of his practical interpretation of verisimilitude. The counterfeiting of history raised two great problems, however. One (which we shall consider in the second section of this chapter) is that which so perplexes him in his last novel: may not the novelist take advantage of the fact that truth is sometimes stranger than fiction? The other is: will not the novelist run the risk of deceiving the reader, or at least of prejudicing his apprehension of the truth with lies? Cervantes was writing for the simple as well as the enlightened reader, it will be remembered.

The inventor of the world's most gullible reader of novels was not likely to risk misleading other readers with his own. Notably by means of his handling of Cide Hamete (which we shall examine in Chapter VI), the *Quixote* as history is contained in an envelope of unmistakable fiction. Cervantes did not mix truth and falsehood indiscriminately. (It is the devil himself, says the witch in the *Coloquio*, who 'with one truth mixes a thousand lies'.) Invention and fact had to be mingled in an imaginative work, of course, but theorists of the period were alive to the dangers. Robortelli allowed true things to be mixed with false so long as they led to true conclusions.[1] Carvallo said that poetic fiction must not be

[1] Robortelli, op. cit., p. 2.

written 'with intent to deceive'.[1] Cervantes was less explicit, but knowing as he did that a deception was all the more effective when it made use of the known truth, his views cannot have differed from theirs.

There is an allegory in Gracián's *Agudeza y arte de ingenio*, in which

> When Truth saw that she was being scorned and even persecuted, she turned to Subtlety. . . . Truth opened her eyes and from that moment began to proceed with artifice. She used inventions, she insinuated herself by circuitous ways, conquered with stratagems, depicted as distant that which was close . . . and, by ingenious circumlocution, contrived ever to arrive at the point she had intended.[2]

Spanish literature in Cervantes's last years was entering the Age of Subtlety. The way he deals with the theme of truth and appearances in *Don Quixote* II and the *Persiles* shows no lack of subtlety on his own part, and no doubt Quixote's observation that 'what has a virtuous object cannot and should not be called a deception' (II. 22) has a literary application in his theory; but, though he belonged to it in many ways, he was not a part of that age in several major respects. Above all, where truth and fiction were concerned, he took pains to leave his reader with no risk of misapprehension. His very mystifications are indulgent, not oracular. Cervantes did not leave the reader to sink or swim, and indeed maintained towards him a sense of responsibility that by most later seventeenth-century standards would have seemed ingenuous. Moreover, there is good evidence that he became more, not less, scrupulous in the course of his career. The Porras manuscript of the *Celoso extremeño* ends with the words, 'Though it appears to be a fabulous fiction, this affair was true.' They are removed from the published edition of 1613. It was one thing for invented characters to make such assertions, but quite another for the author to do so.[3]

---

[1] Carvallo, op. cit., fol. 22ʳ.

[2] B. Gracián, *Agudeza y arte de ingenio* (ed. Madrid, 1944), pp. 578–9.

[3] Amezúa, op. cit. ii. 243–4, believes the remark to be literally true (though possibly an interpolation of Porras de la Cámara) and to have been removed by Cervantes lest it give offence, perhaps, to living persons. Given that such claims were the stock-in-trade of sixteenth-century writers of fiction, the clear literary antecedents of the *Celoso extremeño*, and the lack of any evidence for a historical basis to the story, this explanation seems to have less to recommend it than the one I have offered.

The modern reader may feel at times that the continual harping of Cervantes on truth and fiction borders on the eccentric. One remembers poor Tasso, his brain going. But even allowing for what in Cervantes's preoccupation was peculiar to himself, the problem needs to be seen against the background of ideas in the sixteenth century and in relation to those of the seventeenth. Complete indifference to whether one was dealing with fact or fable was a survival of an old habit of mind coming to be regarded as intolerable by the time that he was writing; and he was not prepared, as later writers were, to make it wholly the reader's responsibility to use his wit to discriminate. He parodied in the *Quixote* the confusion of the chivalresque authors, not reproducing that confusion but illustrating by it the complexity of the relationship between the poetic-universal and the historical-particular.

It remains to try to reach some conclusions about the place of the novel with regard to history and poetry. Certain conclusions follow from Cervantes's treatment of these two in *Don Quixote*. Unfortunately he did not put them into words, so we can only guess how far he arrived at them consciously. He gives history a much fairer share of attention than did the theorists of the time for the most part. Concentrating on the ideal truth of poetry, they were inclined to neglect history. But history could not be kept out of poetry, and even in theory it refused to be ignored and was always making itself felt. Thus Castelvetro, while carefully distinguishing between them, especially as regards their ends, makes the art of poetry heavily dependent on the art of history. He holds that one cannot expect to be able to use 'the art of poetry for the perfect and proper understanding of poetry . . . if one does not first have a clear and complete knowledge of the art of history'.[1] Tasso reminds us that universal truths are derived from the experience of many particulars.[2] El Pinciano points out the curious fact that theoretically a single work could be poetry and history at the same time:

[1] '. . . non si dee potere avere perfetta e convenevole notizia della poesia per arte poetica . . . se prima non s'ha notizia compiuta e distinta dell'arte storica' (*Poetica*, p. 5).
[2] T. Tasso, *Lezione . . . sopra il sonetto, 'Questa vita mortal', ec. di Monsignor della Casa*. In *Opere* iv. 243.

Imagine that an author in Spain composed a book on an action which, at the time when he was composing his fiction, was really taking place in Persia or India . . . the man who was writing in Spain would be a poet, and someone writing of it in India, or wherever it occurred, would be a historian.[1]

Cascales contradicts El Pinciano, arguing that the author in India would still be a poet if his account corresponded in every respect with what the poet in Spain, following the principle of verisimilitude, had written.[2] Whoever was right, one thing is clear: the relationship of history and poetry was certainly more complex than a simple statement of the dichotomy would lead one to suppose.

Cervantes's repeated allusions to the necessity of being historically exact, however playful, buttress the fact that history is an integral part of *Don Quixote*. The two heroes cannot be detached from particular history, which belongs to them as much as they belong to it. The time and place have to be Spain, 16—. Their imaginary adventures have to be such as might have occurred without doing violence to these. Yet Quixote and Sancho are not complete as human beings until universals can be predicated as part of their experience. *Don Quixote*, the first great 'novel of character', centres in these two human beings and embraces both historical and ideal poetic truth. Cervantes's achievement corresponds to what El Pinciano, in a passage whose importance modern scholars have underlined, describes as the object of poetry:

> The object is not falsehood, which would be to fall into sophistry; nor is it history, which would be treating the matter historically. So as it is not history because it deals with fables, or falsehood because it touches history, its object is what has verisimilitude, which embraces everything.[3]

There is in the *Quixote* a practical solution to the problem which taxed the wits of Italian theorists of the Counter-Reformation: how to bring the universal and the particular into harmony.

---

[1] El Pinciano, op. cit. ii. 10–11.

[2] Cascales, *Tablas*, p. 27. Cf. Aristotle, *Poetics*, 1451B.

[3] '. . . el objeto no es la mentira, que sería coincidir con la sofística, ni la historia, que sería tomar la materia al histórico; y, no siendo historia, porque toca fábulas, ni mentira, porque toca historia, tiene por objeto el verisímil que todo lo abraza' (op. cit. i. 220). El Pinciano owes a debt to Piccolomini here: see F. V. Cerreta, 'Alessandro Piccolomini's Commentary on the *Poetics* of Aristotle', *SRen* iv (1957), 148.

Here, for the first time, the novel triumphantly shows its range. It is not history and not poetry : its centre is somewhere in between and it includes both of them.

During the first half of the seventeenth century it came about that 'the true, in the meaning of the word in which history attempts to treat the true, was no longer an important element in poetry'.[1] It was at this point, with *Don Quixote*, that the novel diverged from poetry and became what was to be, in essentials and along the main stream of its course, the *modern* novel, in which the true, in the meaning of the word in which history attempts to treat it, has been persistently an important element. A whole complex of ideological and temperamental impulses prompted Cervantes's new departure in prose fiction, but it may be noted that even sixteenth-century poetic theory offered a cue. Poetry, and epic in particular, was held to be—in Bacon's words— 'feigned history'.[2] Cervantes honoured this dictum not only by scrupulously respecting the rights of historical truth but by putting the dictum into practice in the most literal but undeceptive way.

There remained a problem to which we have referred. Were not the exceptional, the marvellous, and the incredible part of history ? Such things furnished a large part of the pleasure and no inconsiderable part of the instruction to be had from poetry. How were they to be handled by the novelist, who had not the full licence of poetry, who must not make excessive demands upon the co-operation of the willing yet critical reader ? What did verisimilitude admit and what did it not ? We shall find the answer to this in *Persiles y Sigismunda*, the book which many of the best modern critics have dismissed for its incredibility.

[1] J. A. Mazzeo, 'A Seventeenth-century Theory of Metaphysical Poetry', *RR* xlii (1951), 255.
[2] Francis Bacon, extract from *The Advancement of Learning* II, in *English Critical Essays (Sixteenth, Seventeenth and Eighteenth Centuries)*, ed. E. D. Jones (London, 1947), p. 89. Cf. Castelvetro, op. cit., p. 28; El Pinciano, op. cit. iii. 216.

2. *Verisimilitude and the Marvellous*

> . . . an age half scientific and half magical, half sceptical
> and half credulous, looking back in one direction to
> Maundeville, and forward to Newton. BASIL WILLEY

> . . . either criticism can never be in agreement with Cervantes over
> what are absurdities and lies, or else we must accept as possible all the
> episodes in *Persiles y Sigismunda* and the *Novelas ejemplares*, which is too
> much to ask. Clearly, Cervantes did not in his heart worry at all about
> what was 'true', but preferred to pay attention to the pleasantness and
> charm of his narrative and its style.

Cervantes would have been pained by this judgement of Schevill
and Bonilla, which fairly expresses the most common modern
opinion.[1] The verisimilitude that he harps on is not indeed what
we understand by the word, but it is perfectly comprehensible.
Misunderstanding of it has been responsible for many unfortunate
judgements on his last work. The *Persiles* is not a good novel; but
it is not a symptom of senile decay either, nor (as has even been
seriously argued) is it really his immature first novel and not his
last, nor did he drop all his literary principles when he wrote it
and give himself up to romantic day-dreams. If he had dropped
some of them it might even have been a better book. To arrive
at a reasonably clear notion of what Cervantes meant by verisimilitude we shall have to examine his practice, since his
statements on the subject, though important, by no means make
everything clear.

The first reason for the modern misunderstanding of Cervantes's conception of verisimilitude has been the failure to recall
how insistent were the claims of the marvellous in poetic theory—
claims which ran directly counter to those of verisimilitude.
Against Scaliger's or El Pinciano's emphasis on the latter can be
set contemporary declarations of the importance of arousing
wonder. 'But who does not know that the object of poetry is the
marvellous?' asked Minturno.[2] 'Poetry . . . without marvels can
win no praise', said Muzio.[3] There was general agreement that

[1] Schevill and Bonilla, ed. *Novelas ejemplares*, introd., iii. 373. Cf. *Persiles*, introd.,
i, pp. xvi–xvii. Castro too calls the book 'conscientemente inverosímil de la cruz
a la fecha' and quotes Ortega: 'El *Persiles* nos garantiza que Cervantes quiso la
inverosimilitud como tal inverosimilitud' (*Pensamiento*, p. 95).
[2] *L'Arte poetica*, p. 120. [3] *Arte poetica*, fol. 80ᵛ.

both qualities were necessary in poetry, that they must be recon-
ciled, and that this was very difficult.

> The two natures of the marvellous and of verisimilitude . . . are
> very different, and different in such a way that they are almost contrary
> to each other; none the less each one of them is necessary in a poem,
> and the art of an excellent poet needs to be such as will bring them into
> harmony.[1]

Tasso got into deep water over this and changed his mind in
successive writings, but most Aristotelians agreed that one could
not marvel at what was not credible.

> To create wonder, then, good poets are in the habit of making
> their fictions out of probable and plausible [*verisimiles*] things; for if the
> matter is not probable, who will marvel at what he does not approve?[2]

When Cervantes tussles with the problem of credibility in prose
fiction it is with the more extravagant forms of the extraordinary
that he is dealing. There is one major exception to this: the
Priest's criticism of the *Curioso impertinente*.

> I think . . . this *novela* is good, but I cannot persuade myself that it
> is true. And if it is fictitious, then the author's fiction is at fault, because
> one cannot imagine a husband so foolish as to attempt such a costly
> experiment as Anselmo did. If the case were one of a gallant and his
> lady, one might accept it; but as between husband and wife, there is
> something impossible about it. (*DQ* I. 35)

This is a more rigorous criticism than most twentieth-century
readers would level at the story, I suspect. Who nowadays,
moderately acquainted with novels, films, and plays, would be
shocked by an urgent psychiatric case like Anselmo? The Priest's
criticism, however, is unusual because Cervantes almost never
worries about this kind of improbability.

If in *Don Quixote* I. 6 Cervantes had not spoken through the
Priest, and if his words had been a shade less equivocal, we might
have been able to draw some conclusions about the evolution of
his ideas on verisimilitude from his treatment of the *Jardín de flores
curiosas*, a miscellany of strange information by the author of

---

[1] 'Diversissime sono . . . queste due nature, il maraviglioso e 'l verisimile, e in
guisa diverse che sono quasi contrarie fra loro; nondimeno l'una e l'altra nel poema
è necessaria, ma fa mestieri che arte di eccellente poeta sia quella che insieme l'accordi'
(Tasso, *Del poema eroico* ii. 57).

[2] Cascales, *Tablas*, p. 147. Cf. El Pinciano, op. cit. ii. 62.

Don Olivante.[1] This work, apparently condemned by Cervantes in 1605, is extensively used in the *Persiles.* The fact that his patrols into the hazardous realms of fantasy in that novel and the *Coloquio* are without precedent in the earlier novels also suggests a broadening of his concept of verisimilitude. But again, the inclusion of a little astrology and necromancy in the ideal romance is envisaged at least as early as *Don Quixote* I. 47, so we cannot be sure. Nevertheless, it remains likely that a wider reading of epic theory and of books of travel and exotic information, increased confidence in his powers as a novelist, and a growing sophistication among the novel-reading public contributed to Cervantes's experiments in controlled fantasy toward the end of his career.

The difference between his use of the extraordinary and that in the romances he condemned is the difference between controlled and uncontrolled fantasy. Lack of control manifests itself in a disregard for the reactions of the reader's intelligence. No reader who stops to consider their extravagances judiciously can derive from the romances the pleasure that, like the ancient Milesian fables, it was their aim to impart. The comparison in *Don Quixote* I. 47 recalls El Pinciano:

fictions wanting in imitation and verisimilitude are not fables but absurdities, like some of those known in ancient times as Milesian and nowadays as books of chivalry, which contain happenings devoid of any good imitation and resemblance to truth.[2]

For how, asks that rational reader the Canon, can there be any pleasure in hearing of an adolescent slicing in two a giant as big as a tower, or of a single hero defeating an army of a million men, and so on? This passage resembles one in Vives:

Now when they tell a story, what pleasure can there be in things which are so openly and foolishly fabricated? Here one man kills twenty single-handed; another, thirty; another is riddled with six hundred wounds, and, having been abandoned as dead, straight away

---

[1] A. de Torquemada, *Jardín de flores curiosas* (ed. Madrid, 1943). It was published in English in 1600 under the title of *The Spanish Mandeville.*

[2] '. . . las ficciones que no tienen imitación y verisimilitud no son fábulas, sino disparates, como algunas de las que antiguamente llamaron milesias, agora libros de caballerías, los cuales tienen acaecimientos fuera de toda buena imitación y semejanza a verdad' (op. cit. ii. 8). Cf. also Venegas's foreword to *El Momo* and the prologue to his *Diferencias de libros.* The distinction of fables belongs to an old form of literary classification (recalled by El Pinciano, op. cit. ii. 12) which may be seen in St. Isidore, op. cit. i. xl.

gets up and on the next day, restored to health and strength, he lays low two giants in single combat; then he proceeds on his way loaded with more gold, silver, silk and gems than a bullion ship could bear. What madness is it to be gripped and carried away by these things?[1]

An intelligent pleasure in fiction is impossible without verisimilitude. And, though made by a man whose own greatest defect had been the lack of any sense of verisimilitude where chivalry was concerned, Don Quixote's observation that 'fictitious stories are good and delightful to the extent that they approach the truth or the semblance of it' (II. 62) remains the basic principle.

The remoteness of pastoral from everyday life is not so extreme as that of the novel of chivalry, and its idealistic improbability does not arouse Cervantes to nearly such serious criticism. But when Montemayor makes promiscuous use of magic as a *deus ex machina* in the *Diana*, the Priest exercises his censorial authority and recommends the removal of all the part dealing with the wise Felicia and the enchanted water (*DQ* I. 6).[2] Cervantes has critical doubts about literary idealism, but he reserves outright censure for the fantastic.

Verisimilitude does not simply exist in the material of the work. It depends upon the establishment of a special rapport with the reader, upon a delicate adjustment of the writer's persuasiveness to the reader's receptiveness. In no respect does Cervantes more clearly conceive of literature as a communication than in this—

the falsehood is better the truer it looks, and the more it contains of the doubtful and the possible the more pleasing it is. Fabulous plots must be wedded to the reader's intelligence, and written in such a way that the impossible is made easy, enormities are smoothed out, and the mind is held in suspense, amazed, gripped, exhilarated, and entertained.[3]

---

[1] 'Iam quum narrant, quae potest esse delectatio in rebus, quas tam aperte et stulte confingunt? Hic occidit solus viginti, ille triginta; aliu[s] sexcentis vulneribus confossus, ac pro mortuo iam derelictus, surgit protinus, et postridie sanitati viribusque redditus, singulari certamine duos gigantes prosternit; tum procedit onustus auro, argento, serico, gemmis, quantum nec oneraria navis posset portare. Quae insania est, iis duci aut teneri?' (*De institutione feminae christianae* i, *Opera* ii. 658).

[2] Cf. Berganza in the *Coloquio*, p. 165.

[3] '... tanto la mentira es mejor cuanto más parece verdadera, y tanto más agrada cuanto tiene más de lo dudoso y posible. Hanse de casar las fábulas mentirosas con el entendimiento de los que las leyeren, escribiéndose de suerte, que, facilitando los imposibles, allanando las grandezas, suspendiendo los ánimos, admiren, suspendan, alborocen y entretengan' (*DQ* I. 47; iii. 349).

The force of the contrast between the marvellous and the novelistically acceptable in this often-quoted passage has been weakened
by many editors and translators. Some editors, like Hartzenbusch
and Schevill and Bonilla, would replace the word *dudoso* ('doubtful') in the first sentence by the tautologous *gustoso* or *deleitoso*
('pleasing', 'delightful'); others, like Clemencín and Rodríguez
Marín, misinterpret its sense as *verosímil*. But 'doubtful' stands in
antithesis to 'possible'—the most pleasing fiction is that which
contains most of what is so strange as to inspire doubt and yet
is possible. The antithesis is sharpened to the point of paradox
a moment later when Cervantes speaks of making impossibilities
easy. The writer is not going to exclude extraordinary things from
his work: he is going to do all he can to make them acceptable
to the reader. With this object, a harmonious relationship must
be established between the mind of the reader and the events
related:

its actions should be devised with such niceness, taste, and verisimilitude
that, in spite of the falsehood, which makes a discord in the mind,
a true harmony is created.[1]

It is rare to find among contemporary theorists a penetration
into the actual working of verisimilitude comparable with that in
these Cervantine passages, brief as they are. Piccolomini's perci-
pient observations on the suspension of disbelief come first to
mind. The effect of being carried away by reading what one
nevertheless knows to be quite untrue, he attributes to the impact
of the images conjured up by the author's words on the mind of
the reader, before it stops to weigh the truth or falsity of the
matter. The effect endures no longer than the time spent in reading, and is dissipated as soon as the mind ponders the untruth.[2]
One recalls how the Canon of Toledo had said that he could enjoy
the novels of chivalry until he stopped to consider that they were
'all lies and frivolity'. Cervantes sees it as the novelist's business

---

[1] '. . . conviene guisar sus acciones con tanta puntualidad y gusto y con tanta
verisimilitud que, a despecho y pesar de la mentira, que hace disonancia en el entendimiento, forme una verdadera armonía' (*Persiles* III. 10; ii. 100).

[2] *Annotazioni*, pp. 150-1. I refer particularly to the passage: '. . . le quali im-
magini, offerendosi all'intelletto prima ch'ei si rifletta a considerare o a giudicare
se verità o se falsità n'apportano, fan quello effetto che detto abbiamo; il quale
pochissimo tempo dura, cioè tanto a punto quanto dura la lettura o la narrazione;
e come prima s'avvertisce e si considera e si pesa con l'intelletto la falsità del fatto,
subito il detto effetto si disperde e diventa vano' (p. 151).

to forestall such reactions on the part of the reader, and procure his willing suspension of disbelief by doing everything he can to accommodate the fiction to the reader's intelligence—by meeting him half-way, in fact.

We must now see what forms of the marvellous there were and in what ways the writer could make them amenable.

The most fertile source of *admiratio* in the *Persiles*, as in Cervantes's *novelas*, is not the prodigious and the supernatural but surprising events in the course of human affairs. They are not enough for him in the end, but they are the principal means whereby he seeks to give pleasurable surprise. Here the modern reader must put realistic criteria out of his mind and accept the fact that none of the accidents and coincidences that fill the stories of Cervantes is in itself impossible or outside the order of nature.

The *peripety*, or 'change from one state of things to its opposite', and the *anagnorisis*, or 'discovery', were recognized in Aristotelian theory as two of the best means of ensuring pleasurable surprise.[1] Lugo y Dávila, applying them to prose fiction, said the finest virtue of the action of a *novela* was to arouse *admiratio* by means of a happening that depended on chance while containing nothing repugnant to belief.[2] Of course, such devices are fundamental to story-telling, and Cervantes would certainly have used them if he had never read a line of literary theory; nevertheless, they figure recognizably in his own theory of the novel. One wonders, moreover, whether it is a mere coincidence that the opening chapters of the *Persiles* resemble the story of Iphigenia, used for illustrative purposes in this connexion by Aristotle and summarized by El Pinciano[3] and others, even more than they do the *Ethiopic History*.

The doctrine carefully expounded by Aristotle had long ago come to be more crudely interpreted. The peripety had become,

---

[1] Aristotle, *Poetics*, 1452A. See El Pinciano, op. cit. ii. 28; Cascales, *Tablas*, p. 23.
[2] Lugo y Dávila, op. cit., introd., p. 23.
[3] 'A maiden about to be executed as a sacrifice was abducted from those who were going to sacrifice her and taken off to be a priestess in a remote region where it was the custom to sacrifice the strangers who were taken there. It happened that after a few days a brother of the young priestess landed in that country; he was made captive and taken, according to the custom of the place, to be sacrificed by the hand of his sister; and at the moment when he was going to be sacrificed they recognized each other, which resulted in the salvation of the brother' (op. cit. ii. 18–19).

popularly, a simple vicissitude of fortune. I do not think it means anything more than this for Cervantes. It is certainly not as a rule 'in the probable or necessary sequence of events'. Generally it is a change from adverse to favourable circumstances, and Cervantes seems satisfied if both his peripeties and his discoveries are not impossible. The 'happy and unexpected occurrence' mentioned by the Canon as a constituent of the ideal romance (*DQ* I. 47) is a peripety or vicissitude of fortune in a favourable sense, more often than not combined with a discovery. Cervantes's understanding of the term is plain, for when in the *Persiles* Transila is unexpectedly reunited with Mauricio and Ladislao, the event is referred to in precisely the same words as the Canon had used.[1]

These devices are little to modern taste. Those lucky encounters in remote and unlikely islands of the northern seas seem highly improbable to us. It is curious that whereas the modern reader is generally much readier than Cervantes was to accept fantasy uncritically, he cannot swallow the artificialities of ancient plots. For Cervantes and his contemporaries these were high-lights of fiction, extraordinary but not incredible. His *Novelas* too are full of them: in *Las dos doncellas* they are a positive abuse. What, like so many other writers of the time, he does not seem to have remembered is that coincidences are of their nature rare, and that when they occur in rapid succession the cumulative effect is one of inverisimilitude—though El Pinciano gave warning of this, noting that it was a sin of dramatists in particular.[2]

Cervantes's reconciliation of the rare with the possible by these and other means conforms with Bargagli's idea of the *novella*, which should, he said, contain something new and notable and a certain *verisimil raro*: 'that is to say, something that can plausibly occur but rarely does happen'.[3] The best comparable comment in Cervantes on the nature of the *novela* is Don Fernando's on the Captive's tale, a story about which not even the Priest is able to entertain any doubts: 'Everything in it is rare [*peregrino*] and unusual and full of chance happenings which grip and amaze the listener' (*DQ* I. 42). The word *peregrino*, so frequently used by

---

[1] '. . . alegres y no pensados acontecimientos' (*Persiles* I. 12; i. 83).
[2] El Pinciano, op. cit. ii. 70.
[3] '. . . cioè che verisimilmente possa accadere, ma che però di rado addivenga' (op. cit., p. 210).

Cervantes, is the word that best sums up this quality of credible rarity.[1]

Before coming to the more spectacular forms of the marvellous, a special case must be briefly considered. It concerns that type of impossible fiction of which the main purpose is allegorical or symbolical. In the *Curioso impertinente* Lotario, speaking of the magic-cup episode in Canto XLIII of the *Orlando furioso*, justifies the unbelievable poetic fiction by the worthy 'moral secrets' contained (*DQ* I. 33). 'Moral secrets' were also the *raison d'être* of allegory. Nevertheless, Cervantes (who evidently derived some inspiration from Ariosto's episode but used no magic in his own prose story) seems to have come to have doubts about the suitability of this venerable form of fiction in the novel (as distinct from poems and plays). He uses it only once in a straightforward conventional manner: in connexion with the *Canto de Caliope* in his earliest novel, the poetic *Galatea*. And even there the miraculous appearance of the Muse has nothing to do with the plot of any of the stories contained in the novel: it is simply for the purpose of celebrating Spanish poets.

The only other instance of its occurrence in his novels is in the *Persiles*, where it takes an abortive and highly equivocal form. Periandro learns, by hearsay, of an amazing picture gallery in Rome, where celebrities of the future are commemorated. The names on the labels are there; it only remains to add the portraits. Periandro receives this information with a singular lack of enthusiasm:

> I find it hard to believe that anyone should have taken the trouble so long ago to prepare tablets on which people yet to come would be depicted. Indeed, in this city and capital of the world there are other and greater marvels to be wondered at. (IV. 6)

This perfunctory handling of an ancient device, which is in the Homeric and Virgilian tradition of those contrivances for conventional or prophetic commemoration common to epic, romance, and pastoral, betrays a strong Cervantine suspicion that it was unsuited to the new prose epic, to the reasonable romance. A rationalization of his doubts, maybe even the cause of them, can

[1] Thus *DQ* I. 2; i. 105. I. 47; iii. 345. II. 63; viii. 112. *Persiles* I. 6; i. 54. I. 17; i. 292. II. 21; i. 323.

be found in El Pinciano, who made the point that whereas poetic perfection is mainly achieved through imitation and verisimilitude, the poet who uses allegory composed of fantastic fictions gives his work a chiefly doctrinal, philosophical value.[1] Cervantes was never prepared to shift as much weight as this from the pleasure-giving function of the novel to the instructional. However edifying the *Persiles*, it remains a romance, not a moral tract.

Don Quixote is not a novel of wonders as is the *Persiles*; nor is it based on a miraculous occurrence as is the *Coloquio de los perros*; it is about a man whom the reading of novels full of wonders and miraculous occurrences drove out of his wits. It contains plenty of mysteries and odd happenings, but all of them are rationally explained to the reader sooner or later, with the exception of three. These are the question of Benengeli's reality, that of Avellaneda's Quixote and Sancho, and the incident of Montesinos Cave. The first is one of those calculated absurdities for which Cervantes's theory makes significant provision—but which nevertheless, with very rare exceptions, he prefers entrusting to an intermediary for narration—and even this patent absurdity lies outside the story proper. The second is a disconcerting introduction into the fiction of what is none the less a historical fact: namely, that another author wrote about a Quixote and a Sancho who were not those of Cervantes. The third is left unexplained, a deliberate mystification. Even Benengeli washes his hands of the matter and thrusts responsibility for the story on to Don Quixote who told it. Cervantes strews contradictory clues about, hedges the incident around with talk, and finally leaves the reader to judge for himself (II. 24). It is useless to ask if what Quixote related was a dream, a wilful fabrication, or anything else. Cervantes never intended us to know.

The adventures and wonders of *Persiles y Sigismunda* are designed to be acceptable to the reasonable reader of the seventeenth century. Besides being so richly equipped with surprise encounters and changes of fortune, the novel is studded with marvels. These are principally of two sorts: natural marvels, which may either

---

[1] '. . . el que, dejando [la perfección poética], va tras la alegoría guarda más la filosófica doctrina' (op. cit. ii. 95). He adds that to combine imitation (i.e. imitation that has verisimilitude) with allegory is 'miel sobre hojuelas' and the very perfection of art (p. 96).

be odd occurrences that have a rational explanation, or strange yet attested facts about the real world; and secondly, supernatural phenomena. This division corresponds closely enough to that which Cervantes, in the manner of a Pomponazzi or a Torquemada,[1] makes himself:

miracles occur outside the order of nature, and mysteries are those things which look like miracles and are not, but rather are events that rarely occur. (II. 2)

The *Persiles* is remarkable for its rationalizing. When a lady is observed floating to earth from the top of a high tower, Cervantes informs us that her clothes have acted as a kind of parachute (a 'winged bell') and that this is 'a possibility without being a miracle' (III. 14). It is carefully pointed out, when the pilgrim party emerges from a gloomy cave into an unexpectedly charming countryside, that this is not magic (III. 18). When, on the way to Rome, they find a portrait of Auristela hanging on a tree, and then another in the city, this too is naturally accounted for (IV. 2, 6). The miraculous dissolves into rationalistic anticlimax when a church that might have been expected to burn down does not do so— 'not by a miracle', but because the doors are iron and the fire really nothing much to speak of (III. 11)!

When it comes to the natural wonders of the world, allowance must be made for Cervantes's acceptance of some things that the modern reader rejects. He could not know that while such curiosities as ski-ing (II. 18) were authentic, the accepted version of the natural history of the barnacle goose (I. 12) was fabulous. Such ill-assorted information was regularly to be found within the covers of a single authoritative work. It was indeed easier in the early seventeenth century to believe the story of the barnacle goose than in the bizarre proportions of day and night in the Arctic regions, which could be accounted for by mathematical demonstration (IV. 12). No less incredible to the inexpert were those cosmological facts of which Bartolomé the baggage-boy expresses his disbelief. (Periandro laughingly reassures him.) Bartolomé finds it hard to credit 'the size of this sun which gives us light and which, though it looks no bigger than a shield, is many times larger than all the earth' and the idea that 'beneath us there are other folk whom they call Antipodes, on whose heads

[1] Cf. Torquemada, *Jardín*, pp. 14–15, 18.

we, who are walking about up here, have got our feet planted: a thing which seems impossible to me'.[1]

The fact that the passage must have been written just when the problem of the Copernican cosmology was coming to a crisis and the storm-clouds were gathering around Galileo prompts some fascinating speculation. But this exchange in the *Persiles* has a longer history behind it—not least because Augustine and Lactantius had denied the existence of the Antipodes. As usual it is hard to ascertain Cervantes's source. Schevill and Bonilla point out in their note on the passage the close similarity with part of Pedro Mexía's *Coloquio del sol*. But it is worth noting too that El Pinciano cites the example of the sun being larger than the earth as a possibility unconvincing to the majority of men.[2] Yet more strikingly, both the observations of Cervantes's 'rustic astrologer' Bartolomé quoted above appear in Piccolomini's commentary on Aristotle's *Poetics*:

that the sun is much larger than the earth, and that there are people in the opposite hemisphere to our own who have the soles of their feet turned towards the soles of our feet, and other similar truths which the ignorant have difficulty in believing.[3]

The strange yet familiar may be found too among the reasonable marvels of the *Persiles*. Cervantes remarks on the way one's teeth are set on edge by the sound of a knife cutting cloth; at the way one man will tremble at a mouse, another at the slicing of a radish, or that another cannot abide the presence of olives on a table (II. 5). And, finally, he reminds us of the marvellous nature of the continuous cycle of human existence (III. 21), and of love, that works the greatest miracles (I. 23).

There remain the most fabulous features of the book, the monstrous and the supernatural, which also figure in the *Coloquio de los perros*. In both works Cervantes surrounds his fiction with safeguards. In the *Persiles* he treats his fabulous denizens of strange

---

[1] '. . . la grandeza de este sol que nos alumbra, que, con no parecer mayor que una rodela, es muchas veces mayor que toda la tierra . . . debajo de nosotros hay otras gentes a quien llaman antípodas, sobre cuyas cabezas los que andamos acá arriba traemos puestos los pies, cosa que me parece imposible' (*Persiles* III. 11; ii. 111). [2] El Pinciano, op. cit. ii. 69.

[3] '. . . ch'il sole sia molto maggior della terra; e che genti si truovi nell'opposto emisperio al nostro che tenga volte le piante dei piedi in contra alle piante dei piedi nostri; ed altre così fatte verità dagli imperiti con difficoltà credute' (op. cit., p. 392). The source of the passage on the Antipodeans, however, is Cicero's *Somnium Scipionis*.xx.

islands, his werewolves, witchcraft, and astrology, strictly in accordance with the recommendations of contemporary epic theory. Indeed he goes beyond the most conscientious epic poet in his precautions.

All but the sorcery of Julia, the bewitched shirt in Claricia's story, and some of the astrology occurs in Books I and II: that is, in distant and little-known places. There is a difference between these and the absolutely fictitious regions invented by the chivalresque romancers—'lands . . . undiscovered by Ptolemy and never seen by Marco Polo' (*DQ* I. 47). They are parts of the world unknown indeed to Cervantes and most of his public, but about which there was some evidence from recognized authorities, however absurd it may appear today. On this evidence it was not impossible that there should be countries, people, and phenomena of the sort he describes there. These latitudes, where sorcery was popularly supposed to flourish, were latitudes of the poetically probable. Tasso, who set his own *Torrismondo* in the mysterious north, says this about them:

among distant peoples and in unknown countries we can easily set many fictitious things without detracting from the authority of the tale. Therefore the material of poems of this sort must be taken from Gothland and Norway and Sweden and Iceland, from the East Indies or lands newly discovered in the vastness of the ocean beyond the Pillars of Hercules.[1]

Piccolomini judges the 'actions of persons in far-off lands, when related by someone whom we judge to be worthy of credence', a type of material suitable for the poet.[2] El Pinciano says of Heliodorus that 'by inventing a queen and a princess of unknown lands the poet observed verisimilitude, because no one could say that there was no King Hydaspes or Queen Persina of Ethiopia'.[3] Cervantes's use of the age-old device of remoteness, which he used not for justifying the totally impossible but as an aid to making the extraordinary credible, was recognized epic procedure.

What is striking is not the absurdity, from a strictly modern point of view, of Cervantes's narrative, but the conscientious care

---

[1] '. . . fra popoli lontani e ne' paesi incogniti possiamo finger molte cose di leggieri senza togliere autorità alla favola. Però di Gottia e di Norvegia e di Svevia e di Islanda, o dell' Indie Orientali o di paesi di nuovo ritrovati nel vastissimo oceano oltre le colonne d'Ercole, si dee prender la materia de' sì fatti poemi' (*Del poema eroico* II. 63).   [2] Op. cit., p. 150.

[3] Op. cit. ii. 331–2.

with which he documented it. The *Persiles* is his most studied work, the one for which he did most research. He based his story precisely on the best authoritative knowledge available to him. Beltrán y Rózpide has observed how closely the geography of Books I and II corresponds with the existing maps and the descriptions of geographers.[1] Schevill and Bonilla have noted that he uses some, if not all, of the geographical accounts, travel histories, and miscellanies of Niccolò Zeno, Quirino, Olaus Magnus, Torquemada, Solino, Thámara, Mexía, and the Inca Garcilaso. The sea monster—the *fisiter* or *náufrago*—is mentioned by Torquemada 'and almost all the miscellanies of the sixteenth century, Solino, Thámara and others', say his editors.[2] It is hard to see how Cervantes could have known they were all unreliable, or how he could have been more scrupulous in inventing a story of distant parts. It is absurd to reproach him for not being blessed with a twentieth-century sense of verisimilitude.

Amezúa, De Lollis, Castro, and others have examined his views on witchcraft, astrology, and lycanthropy in the general context of his thought and that of the age. The presence of these things in his book should also be considered in the light of epic theory. The marvellous was necessary to epic; but since this could no longer be conveniently supplied by the old heathen deities, it must be furnished by supernatural agencies recognized among Christians—angels, devils, or beings endowed by God or Satan with extraordinary powers, such as saints, wizards, and fairies.[3] These, of course, had to be handled with circumspection, but poetic recognition of necromancy did not necessarily imply that the writer believed in it. Aristotle and the highest literary authorities permitted the inclusion of what was not necessarily true, but in accordance with popular belief. Tasso, speaking of these matters, said that the poet should set aside the exact truth about things which learned men rightly called impossible; it was enough for him to adhere to popular opinion in such cases.[4] The witchcraft, werewolves, and astrological divinations in the *Persiles* were objects of this sort of popular belief.

[1] R. Beltrán y Rózpide, *La pericia geográfica de Cervantes demostrada con la 'Historia de los trabajos de Persiles y Sigismunda'* (Madrid, 1924).

[2] Schevill and Bonilla, ed. cit. i. 348, note.

[3] Thus Tasso, *Dell'arte poetica* I. 13; cf. Carvallo, op. cit., fol. 134ᵛ; Balbuena, *El Bernardo*, prol., p. 146; Cascales, *Tablas*, p. 132.

[4] Tasso, *Dell'arte poetica* I. 13–14.

Cervantes prevaricates less about astrology than about magic. Though he subjects it to his doubts and questionings, predictions are made and fulfilled in the *Persiles*. Black magic he introduces in a more hesitant manner, in spite of the sanction of popular belief. Reluctant to permit his prose fiction the licence of poetry, he not only surrounds witchcraft with discussion, he takes further precautions. He presents people who are said to be witches, call themselves witches of one sort or another, look like witches, and behave as witches are expected to behave, going into trances (in the *Coloquio*) and manipulating supposedly devilish concoctions. But he does not, *in propria persona*, show them performing any miracle more spectacular than causing people to fall ill, and recover, which is trifling compared with the claims made by Zenotia in *Persiles* II. 8, for instance. These powers he permits them—or rather, as he takes pains to explain, God permits them (IV. 10). He sees witches above all as mistresses in deception, and, while he grants them possession of certain secrets (which in fact can be rationalized, in modern terms, as a knowledge of drugs and hypnosis), he never personally depicts them changing men into animals, flying through the air, or the like.

Cervantes carefully entrusts the more extreme manifestations of the marvellous in the *Persiles* to intermediaries for their narration. The sea monster, the werewolves, the flight through the air from Italy to Norway, all occur in second-hand accounts. They are nothing more in the action of the novel than tales that are told, which the audience, let alone the reader, is at liberty to believe or disbelieve. Numerous authorities, ancient and modern, recommended this or analogous procedures. Aristotle said that an unavoidable improbability should be outside the plot; Horace, that marvellous things should be narrated, not shown on the stage; Lucian, that an extraordinary story should be thrown down without guarantee of its truth for the reader to make what he can of it, the writer taking no risks and showing no preference.[1] Similarly the theorists of the sixteenth and seventeenth centuries: Robortelli gives narration by a third party as one way of dealing with the supernatural;[2] and Balbuena's words on his *Bernardo* are admirably to the point:

---

[1] Aristotle, *Poetics*, 1460a; Horace, *Ars poetica*, verses 179–88; Lucian, *The Way to Write History*, § 60. Cf. Dio Chrysostom, *Discourses* XI. 34.

[2] Robortelli, op. cit., p. 87.

I tried to have the author speak as little as possible in his own person, by which means the story could also be made more delightful, for in this way it would be permissible for him to include more astonishing things without loss of verisimilitude. For if the poet were personally to tell of the monsters of Crete or the origin of the city of Granada, the appearance of truth would be lacking in each case. But when these things are related by a third party they retain all their wonder and the author remains within the bounds of verisimilitude. It is not plausible that Gravinia should be changed into a tree and Estordián into a silk-worm, but it is plausible, and very possible, that those tales should circulate among the men of those parts.[1]

In the case of the most fabulous story of all in the *Persiles*, Rutilio's aerial trip across Europe (a type of feat that witches greatly prided themselves upon), Cervantes takes care to show that the character of the narrator was not such as to inspire confidence. Only at the end, we are told, did he mend his ways, 'because he wished to end well his hitherto wicked life' (II. 21).

The doubt that surrounds the integrity of Rutilio detracts nothing from that of the author who invented him. Rutilio told a fantastic tale, but since the possibility that he was a liar is left wide open, the verisimilitude of the novel is in no way impaired. The same possibility exists with regard to every invented character who tells an extraordinary story. But what are we, and Periandro's audience, to make of it when the noblest of heroes tells a frankly unbelievable tale of a miraculous leap on horseback (II. 20)? Cervantes mischievously imposes on audience and reader the awkward dilemma of accepting the incredible or disbelieving someone who enjoys the highest credit. As in the case of Montesinos Cave, the mystification is complete.

Cervantes's method provokes all sorts of quasi-literary problems of credit and authority,[2] persuasion and belief, into which he probes no less in *Don Quixote* II than in *Persiles y Sigismunda*.

---

[1] '. . . procuré que la persona del autor hablase en él lo menos que fue posible, con que también se pudo añadir a la fábula más deleite; siéndole por esta vía permitido el extenderse a cosas más admirables, sin perder la verisimilitud; porque si la persona del poeta contara los monstruos de Creta o el origen de la ciudad de Granada, careciera lo uno y lo otro de apariencia de verdad; mas referidos estos casos por tercera persona, queda con todo lo admirable, y el autor no fuera de lo verisímil; porque, si no lo es que Gravinia se convirtiese en árbol, y Estordián en gusano de seda, eslo, y muy posible, que aquellos cuentos anduviesen en las bocas de los hombres de aquel mundo' (*El Bernardo*, prol., p. 148).

[2] Vives discusses these subjects in *De instr. prob.*, pp. 626 ff.

There are true things in the world, he remarks, which the imagination could not visualize in advance of their occurrence, if it tried; and if they are not to be regarded as apocryphal, they must be helped out with oaths of their veracity or at least by the good credit of their narrator (*Persiles* III. 16). Yet he makes it quite clear that neither of these aids offers any guarantee of truth. Periandro placed a severe strain on the courtesy of his listeners, in the opinion of one of them, and courtesy, it is several times remarked, is something on which story-tellers must often place a good deal of reliance. A judicious audience with some experience of the world is most likely to offer it. Readiness to believe indeed may reflect credit on the listener; doubts, suspicions, scepticism are often unattractive. The nobility of Don Quixote in Part II is not lessened on those occasions when he apparently prefers being hoodwinked to accepting the distasteful consequences of disbelief. Though not directly referring to literature, these Cervantine considerations show how much he was concerned with the reciprocity which is a necessary part of literary fiction.

The many assertions made by fictitious characters that a story is amazing but true serve to remind the reader that sometimes truth really is as strange as fiction. The fiction thereby becomes easier to swallow, and in any case, if the reader is going to object, he can merely make the futile complaint that a fictitious character is a liar. Here is the Canon of Toledo's verisimilitude in action in a somewhat unexpected way. The author needs the compliance of the reader, so it is as well to remind him from time to time that, as Aristotle put it, 'there is a probability of things happening also against probability'.[1]

Thus in recounting the really fantastic events of the *Persiles* Cervantes safeguards himself in one, or often all, of three ways. He places the event in a little-known region where, from his reading of the authorities, such a thing might, in default of evidence to the contrary, possibly occur; he recounts what is in accordance with popular belief; he puts the account into the mouth of one of his invented characters. This use of the supernatural, far from indicating indifference to the truth of history, betrays a reverence for it surpassed by no epic poet of the time.

Bargagli was thinking along the same lines as Cervantes when he conceded less licence to the *novella* than to poetry: the supernatural

---

[1] Aristotle, *Poetics*, 1461B.

was all very well in poems, but those *novelle* 'that contain witches, magic and enchanted things are held to be less beautiful and less perfect', he said.[1] Cervantes tried to find a way to retain the old magic in a genre where historical truth must be respected. It is true that his handling of the matter was not always very skilful: he overdid his use of the marvellous and then betrayed too many doubts about it. This and, even more, the excess of every kind of incident seem to me to be the great faults of the book— but certainly not a lack of verisimilitude as Cervantes understood the term.

The modern reader is little bothered by the incredibility of the *Coloquio de los perros*. Cervantes quite clearly was. It is the only one of his novels based on what is, not to put too fine a point upon it, an impossibility. He uses at least three safety devices, and even so he seems hardly satisfied.

Dogs do not hold conversations in Spanish. The phenomenon must be accounted for. There are three possibilities. First, that, despite everything, Campuzano is in fact telling the truth. If so, witchcraft has almost certainly been at work—otherwise, as Cipión suggests at the beginning of the colloquy, this must be one of those things called portents. Secondly, that Campuzano, sweating out his fever in the hospital, dreamed or deliriously imagined the whole thing. Thirdly, that he invented it, either with malicious intent to deceive or simply as a pleasant tale to pass the time. None of the possibilities, which recall those relating to Montesinos Cave, can be verified conclusively, and so again there is complete mystification. The fantasy can be justified either by its association with popular superstition, or as a possible dream, or else as a story told by a fictitious character of doubtful integrity. The fact that Cervantes did not take the simple and obvious way out is very revealing of his scrupulousness over literary truth. All he had to do to justify it to his contemporaries' satisfaction was to call it a moral fable. Even Castelvetro allowed that animal fables, devoid of both literal truth and verisimilitude, could easily delight and instruct.[2]

The *Coloquio*, uniquely in the *Novelas ejemplares*, is linked with, and attributed to the protagonist of, another tale, a circumstance

---

[1] '. . . men' belle e meno perfette si tengono quelle che maghe, incanti e cose fatate contengono' (op. cit., p. 211).   [2] *Poetica*, p. 24.

which has provoked a good deal of critical comment. Whatever other reasons Cervantes may have had for doing this, there was one good motive. He needed a party other than himself to tell such an outrageously implausible story. The teller would also have preferably to be someone like Rutilio whose trustworthiness was questionable. This fact would have to be established, and by any other method than the one Cervantes used would probably have required a good deal of extra marginalia.

In the preamble and at the beginning of the colloquy there is much discussion of the credibility of the event, which plays its usual part of making the fiction more acceptable and seem more exciting. There are typical Cervantine sidelights on the problem of truth. Campuzano is ready to resort to oaths, and his insistence drives Peralta toward disbelief of the more plausible story of the *Casamiento engañoso*. There are comically dubious notes like 'I heard and *almost* saw these two dogs with my own eyes', and 'the next day I wrote it down using *almost* the very words I had heard'. Later there is an alarming Lewis Carroll-like suggestion that the *dogs* are dreaming the whole thing.[1] Moreover, Campuzano goes to sleep while Peralta reads his manuscript and wakes the moment he has finished. The *novela* is wrapped in mystery, doubt, and dream.

During the preamble to the story both disputants give ground. The Subaltern stops insisting on its veracity and the Licentiate agrees to accept it on those conditions. Within the compass of a piece of fiction we have seen enacted that delicate struggle between author and reader to come to terms, which so engrossed Cervantes. Campuzano then goes so far as to refer to his efforts as 'those dreams or bits of nonsense which have nothing better to be said for them than that they can be put aside as soon as they become tiresome'.[2] Even as reported speech, this is strong language for Cervantes to use of one of his own compositions. Despite all his rationalization and mystification he seems still unable to stomach without qualms the fantasy he has such a taste for. In the brief discussion at the end of the tale, however, Peralta mitigates the severity of this remark and judges the story to have been well enough composed, even if it was all invented

---

[1] '. . . vengo a pensar y creer que todo lo que hasta aquí hemos pasado y lo que estamos pasando es sueño, y que somos perros' (*Coloquio*, p. 228).

[2] '. . . esos sueños o disparates, que no tienen otra cosa de bueno si no es el poderlos dejar cuando enfaden' (*Casamiento engañoso*, p. 152).

and never happened, for the Subaltern to proceed to write the sequel. He acknowledges its *artificio* and invention (terms associated specifically with fiction and not history) and admits to having derived from it mental recreation. With an effort Cervantes seems to have arrived at the point of accepting his own story as nothing more than a well-made piece of fiction, like the far less troublesome 'dreams' of pastoral—an obvious enough conclusion for the modern reader, but not such a simple matter for him.

Fantasy is on the borderland of art where dream easily evades the 'alert sentinel' of reason.[1] The creator of Don Quixote, Tomás Rodaja, Carrizales, and Anselmo knew what madness and neurotic obsessions meant, and the hypnotic fascination of the monsters that lurk in the Montesinos' caverns of the mind. Reason, Vives said, uses phantasms but does not mix with them.[2] 'All that happens in our fantasy does so with such intensity that there is no way of distinguishing it from when we are really and truly present', says the witch in the *Coloquio*. The danger of fantasy, of course, is that indulgence in it reduces the rational power to distinguish what is real from what is false. If Cervantes seems to clutch obsessively at historical reality sometimes, he does so for a healthy reason.

Two hours or more I slept at my discretion, without vapours or imaginings disturbing my brain. Unleashed fantasy set me down in a flower-filled meadow that breathed the scents of Panchaia and Saba. This pleasant place captivated the eye, whose vision was much keener sleeping than awake, as far as it could see. Palpably I saw . . . But I do not know whether to write it down, for my pen has always shied away from things that smack of the impossible. (*Parnaso* VI)

We have discerned two orders of the fabulous in Cervantes's theory of prose fiction: the fantastic and the idealized (the grotesque may be regarded as the antipode of the latter). He allows the idealized to be its own justification—though not without showing those doubts which we discussed in Chapter V and to which we shall return in a moment. He does not allow this of fantasy. Lope de Vega on one occasion makes the same distinction much more explicitly. When we look at a picture of nymphs, he says, what delights us is the portrayal of the beauty of women, a matter of

---

[1] '. . . despierta centinela . . . la razón, que corrige y enfrena nuestros desordenados deseos' (*Galatea* IV; ii. 64).   [2] Vives, *De anima et vita* II. 521.

which we have first-hand experience. But what pleasure is there in some monstrous fantasy, such as a depiction of the war of the Titans, except what is to be had from contemplating the colours and the technical skill of the painter?[1] Ignoring symbolical meanings, as Lope himself does here, the answer is, of course, that the monstrous and the supernatural charm by their very strangeness—which Lope in less rationalistic mood knows very well. Cervantes knows it too, though he shares this view of Lope's. What he therefore seeks to do in the *Persiles* is to retain the charm of the supernatural but to divest it of authority.

His uneasiness over the enhancement of historical reality implicit in idealization, however, betrays a concern with a problem really more crucial to the novel than that posed by fantasy. This problem springs from the potential discrepancy between the ideal and the possible—a discrepancy that was simply disregarded in the concept of verisimilitude inherited from Antiquity. Nothing is more typical of the old world that was dying in the time of Cervantes than the failure to take account of the difference between what ought to be and what could be. *Don Quixote* is— among so many other things—about this very difference.

His concept of verisimilitude is difficult because it is really of two sorts. According to one of them, the invention should not conflict with an intelligent man's apprehension of reality, in which there is much that may be taken as certain (though prudent interpretation may be necessary), and in which there are things that are dubious, such as forms of the supernatural. These must be presented as dubious. According to the other, the invention should correspond to an ideal world-picture composed on paralogical principles. In this the supernatural occupies a place no different from that in the previous interpretation. The division between the two types of verisimilitude, which in a fragmentary manner involves the division of styles, may be seen all through his novels in different forms. But *Don Quixote* is the one major work in which he really brings them into harmony and puts the two sorts of verisimilitude into their only possible relationship in this world, and for the modern novel. His all-embracing verisimilitude includes 'what ought to be' as part of an experience that 'could be'.

---

[1] Lope de Vega, *El peregrino en su patria* IV, *Obras sueltas* (ed. Madrid, 1776–9), v. 299.

The concept is also difficult because in some respects it is excessively broad, so that the word almost comes to refer simply to what is not impossible, and results in his abuse of the accidental. In others it is excessively narrow, which drives him not only to recognized methods of making marvels intellectually palatable, but to the less conventional subterfuge of treating the problem on the historical level by what, as Castro rightly observes, are 'intellectual, and really extra-aesthetic, procedures'.[1]

Cervantes's obsession with literary truth and falsehood, which was in its way the 'ancient quarrel' of poetry and philosophy, was inseparable from the ideological crisis of the age, with its desperate faith and agonizing doubts. It was part of a bigger question as enigmatic for him as the case of the oath and the gallows was for Governor Sancho. The conflict in his writings between the claims of the marvellous and the credible also corresponded to that in his own temperament which made the creation of Don Quixote and Sancho possible. Behind the literary problem lay not merely a love of truth and a devotion to art but a deep concern for human beings, whom it was unforgivable to mislead.

[1] Castro, *Pensamiento*, p. 96.

VI

HEROES, AUTHORS, AND RIVALS IN
DON QUIXOTE

1. *The Heroes Commemorated*

> He was singing of famous men and accompanying himself
> on a tuneful lyre.   HOMER, *The Iliad*

THE literary celebrity of Don Quixote and Sancho offers the
most remarkable example of the interplay of literature and
life in Cervantes's work. The Knight, in particular, aspires
to be celebrated in writing, lives to see this come literally true, and
continues his fictional career acclaimed as the hero of what was
in real life a best-selling novel. The idea is startlingly original and,
on the scale on which Cervantes used it, unique in fiction as far
as I know (there is a suggestion of it in the later stories of Father
Brown by G. K. Chesterton). In this, as in the other two subjects
of this chapter, the boundary between literary theory and imaginative writing vanishes, but the complicated game Cervantes plays
with literature and life gains in meaning when seen against the
theoretical background.

Probably the most ancient of all literary doctrines was the one
that declared the main purpose of poetry to be the celebration of
great men and their deeds. Linked with the idea of exemplariness,
it was still surprisingly vigorous in the sixteenth and seventeenth
centuries. According to De Nores, the heroic poem was invented
for the praise and exaltation of good and lawful princes and to
offer thereby a model to others.[1] For Herrera, poetic commemoration was a 'second life', resistant to time and the dark
silence of oblivion.[2] Poetry itself was generally held to be the
more honourable for thus honouring others. Memorable public
events,[3] together with the heroic virtues of men and the beauty

---

[1] Quoted by Toffanin, *Fine dell' umanesimo*, p. 145.
[2] Herrera, *Anotaciones*, p. 337.   [3] Suárez de Figueroa, *Constante Amarilis*, p. 44.

and goodness of women,[1] were held to be the principal subjects of celebration, though there was more besides.

That Cervantes accepted and put the doctrine of poetic celebration into practice is obvious. He wrote the *Canto de Caliope*, the *Viaje del Parnaso*, and the *Numancia*. What makes his attitude to the subject interesting are the hinted reservations, the implicit contradictions, which spring from his awareness that the doctrine took no account of niceties of distinction between historical fact and poetic fiction. Commemoration meant fictionalizing history to a greater or lesser extent by the decorative and eulogistic means that disturbed him. Rhetorically transfigured, idealistically groomed, it was certainly not plain history, but it took upon itself some of history's prerogative to record. In return, it may be added, the art of history could not yet quite shake off the old idea of celebration, which was almost always reflected at least in the choice of material. The historian rarely concentrated on matters which were not by universal consent and in the popular sense memorable. His business was 'the narration of public affairs or private actions—remarkable and famous, not commonplace, ones'.[2]

The trouble for Cervantes was not the commemorating itself, but the almost inescapable attendant dangers of exaggeration, of flattery. He observes at the end of *Las dos doncellas* that the poets of the day 'exaggerate' the beauty and exploits of the two damsels they have occasion to commemorate. Cervantes seems never to have quite shed his doubts about the legitimacy of flattery, even in verse. In the *Parnaso* IV Mercury, the smooth-tongued, excuses it when contrived with elegance and *artificio*; Apollo, on the other hand, forbids flattery and adulation to cross his threshold (*Adjunta*). Cervantes almost certainly sympathized with them both.

Inevitably he takes refuge in irony and humour. There are frequent allusions in *Don Quixote* which poke fun at the pompous and time-worn cliché of artistic immortalization. The beauty of Dulcinea demands to be depicted on tablets, marbles, and bronzes by the brushes and burins of Parrhasius, Timanthes, Apelles, and Lysippus, and lauded with all the rhetoric of Cicero and

---

[1] *Discurso en loor*, fol. 25ʳ.
[2] Suárez de Figueroa, *El pasajero*, p. 56. In the *Plaza universal*, fol. 167ʳ, this statement is attributed to Robortelli.

Demosthenes (II. 32). Don Quixote, with more loyalty than truthfulness, commends the neatness and frugality of Sancho's eating habits as worthy of equally durable commemoration (II. 62). Allusions to 'events worthy of record and eternal remembrance' abound. Burlesque encomiums in verse open and close Part I of the novel. But more remarkable and ironic than any of these is the fact that throughout the book a conventionally encomiastic history of Don Quixote exists, in all its comic inadequacy, unwritten but omnipresent. Without this history the story of Don Quixote that we read would be something quite other than Cervantes's novel, because, although unwritten, it exists in the mind of the Knight himself and shapes his actions.

The fact that the basis of poetic commemoration had originally been historical was never any deterrent to writers of pure fiction. Indeed it served the purpose of the authors of romances by giving an added semblance of history to their inventions. They made believe that they were perpetuating the names and exploits of their heroes as though these had in fact existed.[1] Cervantes imitates them in this, but introduces several complications. First, he makes Don Quixote firmly convinced in Part I that he is being so commemorated. Secondly, he confronts Quixote and Sancho in Part II with evidence, as irrefutable to the reader as to them, of their literary celebrity. He thus introduces the historical fact of the fame of the first part of the novel into the fiction of the sequel, and in so doing he lops away the frame that separates the world inside his work of art from the living world outside it. Lastly, he draws a contrast, without ever directly mentioning it, between the book Don Quixote imagines is being written about him and the one that actually is written about him, which supplies the supreme irony—and the comedy and the tragedy—of Cervantes's work.

Like all epic heroes Don Quixote seeks fame. But one of the things that distinguishes him is the peculiar attraction that being immortalized in print has for him. This is because his own inspiration proceeds almost entirely from books. He sees himself through the same medium as his heroes. His perpetuation in print will be tangible proof of his own fame.

'One of the things', Don Quixote said at this point, 'that should

---

[1] Thus in *Amadís de Gaula*, Montalvo's prologue, p. 309; *Tirante*, prol., pp. 1060-1; *Amadís de Grecia*, prol.; *Orlando furioso* xxxv. xxii ff.

give most satisfaction to a virtuous and eminent man is to see his good name spread far and wide by the printed and published word.' (II. 3)

From the moment he first sets out in I. 2 he is convinced that his great deeds (worthy also of permanent conservation in bronze, marble, and paint) are being recorded by a wise enchanter. The idea of literary celebrity, and later the evidence of it, have a decided effect on his character. Self-consciousness is apparent in most of his actions. Having a role to play adds that touch of wilfulness to his madness. At the beginning of the second book, when he learns that he really is famous far and wide, he receives the news with eager curiosity (II. 2); but with that prudence which he sometimes shows when his illusions run some risk of assault from reality, he never asks to read the book that has been written about him—an act, indeed, that would have produced formidable complications. The confirmation that he is a literary hero adds perceptibly to his self-conceit, and he boasts to Don Diego that he is known in nearly all the nations of the world through some thirty thousand published copies of his story (II. 16).

The effect of literary fame on Sancho is even greater. If he is not interested in glory in the way Quixote is—and Castiglione had pointed out that the man who is uneducated cannot, for that reason, appreciate the fullness of glory[1]—he is by no means averse to a little publicity, once he gets used to the idea (I. 21). When he learns that he, Sancho, has been mentioned in Benengeli's history and that there are indeed some who enjoy his talk more than anything else in it, his vanity is tickled and he is 'infinitely pleased' that the author has not spoken badly of him (II. 3). In II. 8 he shows some apprehension, begging abjectly for merciful treatment by historians, and then, relapsing into real or affected indifference, asserts his independence of them. But the consciousness of being represented in print has evidently affected him. He becomes pert, cocksure, and more talkative than ever, a process that is fortified by the encounters of Part II. His conceit swells when affirming his identity to Don Álvaro Tarfe as 'the real Sancho Panza, who says more funny things than there are raindrops that fall from the sky', who cannot help making everyone laugh (II. 72). But this new vanity is not unmixed with good. He

[1] 'Ma chi non sente la dolcezza delle lettere, saper ancor non può quanta sia la grandezza della gloria cosí lungamente da esse conservata' (op. cit., p. 108).

acquires with it a new self-awareness and is capable of observing and describing himself as though he were another person:

It's true that I am rather sly and that I have a bit of the rogue in me, but it is all covered up with the great cloak of my simplicity, which is always natural and never artificial. (II. 8)

He undergoes at least a partial disillusionment in Barataria, where he learns the truth of Don Quixote's counsel to know himself, and his limits. Consciousness of his literary personality I think can be said to have played a part in planting in him the seeds of a sense of duty towards himself.

The literary fame the two heroes acquire as a result of the popular success of the novel of 1605, then, has an influence on their characters. The effect is more marked in the case of Sancho, to whom it comes as a greater surprise than it does to Don Quixote. It has a profound influence on their adventures (and so, indirectly, again on their characters), for a large proportion of the incidents in the second book could not have occurred if the people involved in them had not previously heard of Quixote and Sancho, been able to receive them as celebrities, and known what to expect of them. The consequences here are more serious for Don Quixote, because his celebrity is his own undoing. Part II tells the wonderfully comic and infinitely sad story of his disillusionment. He is repeatedly treated, especially at the Duke's palace, in a way that is a nightmarish parody of what, thanks to the previous book, he is known in advance to expect. He is treated with a humiliating mock deference to his own version of his own story, known to people through the real Part I. Part I had 'commemorated' him not as he wished to be commemorated, but as he was—as a man who took himself, and who wished to be taken, for other than he was. Never was the traditionally flattering, poetically commemorative, version of a man's life more mercilessly juxtaposed with the brutal facts. Yet those facts were in large measure shaped by the poetical version of them with which the man's mind was filled.

Don Quixote contains within itself several other books. The one we have been considering celebrates the hero in the conventional idealizing sense usual in epic and the chivalresque romances. Cervantes's novel pretends to do this too, but it tells, rather, the 'whole truth' about him. In this proto-Pirandellian work the frame that separates it from the world of the reader is removed, further exposing what William Empson has called the 'skyline beyond skyline' of Cervantes's irony.[1] Don Quixote achieves literary fame, but not the sort he bargained for. Yet in the end he eclipses his heroes and wins for himself a fame as durable as any in literature.

2. *The Fictitious-Authorship Device*

> . . . though I seem to be the father, I am the stepfather of
> Don Quixote. CERVANTES

If Cervantes's pretence that the story of Don Quixote was the work of an Arab scholar called Cide Hamete Benengeli had no more interest and significance than that of being a parody of a well-worn device, there would be little to say about it here.[2] Its effect, however, is to add much to the remarkable depth of the book. It also throws some more light on his theory of the novel. In his hands, an ancient device of prose fiction reveals unexpected possibilities. Benengeli is, of course, related to the pseudo-authors of the chivalresque romances and of Ginés Pérez de Hita's *Guerras civiles de Granada*,[3] but he is used by the true author with an awareness of literary principle in comparison with which that of the romancers was rudimentary. Although Cervantes makes him deliberately absurd, he is a great refinement upon, for instance, Montalvo's Maestro Elisabat, who at one point is disconcertingly discovered taking down adventures by dictation while on a sea voyage with the heroes.[4]

Benengeli is also related to the many intermediaries, the simple tellers of tales, that abound in Cervantes's novels and which he puts to good use, as we have seen. No one is for an instant deceived into thinking that the responsibility for the fiction is not the real author's, but the reader is easily beguiled into accepting the pretence, and consequently the fiction, as fiction. Cervantes is very careful to show that it is a deception and draws the reader in to share the joke.

[1] W. Empson, *Some Versions of Pastoral* (London, 1935), p. 198.
[2] It is all that can be said of the sage in Avellaneda's *Quixote*. Avellaneda actually abandons Benengeli, and his book is introduced by one Alisolán (op. cit., p. 15).
[3] '. . . ahora nuevamente sacado de un libro arábigo, cuyo autor de vista fue un moro llamado Aben Hamin, natural de Granada' (G. Pérez de Hita, *Guerras civiles de Granada*, BAE iii. 513).
[4] Montalvo, *Esplandián*, p. 453.

With such precedents, it is highly unlikely that the device of
fictitious author ever occurred to Cervantes as a result of his
reading of literary theory. But the advantages of relating events
through another person were pointed out by theorists, some of
whom he almost certainly did read. Several of them made a good
deal of the virtues of detachment and impartiality. Castelvetro
offered the narrator the choice of being an interested party
(*passionato*) or impartial like the ideal historian, making it obvious
which was to be preferred.[1] El Pinciano noted amongst other
things that an author could much more decently express his
opinions through a third party than he could in his own voice.[2]
And here is what Piccolomini had to say:

it does not seem right that the poet, having shed his poet's garb, should
reveal himself as interested and as adhering more to one thing than
another and more to one person than another in what he narrates;
consequently the credibility and trustworthiness of what he has to say
in this way suffer detriment and harm. Besides which, he is acting
arrogantly in thus taking upon himself what belongs freely to the
readers and the audience: namely, discussion, judgement, praise,
blame, and anything that pertains to those who are reading. For the
poet must appear neutral and leave other people free to exercise
judgement on the things which he relates in his imitation. The poet is
not imitating then, and therefore is not a poet, as long as he is speaking
not as a poet but as one offering judgement, advice, and the like.[3]

Cervantes's repeated use of intermediaries was undoubtedly
made with a keen awareness of the advantages of authorial detachment, whether or not it was done in conscious obedience to
a literary principle. He made such good use of the device in *Don
Quixote*, indeed, that he was unable to dispense with it properly
in the *Persiles*. There he vacillates uncertainly between intervention in the first person and the third, calls the book, once,

---

[1] *Poetica*, p. 55. See also ibid., pp. 148, 545.

[2] *Filosofía antigua poética*, iii. 208-9.

[3] '... non parendo ben fatto che il poeta, toltosi l'abito del poeta, si scuopra come
interessato, ed aderente più ad un fatto che ad un'altro e più ad una persona che ad
un'altra, in quel che narra; e per conseguente deroghi e nuochi in questa guisa alla
credibilità ed alla fede di quel che ei dice. Oltra che in tal guisa vien' a mostrar
superbia in attribuire a se quello che ha da esser liberamente dei lettori e degli
ascoltatori: cioè il discorrere, il giudicare, il lodare, il biasimare o altra cosa fare che
appartenga a coloro che leggono; dovendo il poeta apparir come neutrale e lasciar
libero il giudizio agli altri sopra le cose che egli imitando narra. Non imita dunque
il poeta, e per conseguente non è poeta, mentre ch'ei parla non come poeta ma come
giudicante, consigliante e simili' (op. cit., p. 386).

a 'translation' (II. 1), intrudes his novelistic difficulties into the narrative (as in II. 2), and now and then allows an unsuitable comic irony to break through—as when (in a passage very like one in the ancient novel of Apuleius) he comments: 'I do not know how it came to be known that she had spoken these words, or similar ones, to herself in solitude.'[1] The reason for Cervantes's uncertain procedure, which is no exoneration for his writing badly, is clear. He could neither dispense with the advantages of using a device of the type of Benengeli, nor find a way of meddling with a fictitious narrative without resort to comic irony. Irony that was not comic would run the unthinkable risk of deceiving the reader—and the *Persiles* was not a comic novel.

Cide Hamete occupies a peculiar position in *Don Quixote*. He is at once peripheral to the story and central to the book. He stands between the real author and the story and between the story and the reader. Cervantes relegates himself to second place as Quixote's literary 'stepfather', not his 'father' (I, prol.), as 'the second author' (I. 8), as 'the painstaking one who took it upon himself to have [the story] translated' (II. 3), or simply as 'the translator' (II. 18). The actual translator is the Spanish-speaking Moor of I. 9, who translated Benengeli's manuscript. We never hear of him again, but strictly he constitutes yet another intermediary, and with every one of these the 'certainty' of Don Quixote's adventures recedes a little farther from the reader. Altogether, a surprising number of agents have a hand in *Don Quixote*, for in addition there are the unspecified authors mentioned in the early chapters, and in the very last chapter the Moor's pen comes to acquire an identity singular enough, perhaps, to be included.

Cide Hamete is much the most important of them. He is narrator, intermediary, and, in his own right and his own way, a character. He need not concern us as a story-teller. In his second capacity, he sometimes detaches himself from the story, like Cervantes, to make marginal comments, which may be to prepare

---

[1] '. . . no sé cómo se supo que había hablado a solas estas ú otras semejantes razones' (*Persiles* III. 17; ii. 164). Cf. Apuleius in the early Renaissance translation Cervantes very likely knew: 'Aquí, por ventura, tú, lector escrupuloso, reprehenderás lo que yo digo y dirás así: — Tú, asno malicioso, ¿dónde pudiste saber lo que afirmas y cuentas que hablaban aquellas mujeres en secreto, estando tú ligado a la piedra de la tahona y tapados los ojos?' (*La metamorfosis o El asno de oro*, trans. Diego López de Cortegana (?), ed. Madrid, 1920, p. 288).

the reader for something, and perhaps whet his appetite (II. 10, 17), or to draw the critic's fire from the real author. His anticipation of sentiments sometimes disarms the reader completely. 'Allah be praised!' he exclaims three times when Quixote and Sancho set out on their travels at last after all the preliminaries with which Part II opens (II. 8). The success of this mediation is due not only to Cervantes's lightness of touch, but to his genuine concern for the reader's feelings, a concern which is not impaired by the fact that the author's own ends are being served. Oddly enough, it is by this introduction of a third party that Cervantes establishes that intimacy with the reader so dear to nineteenth-century novelists, without ever relapsing into the dispiriting chumminess to which they were prone. Appeals to the reader were not new to fiction, but the importance that the authors of *Guzmán de Alfarache* and *Don Quixote* evidently attach to making contact with him—in their different ways—marks a significant stage in the evolution of the novel.

The Moorish ghost-author is a suitably mysterious and shady character. He is not allowed to materialize tangibly in the world he is writing about, as do those in charge of the stories of *Esplandián* or the *Lozana andaluza*. But he is rumoured to be a relative of the muleteer who courts Maritornes (I. 16). Quixote is always aware of having a chronicler; Sancho, who apparently begins by picturing him as an ordinary human recorder of their doings (I. 21), comes to accept his omnipresence. They are two characters in possession of an author, whom they accept but in whom they are not much interested so long as he represents them properly. Author and characters respect each other's independence, and the latter do not for a moment regard themselves as Benengeli's puppets. Sancho knows the truth about the theft of his donkey, and if there is any inconsistency in the narrative of Part I, then 'either the chronicler was mistaken or else it must have been a printer's error' (II. 4). Very rarely, Don Quixote credits Benengeli with a certain supernatural influence over them. It must have been the sage who put into Sancho's head the happy thought of calling his master 'the Knight of the Sorry Countenance', he says (I. 19). On another occasion he hopefully leaves it to Cide Hamete to find him a suitable royal pedigree (I. 21). Cide Hamete exists on a plane of his own, and represents yet another of the different levels of being in the book. But in one of his jovial apostrophes

Cervantes brings him together as one of his creatures with the imaginary Dulcinea and the 'real' Quixote and Sancho: 'Oh, most celebrated author! Oh, happy Don Quixote! Oh, famous Dulcinea! Oh, droll Sancho Panza! May each one and all of you live infinite centuries!' (II. 40)

Someone else may be said to have had a hand in the creation of Benengeli in this extraordinary novel. I mean Don Quixote himself, who is himself supposedly fathered by the Moor. In I. 1 Cervantes mentions the unspecified authors who have written about Quixote, but the first allusion to a single sage as the author of the story comes from Don Quixote himself (I. 2). The Knight invents an enchanter-chronicler and proceeds to believe in him. In a sense, then, Cide Hamete springs from Quixote's conviction that such a chronicler must exist. Like Dulcinea he belongs to the supremely literary world Quixote creates for himself. Unlike her, however, he is miraculously realized in fact and presents proof of his existence through the publication of Part I. The implications of this are formidable. It is a vindication of all his beliefs, for it means that chivalresque enchanters do exist outside the Knight's fancy—a point which Cervantes wisely refrains from pursuing, however. Although the specific idea of Benengeli evidently arrived belatedly to Cervantes (he is not mentioned until chapter 9 and only attains his full stature in Part II), an unknown Benengeli certainly existed in the Knight's mind from the moment he first set out on his adventures.

Immanent and transcendent in relation to the world of his story, a creator perhaps created by his creature, this sorcerer who keeps the record has some of the baffling characteristics of divinity. But the poet as a god-like creator was a familiar concept in the sixteenth and seventeenth centuries.

When the book is seen as a whole, the distinction between the true and the supposed author melts away. Cide Hamete, like Cervantes in the first prologue, talks of 'my desire' to discredit the novels of chivalry (II. 74); and the remark, 'whose native village Cide Hamete was unwilling to indicate exactly', merges with Cervantes's first person singular: 'the name of which I do not wish to recall' (I. 1). Which, after all, is as it should be.

The existence of Cide Hamete is a joke—and such a successful one that the significance of his absurdity is almost invariably passed over. He offers the one instance of total inverisimilitude in the book, with the exception of Don Álvaro Tarfe who is a comparably peculiar case; but it is precisely his incredibility which is important. For, by making a patently unbelievable character supposedly responsible for the story, Cervantes wraps his vivid simulacrum of historical reality safely in an envelope of fiction. It is not endangered by the breaches he makes in its fabric. There is no confusion. Cervantes contrives by every means in his power to make Quixote and Sancho as 'real' as he can, but he is equally careful to see that the reader accepts them as the products of 'art'.

Even his use of the phrase 'the history relates', common to the novels of chivalry, which for its part helps to confer a sort of independence on the narrative, probably contains an equivocation. It has been plausibly suggested that the phrase may also be a reminiscence of the Arabic *qāla*, approximately equivalent to 'says the narrator'. This, says R. S. Willis, is 'the vestigial form of the *isnād*, the chain of authorities that introduces and authenticates the text of a *hadith*, or record of an action or saying of the Prophet. . . . The presupposition is, of course, that the most authentic truth is that which emanates from Mohammed, and the chain seeks to reach back as close to him as possible.'[1] The ultimate guarantor of the truth of the story would thus be Mohammed! The idea is well suited to the ironical humour of the real author and the equivocal character of the pretended one.

In Benengeli's case Cervantes bewilders us with a sort of double-talk. The trustworthiness of a story-teller is again in question, and the evidence is completely contradictory. On the one hand he is presented as a model of historians—as 'very painstaking and very exact in all things' (I. 16), a 'trustworthy author' (II. 61), the 'flower of historians' (I. 52), and so on. On the other hand he is a Moor, and it is 'very characteristic of those of that nation to be liars' (I. 9) and there is 'no truth at all to be expected from Moors' (II. 3). Further to dismay us, he swears on one occasion 'like a Catholic Christian' (II. 27). He is therefore a comic paradox, whom we must believe and whom we must not believe. He is no ordinary historian in another way too: he is a wise magician, and from these,

---

[1] R. S. Willis, *The Phantom Chapters of the 'Quijote'* (New York, 1953), p. 101. Clemencín, *Don Quijote* II. 2, note 2, also suggests a possible Arabic origin for the phrase.

as Quixote remarks, 'nothing that they want to write about is hidden' (II. 2).

It has been persuasively shown that when Cervantes chose to call his chronicler 'Cide Hamete Benengeli' he may well have had in mind not only the chivalresque sages or Pérez de Hita's fictitious author, but also the marabouts or holy men of Algiers, where he was for so long a captive.[1] They were commonly designated as 'Cide', venerated as scholars, and credited with necromantic skill. Benengeli shares this title and these distinctions with them. As a sorcerer, he is privileged to know the smallest thoughts and most trivial feelings of his characters. This privilege of the authors of chivalresque histories in general, and Don Quixote's in particular, is several times insisted upon. Every knight errant, says Quixote,

had one or two sages, ready for the purpose, who not only wrote down his deeds but depicted his most trivial thoughts and tomfooleries, however well hidden they may have been. (I. 9)

Later he professes surprise that the author should have introduced alien *novelas* and tales into Part I, when he could have filled a large volume by simply recording the Knight's 'thoughts, sighs, tears, good intentions and undertakings' (II. 3). And when Cervantes reminds us of our debt to Cide Hamete (with some irony, for his words are an oblique reminder of the excess of detail in the romances) he says:

Really and truly, all those who enjoy such histories as this ought to show their gratitude to Cide Hamete, its first author, for the pains he has taken in recounting every detail to us, without failing to bring everything to light, however small it might be. He depicts thoughts, reveals fancies, answers every tacit question, clears up doubts, settles arguments, and finally elucidates the minutest points the most curious could desire. (II. 40)

Now private thoughts, fancies, and intentions belong to that class of things which Castelvetro in his *Poetica* calls 'cose incerte', unverifiable things which cannot be said to have historical truth but are a legitimate part of the action in poetry.[2] For this reason alone the pretensions of Benengeli's narrative to historical certitude are fabulous nonsense. Chroniclers cannot know the secret thoughts of their subjects—unless, of course, they happen also to be magicians.

[1] G. L. Stagg, 'El sabio Cide Hamete Venengeli', *BHS* xxxiii (1956), 221 ff.
[2] Castelvetro, op. cit., pp. 208-10.

Benengeli the magician is Benengeli the poet. But to ignore his other title because he is not writing true history would be a mistake. The persistent reminders of history in *Don Quixote* are whimsical perhaps; they are not perverse. They direct attention towards the substratum of historical fact which must underlie what imaginatively 'could be', in Cervantes's conception of prose fiction. As a chronicler, even a dubious one, Benengeli has a duty towards the truth of history. As a sorcerer he knows those hidden things that go beyond the historical evidence, things that are the poet's province. He works therefore in a terrain encompassing both history and poetry. In other words, Benengeli stands for the novelist, who is part historian, part poet. We have already seen that Cervantes's treatment of history and fiction in *Don Quixote* points to the same conclusion. By presenting Benengeli as a historian Cervantes respects the obligation the novelist has towards history. By discrediting him because he is a Moor he makes it plain that the novel is not something to be believed literally. By treating him as an enchanter he recognizes the novelist's right to operate in extra-historical regions. He makes us sensible of the nature of truth in the novel and of the novel's fictional quality.

So an ancient device, parodied by Cervantes, is much more than that. It allows him to satisfy a temperamental necessity: to criticize his own invention and at the same time to deflect criticism by humorously shifting the responsibility to that 'dog of an author' who must be blamed if the story lacks anything that it ought to have (I. 9). As this caveat suggests, not even Cide Hamete's story is the complete account. It is just one of the books contained in *Don Quixote*.

3. *Avellaneda's* Quixote

> God bless my soul, noble, or perhaps plebeian, reader! How you must be looking forward to this prologue, expecting to find in it vengeance, wrangling, and railing at the author of the second *Don Quixote*—the one, I mean, who was engendered in Tordesillas and born in Tarragona.
> CERVANTES, *Don Quixote* II

Cervantes's reply to the pseudonymous and scurrilous Avellaneda takes several forms. He retorts to the personal abuse and makes some retaliation in kind, excusable enough considering the provocation. He deals with one or two specific matters, such as Avellaneda's comment on the nature of the *Novelas ejemplares*[1] and the alleged attack on Lope de Vega. The rest is criticism, of one sort or another, of Avellaneda's book. Much of this is in the form of opprobrious references which cannot be held to represent considered judgements. Their culmination is in II. 70, in which Altisidora describes her Quevedo-esque visit to hell, where even the devils find the book too repellent to use as a missile in their game of volley-ball.

There is very little detailed or specific criticism. The three observations made by Don Quixote in II. 59 when he first hears of the work and glances through it are negligible as literary criticism, if interesting for other reasons. A comment by one of the two gentlemen at the inn, however, introduces a significant complication. The jousts at Saragossa took place, says Don Juan, 'in a ring lacking in invention, poor in mottoes, very poor in liveries, but rich in stupidities' (II. 59).[2] Is this a literary appraisal or is he criticizing the arrangements of an actual tournament? It depends on whether he accepts Avellaneda's book as fiction or as fact. Cervantes himself deals with the spurious sequel in his own genuine Part II on these two levels: as a work of literary fiction, which it is from his and the reader's point of view; and as a matter of 'fact' to be verified or disproved as far as Don Quixote and Sancho are concerned.

The supreme merit of a work of fiction for Cervantes is its poetic truth. The main issue in this case is the truth of the work. Here as elsewhere the word 'truth' has two possible meanings: historical truth for Quixote and Sancho, poetic truth for Cervantes and the reader. So the question of the 'reality' of the happenings in the sequel is really one with that of its literary quality. The rejection of the former is a rejection of the latter. The case is substantially the same as that of the chivalresque romances, the heroes of which Don Quixote is destined to put in the shade, his historical reality (in the fiction) being equivalent to his greater

---

[1] He thanks Avellaneda for saying that these were good, though more satirical than exemplary, and retorts that they could not have been if they had not contained a little of everything (*DQ* II, prol.; iv. 31–32). This implies that variety is desirable in a collection of *novelas*. Cf. Lope, *El desdichado por la honra*, p. 14.

[2] Cf. Castiglione on the necessity for a good turn-out on such occasions: 'e porrà cura d'aver cavallo con vaghi guarnimenti, abiti ben intesi, motti appropriati ed invenzioni ingeniose' (op. cit., p. 150).

poetic truth (as seen by the reader). Only there is greater urgency about the matter this time, for the falsity of Avellaneda's history remains to be proved. Cervantes leaves it to his own two heroes to shoot down Avellaneda. His major criticism thus lies permanently enshrined in the pages of *Don Quixote*. He could well afford to make a show of restraint in the prologue.

Most unexpectedly Avellaneda has provided the occasion for Cervantes to give another twist to the problem of history and fiction, and to turn a critical matter into matter for the novel. In fact, Cervantes exploits Avellaneda's irruption into his domain so well that one could almost believe that if the spurious sequel had not existed he would have had to invent it. Nevertheless, the whole thing is a kind of literary joke, like the device of Benengeli, and Cervantes, wounded by his imitator's churlishness and offended at his clumsy imitation, takes it farther than he need. His final comic mystification is sufficient neither to disguise his annoyance nor to deflect critical scrutiny.

The major literary criticism is expressed directly or indirectly in three intimately related forms. Avellaneda, it will be recalled, is likened to Orbaneja, who painted 'whatever it turned out to be' (II. 71). The recollection of his book prompts the observation that fictitious histories are good and delightful in the measure that they approach the truth or the semblance of it (II. 62). And we are told that if the work 'were good, faithful and true, it would live for centuries; but if it should be bad, the road from its cradle to its grave will not be a very long one' (II. 70). In a word: the book is artistically bad, it lacks poetic truth, and it will not survive.

It is appropriate that each of these literary comments should come from the true, the poetic Don Quixote; but from his point of view the vital fact to be established is that the history is spurious. In the circumstances, the degree of detachment Cervantes achieves is remarkable. Indeed, there is a certain ironic similarity between the way that Quixote and Sancho now treat Avellaneda and the way they had treated Benengeli in chapter 3. There are comparable objections to points of detail. Neither the honest nor the mendacious author is treated with much indulgence by the heroes. Both authors are compared with Orbaneja (II. 3, 71). Quixote says he does not care who depicts him, so long as he is not maltreated (II. 59).

Whatever Avellaneda relates did not occur to the true heroes. Two questions follow: Did it occur at all? And—a very disturbing one this—if so, to whom? Their natural reaction is to regard Avellaneda as a liar. But Cervantes does not let the matter rest there. From chapter 59 onwards the heroes are haunted by the possibility that impersonators, travesties of themselves, have been at large. One of the most mysterious problems in the whole book, that of personal identity, becomes henceforth of immediate moment to Quixote and Sancho. Not only have they had to contend with false knights, spurious Merlins, bogus duennas, convicts disguised as puppet-masters, lackeys substituted for champions, and Dulcineas transformed and enchanted, but now with simulacra of their very selves. Don Quixote, the great player of romantic roles, finds that someone has been acting the role of Don Quixote. His identity has been challenged, his celebrity threatened. It is hard to imagine anything more disconcerting for the Knight. No malevolent enchanter could have struck a shrewder blow at the heart of his self-esteem.

Although they are no more than dark hints, there are, however, a couple of curious anticipations of the situation that exists from the time that the heroes first hear of their rivals, late in the book. Don Quixote has already had occasion, he believes, to fear the existence of another impersonator. The Knight of the Wood claims to have previously defeated a Don Quixote in combat. Our Knight, on vanquishing the former, adjures him to 'confess and believe' that that other knight 'was not, and could not have been, Don Quixote of La Mancha, but another who resembled him' (II. 14). And Sancho introduces himself to the Duchess in this odd fashion:

and the squire who goes about, or ought to go about, in that history, and whom they call Sancho Panza, is myself, unless I was changed in my cradle—I mean in the press. (II. 30)

Perhaps, as some critics have suspected, Cervantes had heard of Avellaneda's *Quixote* before he came to write chapter 59. Perhaps a later doctoring was responsible for these 'premonitions'. But it is just as likely that neither was the case: that the passages simply illustrate how cunningly Cervantes integrated his criticism of Avellaneda into *Don Quixote* II, contriving out of it a brilliant variation on themes already contained in his novel.

Certain primary distinctions have to be established. The real Knight, as that gentleman hotly informs Don Juan and Don Jerónimo, is not now out of love with Dulcinea (II. 59). Nor is the true Sancho gross and unfunny, a glutton and a tippler, like Avellaneda's (II. 59, 62). More than once they take pains to make it quite clear who they are. And at least they have the satisfaction of never being doubted by those whom they meet, which is an indirect tribute paid by Cervantes to his own superior powers of creation. Don Quixote is immediately accepted by the gentlemen at the inn, and he is also welcomed into Barcelona as the true, and not the false, Don Quixote (II. 61).

The fact that Avellaneda's work is not simply dismissed as untrue owes a good deal, I think, to the fact that Cervantes credits even bad literary fiction with so much force in real life. Bad as it is, the false *Quixote* is a historical fact to be reckoned with: it exists, however untrue its protagonists, and has been read by thousands of people. Its existence is a fact entirely outside, but intimately relevant to, his own fiction. So the book comes to intervene in Part II in the way that his own Part I had done. The true Part I and the false Part II acquire the importance that true history and false romances had enjoyed earlier in the story. The intervention of Avellaneda's *Quixote* is especially dramatic, for the course of the narrative and the Knight's fortunes are decisively altered when he changes his plans and refuses to set foot in Saragossa, simply, we are told, to give the lie to the rival author (II. 60).

Matters do not really come to a head until the meeting with Don Álvaro Tarfe. Until chapter 72 there has been no confirmation that the pseudo-heroes were anything more than malicious inventions. Their existence is not now proven, but the appearance of one of the characters out of the same book certainly introduces a complication, not to say a confusion, that might have been better avoided. The friend of the false Quixote, from this moment at least, 'exists' as much as do the true Quixote and Sancho. No doubt Cervantes felt that the satisfaction of making one of Avellaneda's creations pay homage to his own superior protagonists and deny those of his creator was worth the sacrifice of some logic and verisimilitude. It was tit for tat.

The problem narrows down to the identification of the heroes. It does not take Don Álvaro long to admit the complete dissimilarity of those he has now met and those he knew formerly. As has elsewhere been pointed out, his only criterion for choosing the original Quixote and Sancho as the genuine heroes is aesthetic.[1] They convince; the false Quixote and Sancho do not. Who then were they? Cervantes provides no better answer to this inevitable question than that they must have been the work of enchanters, those Quixotic maids of all work. Tarfe himself advances this solution. He was the victim of some potent form of magical hallucination. Clearly, this will not do. All the other enchanters in the *Quixote* can be explained away, with the single exception of Benengeli. The best one can say is that at least there is a certain analogy here: Avellaneda's *Quixote* is 'outside' the story too. Since the book, whatever its worth, exists as an undoubted fact, it is therefore possible, if not strictly honest, to blame its author for any subsequent confusion.

The true heroes now have a vital witness for their defence. So they ask for a solemn declaration, legally drawn up and sworn before the local mayor, from the friend and patron of the pseudo-Quixote, to the effect that they alone are the true Quixote and Sancho. This is duly furnished,

which made Don Quixote and Sancho very happy, as if such a declaration mattered a great deal to them, and as though the difference between the two Don Quixotes and the two Sanchos were not clearly manifest in their words and their deeds. (II. 72)

The reading public needs no such declaration; the artistic disparity between the two pairs of heroes is sufficient. But the heroes do, for their peace of mind. At any rate they can do no more to lay Avellaneda's ghosts.

Avellaneda's action, more than anything else, drives Cervantes to claim, in his indirect way, the proprietary rights of Quixote's story. Thus Don Juan would have liked it decreed, if possible, that no one save Cide Hamete should dare to write about the great Don Quixote (II. 59). The claim is reinforced in the last chapter, and another legal precaution is taken when the Priest has a notary testify to the death of Don Quixote, to prevent some other author falsely resurrecting him and writing interminable histories of his exploits. There must be no more bad sequels.

Now, although Cervantes's retaliation to his rival takes an

[1] Gerhardt, '*Don Quijote*': *la vie et les livres*, p. 38.

unusual form, there had been a similar case not many years before. The parallel is not exact, but it is too close to escape comment. Mateo Alemán had had the experience of seeing his continuation of *Guzmán de Alfarache* anticipated by one Juan Martí, who wrote under the name of Mateo Luján de Sayavedra.[1] Into the second book of his own Part II (1604) Alemán introduces Martí, thinly disguised as the rogue Sayavedra. Alemán wastes few words on him. He presents him as a liar, who robs Guzmán and fittingly becomes his servant, because he is patently of lesser calibre and has no real business to be a picaroon at all. Sayavedra eventually goes mad on the sea voyage from Italy to Spain, runs about shouting 'I am the ghost of Guzmán de Alfarache!' and leaps overboard and drowns.[2]

Changing times, as well as private mortification, I think, are discernible in the jealousy of Alemán and Cervantes for their creations. This jealousy is related to Tasso's obsessive preoccupation with his *Gerusalemme liberata* and Montaigne's emphatic identification of himself with his *Essais*. It is true that there was scarcely any notion in the early seventeenth century in Spain that an author had special property rights over his material; but a new artistic individualism was gradually encroaching upon that communal and anonymous approach to art and literature that had typified the Middle Ages. It is significant that Avellaneda found it necessary to remind readers that there were precedents for the fact that his sequel to *Don Quixote* I was not by the original author.[3] An increasing sense of the individuality of the writer was the complement to the growing recognition of the reader's or audience's participation in a work. Both were major developments in the history of literary ideas. Both are very apparent in Cervantes, who regarded his novel as his own particular creation, and stamped it as such.

He was confident that his 'true' Don Quixote had a poetic existence denied both to the incredible chivalresque heroes and to

---

[1] The theory, advanced by P. Groussac, that Avellaneda was Martí was effectively punctured by A. Morel-Fatio, 'Le *Don Quichotte* d'Avellaneda', *BH* v (1903).

[2] M. Alemán, *Guzmán de Alfarache* II, in *La novela picaresca española*, ed. A. Valbuena Prat (Madrid, 1946), 491–2.

[3] '... sólo digo que nadie se espante de que salga de diferente autor esta "Segunda parte", pues no es nuevo el proseguir una historia diferentes sujetos. ¿Cuántos han hablado de los amores de Angélica y de sus sucesos? Las *Arcadias*, diferentes las han escrito; la *Diana* no es toda de una mano' (op. cit., prol., p. 13).

Avellaneda's unhappy travesty, 'who wanted to be he, and did not succeed' (*Comedias*, dedic.). To the world of Quixote and Sancho, with its real 'live' characters like the Priest or Maritornes, its semi-literary Grisóstomo and Marcela, its visional Dulcinea, its fabulous Amadises and Belianises, and its peripheral narrator Benengeli, he added two new, shady figures, who hover uncertainly but ominously between fiction and fact. Merely as criticism Cervantes's indictment of his imitator's work is undistinguished. But the way in which he chooses chiefly to convey it is remarkable. The burden of it is that Avellaneda's *Quixote* is artistically bad and lacks poetic truth; his own two heroes are poetically true and therefore 'exist'; Avellaneda's are not and so they do not really exist, although, like the conjurings of a necromancer, they may appear to do so. As a comic mystery the idea is less successful than was that of Cide Hamete, although thematically it could not be better integrated in the novel. It may not represent a coolly considered criticism, but it was the most serious he knew how to make, and, by inevitable comparison with his own work, it is justified.

Three quite different accounts of Don Quixote have been referred to in this chapter: the Knight's own idealized one, Benengeli's history, and the rejected version of Avellaneda. These are quite sufficient to implant in the mind of the reader of the *Quixote* the suggestion that, if they could exist, other authorial approaches are possible too; that there is in fact an infinity of potential versions, interpretations, points of view. Englobed in *Don Quixote*, by allusion or by inference, are all the possible partial accounts of Don Quixote. Speculation on their respective validity and completeness would be meaningless, since their object is pure invention. But Cervantes has succeeded in conferring on his invention the appearance of being independent of them all by the simple device of drawing attention discreetly to the variety of possible interpretations. If few heroes in literature are at once so substantial and so elusive, in such a lifelike way, the effect owes a great deal to the fact that Cervantes, as an integral part of the representation, has occasional recourse to, and repeatedly reminds us of, other points of view than that of the immediate narrator. 'Take note, Sancho,' said the Duchess, 'that one does not see the whole of what one is looking at from a little corner.' (II. 41)

The nearest one can get to seeing the whole of an object at one time is by erecting mirrors that will reflect the sides hidden from view. The extra dimension attained in *Don Quixote* is achieved by the literary equivalent of this. Italian Renaissance painters knew that the mirror image produces a curiously heightened effect of reality; so did Velasquez. Cervantes achieved this effect too, whether or not he was aware of the physical phenomenon. The *Quixote* is a conjuring trick—Benengeli is not a magician for nothing. Among the reflections of reflections (about which Piccolomini speculated), reality and illusion become indistinguishable (or do they?), but as with any good conjuring trick, our awareness of the illusion does not spoil—it enhances—the act.

CONCLUSION

THE theory of the novel that has been pieced together in the preceding pages from Cervantes's critical observations and, when necessary, inferred from his practical application of current poetic principles, is ample though not exhaustive, coherent though not always self-consistent. It suffers from his failure to draw conclusions. His silence on many of the most outstanding features of his own art is also disappointing. He says next to nothing about the nature of the comic (which El Pinciano discussed at some length) or the particular requirements of the short story, let alone the processes that went into the making of *Don Quixote*. There is indeed little in his direct statements of theory to account for that novel—although a few such statements, such as his definition of an episode in Part II, are of immediate relevance. But nothing that he could have said about the sixteenth-century prose romance is nearly as eloquent a statement about its nature as is his story of a man who attempted to translate it into life. This metamorphosis of criticism into imaginative invention represents the final triumph of Cervantes's creative over his critical instinct.

Simply as a literary theorist, he does not rank with Tasso, say; but he was one of the first European writers—perhaps the very first—to have had a theory of the novel of any considerable scope at all. His most original contribution to the subject, to which we will advert presently, took the form of an inference, but it was one of major importance. Some of his other critical observations, too, while not wholly new, acquired in his theory a significance they had not enjoyed before: his views on the calculated absurdity, on poetic hyperbole, and on the way verisimilitude worked, for instance.

Contemporary theorists were, as Cervantes was, a good deal concerned with the reconciliation of conflicting literary principles. The disparate claims of art and nature, originality and the imitation of literary models, the highbrow and the lowbrow, instruction and entertainment, unity and variety, elaboration and simplicity, *admiratio* and verisimilitude, are all very evident in his own theory. Most of them presented him with immediate problems which he had to solve as a novelist: none more so, perhaps, than art and nature—the twofold problem of subjecting creative talent to critical discipline and of making a work of art out of the raw material of life.

The rules and principles laid down in sixteenth-century poetics altered little in the next two hundred years, but the attitude to them slowly changed. As Spingarn reminds us, 'the history of this attitude gives us the history of criticism in the seventeenth and eighteenth centuries'.[1] Those principles continued to be treated as absolute for the most part, but in fact, even in Cervantes's day, literary criticism was gradually becoming more relativistic. (The dominance of 'taste'—an expression of the particular standards of a select audience, masquerading as a norm of universal validity— over the literary ideas of the eighteenth century was symptomatic of the impending breakdown of neo-classical theory.) The widening of critical focus which brought author and reader more fully into the picture is particularly characteristic of Cervantes's theory of the novel. It is implicit in his views on the calculated absurdity and on the functioning of verisimilitude, and evident in his observation of the variety of readers' reactions to the novel of chivalry. Slowly, a work of literature was coming to be judged more by reference to the writer's intentions and the reader's reactions, and less by reference to an abstract concept of genre. In the sixteenth century, concern with the effects of literature on people played a large part in this development.

The central issue in the poetics of the latter half of that century was the relationship of history and poetry. But what emerges most clearly from Cervantes's imaginative version of the problem in *Don Quixote* is that it far transcended critical theory and properly belonged to philosophy. The nature of truth and fiction indeed became in the seventeenth century the primary object of philosophical inquiry.

Cervantes's aptitude for ironic detachment owes much to an acute consciousness of the enigma of this relationship, together with the conviction that the writer must realize a rational purpose in his work. His chief criticism of the chivalresque novelists was for not being properly aware of what they were doing with fiction. His own novels are full of authorial uncertainties, but the difference

---

[1] J. E. Spingarn, 'The Origins of Modern Criticism', *MPh* i (1904), 493.

between himself and the romancers was the degree to which he showed himself conscious of those uncertainties. To know what he is about, the writer must be able to stand back from his work, observe it dispassionately as a spectator, and even watch himself at work. When Cervantes in *Don Quixote*, like Velasquez in *Las Meninas*, in imagination stepped out of himself and stepped back from the work he was doing, and then proceeded to put the whole scene into the work he was engaged on—artist, work, audience, and all—he realized artistically an act of mental detachment which is a distinguishing mark of European thought around 1600. It was a similar act, 'essayed' earlier by Montaigne, that produced the first axiom of the philosophy of Descartes.

The coexistence in Cervantes's fiction of two worlds that are recognizably distinct reflects the potential disparity between the two aspects of verisimilitude, the ideal and the possible. The modern reader is apt to find the unintegrated coexistence of these two worlds within the compass of a single story like *La ilustre fregona* disconcerting. In one of them life is pruned, heightened and, as it were, prearranged according to an ideal plan; in the other, life is represented in the context of more common human experience. The difference between them is only fragmentarily an expression of the traditional doctrine of styles, which as we have seen was only very partially observed by Cervantes, although it is certain that the doctrine greatly complicated matters. The difference between them is really the difference between the *Quixote* and the *Persiles*, and it was not by a casual coincidence that in the former Cervantes most completely upset the stylistic order and also found the most harmonious relationship he ever achieved for the poetically ideal and the historically possible. The congenial modernity of the *Quixote* largely derives from the fact that the novel's centre of gravity is situated in the historically possible. In the *Persiles* Cervantes shifted it to the poetically ideal, reversing the relationship established in the earlier work.

Don Quixote I appeared in the same year as Bacon published *The Advancement of Learning* and Kepler finished writing the *Astronomia nova*. The event of greatest consequence during the lifetime of Cervantes was the rise of science, and the predominant characteristic of European thought in the early seventeenth century was its ideological ambivalence. The medieval universe was beginning to fall apart; its centre had been plucked out and sent spinning round the sun. But the old idealistic design had not yet been replaced by the mechanical Newtonian model. The old world-view was essentially poetic, the one just forming was essentially scientific. The oscillations of Cervantes between his two worlds of fiction in their own way reflect the prevailing uncertainty before these two world-views. Seventeenth-century Spanish thought presently ossified, generally speaking, into a sclerotic if decorative posture of adherence to the former. It may be that *Persiles y Sigismunda* represents the final decision of Cervantes to attach the novel firmly to poetry, for it was poetic truth that mattered most, and the grandeur of epic was a powerful attraction. But knowing his reluctance to take final decisions, and the way he grasps at historical certitude even in this novel, we may more plausibly conclude that, like many of the enigmatic Elizabethans, he was simply obeying the same impulse as prompted Kepler, a scientist, to follow up his revolutionary *Astronomia nova* with *De harmonice mundi*, which (the third law of planetary motion apart) from the scientific point of view is largely idealistic romancing.

Cervantes's principal contribution to the theory of the novel was a product, never properly formulated, of his imaginative-critical method. It was his all but explicit recognition of the fact that the novel must be rooted in the historical stuff of everyday experience, however much it might reach out to the marvellous heights of poetry. Though the novelist could only be truthful in the way that the poet was truthful, he had to take greater cognizance of history than the poet did. More than a mere echo of the rule about verisimilitude, this was an adumbration of a major—an almost indispensable—function of the modern novel: to convey an idea of what Hazlitt called 'the web and texture of society as it really exists'. It is here that the novel and poetry part company.

Cervantes thus took the novel beyond the concept of the prose epic, which, though it long continued to be the main assurance of the novel's respectability, was of limited usefulness, even when sweetened for the popular taste. It led all too naturally to the dead-end of the heroic romance. Only as mock-epic, in the hands of Fielding (who had the example of *Don Quixote* ever before him), did the notion have a literary future. Cervantes's effective revision of the idea was born of a humanistic concern for the sacredness of historical truth, which the great Aristotelian justification of poetic fiction had not succeeded in dispelling. From the same concern germinated the methods of modern scientific inquiry, and whereas the climate of thought in which these flourished was in the long run detrimental to poetry, it was not so to the novel. Bargagli had suggested that the supernatural was out of place in the *novella*, which it was not in epic; but the modern novel owes more to Cervantes than to anyone else for the revised concept of the prose epic, even if it was for his example rather than for his precept, and even if he himself had no more than an intuition of the implications.

The problems of truth and fiction, reality and illusion, that preoccupied the seventeenth century as they did Cervantes, were critical problems for him in one of their aspects. He put his imaginative grasp of their implications to account as a novelist rather than as a theorist. But his awareness of them as critical problems made it possible for him to achieve in *Don Quixote* that extraordinary illusion of human experience which is not a shadow or distortion of human experience, but an illumination of its nature.

LIST OF WORKS CITED

WHAT follows is not a complete list of the printed works consulted, but only of those quoted from or referred to in this study. Works of unknown authorship are given under their title. Prefatory writings not by the author of the book in which they occur will be found under the name of their writer.

ALBERTI, LEON BATTISTA, *see* VENEGAS DE BUSTO.

ALEMÁN, MATEO, *Guzmán de Alfarache*. Ed. A. Valbuena Prat, *La novela picaresca española*. Madrid, 1946.

ALONSO, AMADO, review of W. C. ATKINSON, 'Cervantes, El Pinciano and the *Novelas ejemplares*', *Nueva revista de filología hispánica*, vol. iv (1950).

Amadís de Gaula. Ed. F. Buendía, *Libros de caballerías españoles*. Madrid, 1954.

AMEZÚA, *see* GONZÁLEZ DE AMEZÚA.

APULEIUS, LUCIUS, *La metamorfosis o El asno de oro*. Trans. Diego López de Cortegana (?). Ed. Madrid, 1920.

ARBOLANCHE, JERÓNIMO DE, *Los nueue libros de las Hauidas*. Saragossa, 1566.

ARCO Y GARAY, RICARDO DEL, 'Estética cervantina en el *Persiles*', *Revista de ideas estéticas*, vol. vi (1948).

—— *La sociedad española en las obras de Cervantes*. Madrid, 1951.

—— 'Las artes y los artistas en la obra cervantina', *Revista de ideas estéticas*, vol. viii (1950).

ARIOSTO, LODOVICO, *Orlando furioso*. Ed. Naples–Milan, 1954.

ARISTOTLE, *Nicomachean Ethics*. Trans. H. Rackham. Loeb Classical Library. London, 1925.

—— *On the Art of Poetry*. Trans. Ingram Bywater. Oxford, 1909.

—— see ORDÓÑEZ DAS SEIJAS Y TOVAR.

—— *Rhetoric*. Trans. R. C. Jebb. Cambridge, 1909.

ATKINSON, W. C., 'Cervantes, El Pinciano and the *Novelas ejemplares*', *Hispanic Review*, vol. xvi (1948).

—— 'The Enigma of the *Persiles*', *Bulletin of Spanish Studies*, vol. xxiv (1947).

AUERBACH, ERICH, *Mimesis: the Representation of Reality in Western Literature*. Trans. W. R. Trask. London, 1953.

AVELLANEDA, ALONSO F. DE, *El Quijote*. Colección Austral. Buenos Aires, 1946.

BACON, FRANCIS, extract from *The Advancement of Learning*. Ed. Edmund D. Jones, *English Critical Essays (Sixteenth, Seventeenth and Eighteenth Centuries)*. London, 1947.

BALBUENA, BERNARDO DE, prologue to *El Bernardo*. Ed. J. Van Horne, '*El Bernardo* of Bernardo de Balbuena', *University of Illinois Studies in Language and Literature*, vol. xii (1927).

—— *Grandeza mexicana*. Mexico, 1604.

—— *Siglo de oro, en las selvas de Erífile*. Madrid, 1608.

BARGAGLI, GIROLAMO, *Dialogo de' giuochi che nelle vegghie sanesi si vsano di fare.* Siena, 1572.

BASIL (the Great), ST., *To Young Men, On how they might derive Profit from Pagan Literature. The Letters,* vol. iv. Trans. R. J. Deferrari and M. R. P. McGuire. Loeb Classical Library. London, 1934.

BATES, MARGARET, 'Cervantes' criticism of *Tirant lo Blanch', Hispanic Review,* vol. xxi (1953).

—— *'Discreción' in the Works of Cervantes.* Washington, 1945.

BELTRÁN Y RÓZPIDE, R., *La pericia geográfica de Cervantes demostrada con la 'Historia de los trabajos de Persiles y Sigismunda'.* Madrid, 1924.

BISBE Y VIDAL, *see* FERRER.

BONILLA, ADOLFO, *Cervantes y su obra.* Madrid, 1916.

BROCENSE, EL, *see* SÁNCHEZ DE LAS BROZAS.

CABRERA DE CÓRDOBA, LUIS, *De historia, para entenderla y escrivirla.* Madrid, 1611.

CAMÕES, LUIS, *see* SÁNCHEZ DE LAS BROZAS.

CANAVAGGIO, JEAN-FRANÇOIS, 'Alonso López Pinciano y la estética literaria de Cervantes en el *Quijote', Anales cervantinos,* vol. vii (1958).

CARRILLO Y SOTOMAYOR, LUIS, *Libro de la erudicion poetica.* Ed. Madrid, 1946.

CARTAGENA, ALONSO DE, *Prólogo y dedicatoria del libro de Marcho Tulio Ciceron q. se llama de la retórica.* M. Menéndez y Pelayo, *Historia de las ideas estéticas en España,* vol. i, appendix 2. Ed. Buenos Aires, 1943.

CARVALLO, LUIS ALFONSO DE, *Cisne de Apolo.* Medina del Campo, 1602.

CASALDUERO, JOAQUÍN, *Sentido y forma del 'Quijote'.* Madrid, 1949.

CASCALES, FRANCISCO, 'A don Tomás Tamayo y Vargas'. *Cartas filológicas,* vol. ii. Clásicos castellanos. Madrid, 1940.

—— *Tablas poeticas.* Ed. Madrid, 1779.

CASELLA, MARIO, *Cervantes: Il 'Chisciotte'.* 2 vols. Florence, 1938.

CASTELVETRO, LODOVICO, *Poetica d'Aristotele vulgarizzata et sposta.* Ed. Basle, 1576.

CASTIGLIONE, BALDESAR, *Il libro del Cortegiano.* Ed. Florence, 1947.

CASTRO, AMÉRICO, 'Cervantes y Pirandello', *La Nación* (Buenos Aires), 16 November 1924.

—— *El pensamiento de Cervantes.* Madrid, 1925.

—— *Hacia Cervantes.* Madrid, 1957.

CERRETA, F. V., 'Alessandro Piccolomini's commentary on the *Poetics* of Aristotle', *Studies in the Renaissance,* vol. iv (1957).

CERVANTES, MIGUEL DE, *Comedias y entremeses; Poesías sueltas.* Ed. Rodolfo Schevill and Adolfo Bonilla. 6 vols. Madrid, 1915–22.

—— *Don Qvixote de la Mancha.* Ed. Schevill and Bonilla. 4 vols. Madrid, 1928–41.

—— *El ingenioso hidalgo Don Quijote de la Mancha.* Ed. Diego Clemencín. 8 vols. Madrid, 1894.

—— *El ingenioso hidalgo Don Quijote de la Mancha.* Ed. Francisco Rodríguez Marín. 10 vols. Madrid, 1947–9.

—— *La Galatea.* Ed. Schevill and Bonilla. 2 vols. Madrid, 1914–15.

—— *Novelas exemplares.* Ed. Schevill and Bonilla. 3 vols. Madrid, 1922–5.

CERVANTES, MIGUEL DE, *Persiles y Sigismunda*. Ed. Schevill and Bonilla. 2 vols. Madrid, 1914-15.
—— *The Travels of Persiles and Sigismvnda*. London, 1619.
—— *Viage del Parnaso*. Ed. Schevill and Bonilla. Madrid, 1922.
—— *Viaje del Parnaso; Entremeses*. Ed. Agustín del Campo. Madrid, 1948.
CHAPMAN, GEORGE, Preface to *Seaven Bookes of the 'Iliades' of Homere*. Ed. G. G. Smith, *Elizabethan Critical Essays*, vol. ii. Oxford, 1904.
CICERO, *De Oratore*. Trans. E. W. Sutton and H. Rackham. 2 vols. Loeb Classical Library. London, 1942.
—— *see* CARTAGENA.
CLARK, KENNETH, '*Las Meninas* by Velasquez', *The Sunday Times*, 2 June 1957.
COTARELO VALLEDOR, A., *Cervantes lector*. Madrid, 1943.
COVARRUBIAS, SEBASTIÁN DE, *Tesoro de la lengua castellana o española*. Ed. Martín de Riquer. Barcelona, 1943.
Cronica del muy valiente y esforçado cauallero Platir. Valladolid, 1533..
CUEVA, JUAN DE LA, *El infamador, Los siete infantes de Lara y El ejemplar poético*. Clásicos castellanos. Madrid, 1941.
CURTIUS, ERNST R., *European Literature and the Latin Middle Ages*. Trans. W. R. Trask. London, 1953.

DELICADO, FRANCISCO, *La Loçana andaluza*. Ed. Barcelona, 1952.
DE LOLLIS, C., *Cervantes reazionario*. Ed. Florence, 1947.
DEMETRIUS PHALERIUS, *On Style*. Trans. W. Rhys Roberts. Loeb Classical Library. London, 1927.
DI FRANCIA, LETTERIO, *Novellistica*. 2 vols. Milan, 1924-5.
DIO CHRYSOSTOM, *Discourse XI*, 'Maintaining that Troy was not captured'. *Discourses*, vol. i. Trans. J. W. Cohoon. Loeb Classical Library. London, 1932.
Discvrso en loor de la poesia. In Diego Mexía, *Parnaso antartico de obras amatorias*. Seville, 1608.
DUNLOP, J. C., *History of Prose Fiction*. Revised H. Wilson. 2 vols. London, 1888.

EMPSON, WILLIAM, *Some Versions of Pastoral*. London, 1935.
ENCINA, JUAN DEL, *Arte de poesía castellana*. M. Menéndez y Pelayo, *Historia de las ideas estéticas en España*, vol. i, appendix 5. Ed. Buenos Aires, 1943.
ERASMUS, DESIDERIUS, *Colloquia familiaria et Encomium moriae*. 2 vols. Ed. Leipzig, [1905 ?].
ERCILLA, ALONSO DE, *La Araucana*. 2 vols. Ed. Madrid, 1866.
ESPINEL, VICENTE, *see* VALDÉS, ALONSO DE.
ESPINOSA DE SANTAYANA, RODRIGO DE, *Arte de rethorica*. Madrid, 1578.

FARAL, EDMOND, *Les Arts poétiques du XIIe et du XIIIe siècle*. Paris, 1924.
FARINELLI, ARTURO, *Dos excéntricos: Cristóbal de Villalón, El doctor Juan Huarte*. Madrid, 1936.
FERRER, JUAN, *Tratado de las comedias*. Por Fructuoso Bisbe y Vidal. Barcelona, 1618.

FORSTER, E. M., *Aspects of the Novel*. London, 1927.

FRACASTORO, GIROLAMO, *Naugerius, sive de poetica dialogus*. Trans. Ruth Kelso. *University of Illinois Studies in Language and Literature*, vol. ix (1924).

GÁLVEZ DE MONTALVO, LUIS, *El pastor de Filida*. Ed. Madrid, 1589.

GARCÍA SORIANO, J., 'Carrillo y los orígenes del culteranismo', *Boletín de la Real Academia española*, vol. xiii (1926).

—— *El humanista Francisco Cascales*. Madrid, 1924.

GARCILASO DE LA VEGA, *see* HERRERA.

—— *see* SÁNCHEZ DE LAS BROZAS.

GARZONI, TOMMASO, *La piazza vniuersale di tutte le professioni del mondo*. Venice, 1587.

GERHARDT, MIA I., *'Don Quijote': la vie et les livres*. Amsterdam, 1955.

GILLET, J. E., 'The Autonomous Character in Spanish and European Literature', *Hispanic Review*, vol. xxiv (1956).

GIRALDI CINTHIO, GIAMBATTISTA, *Discorso . . . intorno al comporre de i romanzi*. Venice, 1554.

—— *Primera parte de las cien novelas de M. Ivan Baptista Giraldo Cinthio*. Trans. L. Gaitán de Vozmediano. Toledo, 1590.

—— 'Risposta . . . a Messer G. B. Pigna'. *Scritti estetici, II*. Biblioteca Rara, vol. liii. Milan, 1864.

GONZÁLEZ DE AMEZÚA, AGUSTÍN, *Cervantes creador de la novela corta española*. 2 vols. Madrid, 1956-8.

GONZÁLEZ DE BOBADILLA, BERNARDO, *Nimphas y pastores de Henares*. Alcalá de Henares, 1587.

GRACIÁN, BALTASAR, *Agudeza y arte de ingenio*. Ed. Madrid, 1944.

GRACIÁN DANTISCO, LUCAS, *Galateo español*. Ed. Madrid, 1943.

GREEN, R. H., 'Dante's "Allegory of Poets" and the mediaeval theory of Poetic Fiction', *Comparative Literature*, vol. ix (1957).

GRIFFITH, T. GWYNFOR, *Bandello's Fiction*. Oxford, 1955.

GUERRIERI-CROCETTI, C., *G. B. Giraldi e il pensiero critico del sec. XVI*. Milan, 1932.

GUTIÉRREZ DE LOS RÍOS, GASPAR, *Noticia general para la estimacion de las artes*. Madrid, 1600.

GUZMÁN, JUAN DE, *Primera parte de la rhetorica*. Alcalá de Henares, 1589.

HANKE, LEWIS, *Aristotle and the American Indians*. London, 1959.

HATZFELD, HELMUT, 'Artistic parallels in Cervantes and Velázquez', *Estudios dedicados a Menéndez Pidal*, vol. iii. Madrid, 1952.

—— *El 'Quijote' como obra de arte del lenguaje*. Madrid, 1949.

HAYDN, HIRAM, *The Counter-Renaissance*. New York, 1950.

HEBREO, LEÓN, *Diálogos de amor*. Trans. El Inca Garcilaso de la Vega. Colección Austral. Buenos Aires, 1947.

HELIODORUS, *Historia etiópica de los amores de Teágenes y Cariclea*. Trans. Fernando de Mena. Ed. Madrid, 1954.

HERRERA, FERNANDO DE, 'Contestación al muy reverendo padre Prete Jacopín'. *Controversia sobre sus anotaciones a las obras de Garcilaso de la Vega.* Seville, 1870.

—— *Obras de Garci Lasso de la Vega con anotaciones de Fernando de Herrera.* Seville, 1580.

HERRERO GARCÍA, M., 'Ideas estéticas del teatro clásico español', *Revista de ideas estéticas*, vol. v (1944).

HERRICK, M. T., 'Comic Theory in the Sixteenth Century', *University of Illinois Studies in Language and Literature*, vol. xxxiv (1950).

—— 'The Fusion of Horatian and Aristotelian literary criticism', *University of Illinois Studies in Language and Literature*, vol. xxxii (1946).

HORACE, *Satires, Epistles and 'Ars poetica'.* Trans. H. R. Fairclough. Loeb Classical Library. London, 1926.

—— *see* VILLÉN DE BIEDMA.

HUARTE DE SAN JUAN, JUAN, *Examen de ingenios, para las sciencias.* Ed. Leyden, 1591.

HURTADO DE MENDOZA, DIEGO, *Carta de don Diego de Mendoza al capitán Salazar.* Biblioteca de Autores españoles, vol. xxxvi.

ISIDORE, ST., *Etymologiarum sive originum libri XX.* 2 vols. Ed. Oxford, 1911.

JÁUREGUI, JUAN DE, *Discurso poetico.* Madrid, 1624.

LEBOIS, A., 'La Révolte des personnages, de Cervantes et Calderón à Raymond Schwab', *Revue de Littérature Comparée*, vol. xxiii (1949).

LEÓN, LUIS DE, *Traducción literal y declaración del libro de los Cantares de Salomón.* Biblioteca de Autores españoles, vol. xxxvii.

LEVIN, HARRY, 'The Example of Cervantes', *Contexts of Criticism.* London, 1957.

LOFRASO, ANTONIO DE, *Los diez libros de fortvna de amor.* Barcelona, 1573.

'LONGINUS', *On the Sublime.* Trans. W. H. Fyfe. Loeb Classical Library. London, 1927.

LÓPEZ, FRANCISCO, prologue to *Romancero general.* Madrid, 1604.

LÓPEZ DE ENCISO, BARTOLOMÉ, *Desengaño de celos.* Madrid, 1586.

LÓPEZ ESTRADA, FRANCISCO, 'La influencia italiana en la *Galatea* de Cervantes', *Comparative Literature*, vol. iv (1952).

LÓPEZ PINCIANO, ALONSO, *Philosophia antigua poetica.* 3 vols. Ed. Madrid, 1953.

LUCIAN, *Dialogos.* León, 1550.

—— *Essays in Portraiture defended.* Lucian, vol. iv. Trans. A. N. Harmon. Loeb Classical Library. London, 1925.

—— *Professor of Public Speaking.* Lucian, vol. iv. Trans. A. N. Harmon. Loeb Classical Library. London, 1925.

—— *The Way to Write History. Works*, vol. ii. Trans. H. W. and F. G. Fowler. Oxford, 1905.

LUGO Y DÁVILA, FRANCISCO DE, *Teatro popular.* Ed. Madrid, 1906.

MADARIAGA, SALVADOR DE, *Don Quixote: An Introductory Essay in Psychology.* Oxford, 1935.

MAL LARA, JUAN DE, *Philosophia vulgar.* Seville, 1568.

MALDONADO DE GUEVARA, FRANCISCO DE, 'El dolo como potencia estética', *Anales cervantinos*, vol. i (1951).

MARASSO, ARTURO, *Cervantes: la invención del 'Quijote'*. Buenos Aires, 1954.

MARTORELL, JOHANNOT, *Tirante el Blanco*. Ed. F. Buendía, *Libros de caballerías españoles*. Madrid, 1954.

MAZZEO, J. A., 'A Seventeenth-century Theory of Metaphysical Poetry', *Romanic Review*, vol. xlii (1951).

MEDINA, FRANCISCO DE, prologue to *Obras de Garci Lasso de la Vega. See* HERRERA.

MENÉNDEZ Y PELAYO, MARCELINO, *Historia de las ideas estéticas en España*. 5 vols. Ed. Buenos Aires, 1943.

—— *Orígenes de la novela*. 4 vols. Madrid, 1905–10.

MEXÍA, DIEGO, see *Discvrso en loor de la poesia*.

MINTURNO, ANTONIO SEBASTIANO, *L'Arte poetica*. Venice, 1563.

MONTALVO, GARCI RODRÍGUEZ (or ORDÓÑEZ) DE, *see* RODRÍGUEZ DE MONTALVO.

MONTEMAYOR, JORGE DE, *Los siete libros de la Diana*. Clásicos castellanos, Madrid, 1946.

MOREL-FATIO, A., 'Le *Don Quichotte* d'Avellaneda', *Bulletin Hispanique*, vol. v (1903).

MUZIO, GIROLAMO, *Tre libri di arte poetica. Rime diuerse*. Venice, 1551.

NAVARRA, PEDRO DE, *Dialogos de la differencia del hablar al escrevir*. Tolosa, [1560?].

NEBRIJA, ANTONIO DE, *Gramatica de la lengua castellana* and *Reglas de orthographia en la lengua castellana*. Ed. Oxford, 1926.

Oliveros de Castilla. Nueva Biblioteca de Autores españoles, vol. xi.

ORDÓÑEZ DAS SEIJAS Y TOVAR, ALONSO, *La poetica de Aristoteles dada a nvestra lengva castellana*. Madrid, 1626.

ORDÓÑEZ DE MONTALVO, GARCI, *see* RODRÍGUEZ DE MONTALVO.

ORS, EUGENIO D', 'Fenomenología de los libros de caballerías', *Boletín de la Real Academia española*, vol. xxvii (1947–8).

ORTEGA Y GASSET, *Meditaciones del 'Quijote'*. Ed. Madrid, 1957.

PARKER, A. A. (ed.), CALDERÓN DE LA BARCA, *No hay más fortuna que Dios*, Appendix. Manchester, 1949.

PATRIZI, FRANCESCO, *Della historia*. Venice, 1560.

—— *Della poetica*. Ferrara, 1586.

PÉREZ DE HITA, GINÉS, *Guerras civiles de Granada*. Biblioteca de Autores españoles, vol. iii.

PICCOLOMINI, ALESSANDRO, *Annotationi . . . nel libro della poetica d'Aristotele*. Venice, 1575.

PINCIANO, EL, *see* LÓPEZ PINCIANO.

PLUTARCH, *Comparison of Aristophanes and Menander. Moralia*, vol. x. Trans. H. N. Fowler. Loeb Classical Library. London, 1936.

—— *On the Fame of the Athenians. Moralia*, vol. iv. Trans. F. C. Babbitt. Loeb Classical Library. London, 1936.

PONTANO, GIOVANNI, extract from *Actius*, *see* FRACASTORO.
—— *Opera omnia*. 6 vols. Florence, 1520.
PREDMORE, RICHARD L., *El mundo del 'Quijote'*. Madrid, 1958.
PUTTENHAM, GEORGE, *The Arte of English Poesie*. Ed. G. G. Smith, *Elizabethan Critical Essays*, vol. ii. Oxford, 1904.

QUINTILIAN, *Institutio oratoria*. Trans. H. E. Butler. 4 vols. Loeb Classical Library. London, 1921–2.

RENGIFO, DIEGO GARCÍA, *Arte poetica española*. Salamanca, 1592.
REY DE ARTIEDA, ANDRÉS, 'Carta al illustrissimo marques de Cuellar sobre la comedia'. *Discursos, epistolas y epigramas de Artemidoro*. Saragossa, 1605.
Rhetorica ad Herennium. Trans. H. Caplan. Loeb Classical Library. London, 1954.
RILEY, E. C., '"El alba bella que las perlas cría": dawn-description in the novels of Cervantes', *Bulletin of Hispanic Studies*, vol. xxxiii (1956).
—— 'Episodio, novela y aventura en *Don Quijote*'. *Anales cervantinos*, vol. v (1955-6).
RÍO, ÁNGEL DEL, 'El equívoco del *Quijote*', *Hispanic Review*, vol. xxvii (1959).
RIQUER, MARTÍN DE, 'Don Quijote, caballero por escarnio', *Clavileño*, vol. vii (1956).
ROBORTELLI, FRANCESCO, *In librum Aristotelis de Arte Poetica explicationes*. Florence, 1548.
RODRIGUES LOBO, FRANCISCO, *Corte en aldea, y noches de imbierno*. Trans. J. B. Morales. Montilla, 1622.
RODRÍGUEZ DE MONTALVO, GARCI, prologue to *Amadís de Gaula*. Ed. F. Buendía, *Libros de caballerías españoles*. Madrid, 1954.
—— *Las sergas del muy esforzado caballero Esplandian*. Biblioteca de Autores espanoles, vol. xl.
ROJAS, AGUSTÍN DE, *El viaje entretenido*. Ed. Madrid, 1945.

SAINTSBURY, GEORGE, *A History of Criticism and Literary Taste in Europe*. 3 vols. Edinburgh, 1900-4.
SALAS GARRIDO, S., *Exposición de las ideas estéticas de Cervantes*. Malaga, 1905.
SALILLAS, R., *Un gran inspirador de Cervantes: Juan Huarte*. Madrid, 1905.
SALINAS, MIGUEL, *Rhetorica en lengua castellana*. Alcalá de Henares, 1541.
SÁNCHEZ DE LAS BROZAS, FRANCISCO, prologue to Camões, *La Lusiada*. Trans. L. Gómez de Tapia. Salamanca, 1580.
—— *Obras del excelente poeta Garci Lasso de la Vega. Con anotaciones del Maestro Francisco Sanchez*. Ed. Salamanca, 1581.
SÁNCHEZ DE LIMA, MIGUEL, *El arte poetica en romance castellano*. Alcalá de Henares, 1580.
SANNAZARO, JACOPO, *Arcadia*. Ed. Turin, 1948.
SANTILLANA, MARQUÉS DE, 'A su hijo cuando estaba estudiando en Salamanca'. *Prose and Verse*. London, 1940.
—— *Prohemio e carta*. Ed. Oxford, 1927.
SANVISENTI, B., 'Il passo più oscuro del *Chisciotte*', *Revista de filología española*, vol. ix (1922).
SCALIGER, JULIUS CAESAR, *Poetices libri septem*. Ed. [Heidelberg], 1581.

SENECA, LUCIUS ANNAEUS, *De brevitate vitae. Moral Essays*, vol. ii. Trans. J. W. Basore. Loeb Classical Library. London, 1932.

SIDNEY, PHILIP, *An Apologie for Poetrie*. Ed. G. G. Smith, *Elizabethan Critical Essays*, vol. i. Oxford, 1904.

SILVA, FELICIANO DE, *Cronica del muy valiente y esforçado principe y Cauallero de la Ardiente Espada Amadis de Grecia*. Ed. Seville, 1549.

SOTO DE ROJAS, PEDRO, *Discurso sobre la poetica. Obras*. Ed. Madrid, 1950.

SPINGARN, J. E., *A History of Literary Criticism in the Renaissance*. New York, 1899.

—— 'The Origins of Modern Criticism', *Modern Philology*, vol. i (1904).

SPITZER, LEO, 'Perspectivismo lingüístico en el *Quijote*', *Lingüística e historia literaria*. Madrid, 1955.

STAGG, GEOFFREY, 'El sabio Cide Hamete Venengeli', *Bulletin of Hispanic Studies*, vol. xxxiii (1956).

SUÁREZ DE FIGUEROA, CRISTÓBAL, *El pasagero*. Ed. Madrid, 1913.

—— *La constante Amarilis*. Valencia, 1609.

—— *Plaza vniuersal de todas ciencias y artes*. Madrid, 1615.

TACITUS, *Dialogus de oratoribus*. Trans. W. Peterson. Loeb Classical Library. London, 1914.

TAMAYO, J. A., 'Ideas estéticas y literarias de Cervantes', *Revista de ideas estéticas*, vol. vi (1948).

TASSO, TORQUATO, *Apologia . . . in difesa della sua 'Gerusalemme' agli Accademici della Crusca. Opere*, vol. iv. Ed. Florence, 1724.

—— *Discorsi del poema eroico. Opere*, vol. iv. Ed. Florence, 1724.

—— *Discorsi dell'arte poetica e in particolare sopra il poema eroico. Opere*, vol. iv. Ed. Florence, 1724.

—— *La Cavelletta ovvero della poesia toscana: Dialogo. Opere*, vol. iv. Ed. Florence, 1724.

—— *Lezione . . . recitata . . . nell'Accademia ferrarese sopra il sonetto, 'Questa vita mortal'*, ec. di Monsignor della Casa. *Opere*, vol. iv. Ed. Florence, 1724.

THOMAS, HENRY, *Spanish and Portuguese Romances of Chivalry*. Cambridge, 1920.

TOFFANIN, GIUSEPPE, *La fine dell'umanesimo*. Turin, 1920.

TORQUEMADA, ANTONIO DE, *Jardín de flores curiosas*. Ed. Madrid, 1943.

—— *La historia del inuencible cauallero Don Oliuante de Laura*. Barcelona, 1564.

TRUEBLOOD, A. S., 'Sobre la selección artistica en el *Quijote*: ". . . lo que ha dejado de escribir" (II. 44)', *Nueva revista de filología hispánica*, vol. x (1956).

UNAMUNO, MIGUEL DE, *Vida de Don Quijote y Sancho*. Colección Austral. Buenos Aires, 1946.

URDANETA, A., *Cervantes y la crítica*. Caracas, 1877.

URFÉ, HONORÉ D', *L'Astrée*. Bibliotheca Romanica. Strasbourg, n.d.

VALDÉS, ALONSO DE, *Prologo en alabança de la poesia*. In Vicente Espinel, *Diversas rimas*. Madrid, 1591.

VALDÉS, JUAN DE, *Diálogo de la lengua*. Clásicos castellanos. Madrid, 1946.

VEGA CARPIO, LOPE DE, *Arte nuevo de hazer comedias en este tiempo*. Ed. A. Morel-Fatio. *Bulletin Hispanique*, vol. iii (1901).

—— *El desdichado por la honra*. Biblioteca de Autores españoles, vol. xxxviii.

—— *El peregrino en su patria*. *Obras sueltas*, vol. v. Ed. Madrid, 1776.

—— *La Arcadia*. Biblioteca de Autores españoles, vol. xxxviii.

—— *La Filomena*. Biblioteca de Autores españoles, vol. xxxviii.

—— *Laurel de Apolo*. Biblioteca de Autores españoles, vol. xxxviii.

—— *Respuesta a un papel que escribió un señor de estos reinos en razón de la nueva poesía*. Biblioteca de Autores españoles, vol. xxxviii.

—— *Triunfo de la fe*. Biblioteca de Autores españoles, vol. xxxviii.

VENEGAS DE BUSTO, ALEXIO, prologue to L: B. Alberti, *El Momo*. Trans. Agustín Almazán. Ed. Madrid, 1598.

—— *Primera parte de las differencias de libros*. Ed. Valladolid, 1583.

VERA Y MENDOZA, FERNANDO, *Panegyrico por la poesia*. Montilla, 1627.

VIDA, GIROLAMO, *De arte poetica*. In *Les quatre poëtiques: d'Aristote, d'Horace, de Vida, de Despréaux, avec les traductions & des remarques, par M. l'Abbé Batteux*, vol. ii. Paris, 1771.

VIDART, LUIS, 'Cervantes, poeta épico', *Apuntes críticos*. Madrid, 1877.

—— *El 'Quijote' y la clasificación de las obras literarias*. Madrid, 1882.

VILANOVA, ANTONIO, 'Cervantes y la *Lozana andaluza*', Ínsula, no. 77 (May 1952).

—— 'Preceptistas españoles de los siglos XVI y XVII', in *Historia general de las literaturas hispánicas*, vol. iii. Ed. G. Díaz-Plaja. Barcelona, 1953.

VILLÉN DE BIEDMA, JUAN, *Q. Horacio Flacco poeta lyrico latino: sus obras con la declaracion magistral en lengua castellana*. Granada, 1599.

VIVES, JUAN LUIS, *De anima et vita*. Opera, vol. ii. Basle. 1555.

—— *De cavsis corrvptarvm artivm*. Opera, vol. i. Basle, 1555.

—— *De conscribendis epistolis*. Opera, vol. i. Basle, 1555.

—— — *De institutione foeminae christianae*. Opera, vol. ii. Basle, 1555.

—— *De instrvmento probabilitatis*. Opera, vol. i. Basle, 1555.

—— *De ratione dicendi*. Opera, vol. i. Basle, 1555.

—— *De tradendis disciplinis*. Opera, vol. i. Basle, 1555.

—— *Obras completas*. Trans. Lorenzo Riber. 2 vols. Madrid, 1947–8.

—— *Veritas fucata*. Opera omnia, vol. ii. Valencia, 1782.

WEINBERG, B., 'Castelvetro's Theory of Poetics', in *Critics and Criticism, ancient and modern*. Ed. R. S. Crane. Chicago, 1952.

—— 'From Aristotle to pseudo-Aristotle', *Comparative Literature*, vol. v (1953).

—— 'Robortello on the *Poetics*', in *Critics and Criticism, ancient and modern*. Ed. R. S. Crane. Chicago, 1952.

—— 'Scaliger versus Aristotle on Poetics', *Modern Philology*, vol. xxxix (1942).

WELLEK, RENÉ, *A History of Modern Criticism*. 2 vols. London, 1955.

WILLIS, R. S., *The Phantom Chapters of the 'Quijote'*. New York, 1953.

ZAPATA, LUIS, *Carlo famoso*. Valencia, 1566.

INDEX OF NAMES

INDEX OF TOPICS

INDEX OF REFERENCES TO WORKS
OF CERVANTES

*References to works as a whole, or to matters extending over several chapters,
are not included.*